Computer Supported Cooperative Work

Springer

London
Berlin
Heidelberg
New York
Hong Kong
Milan
Paris
Tokyo

Also in this series

Gerold Riempp
Wide Area Workflow Management
3-540-76243-4

Celia T. Romm and Fay Sudweeks
(Eds)
Doing Business Electronically
3-540-76159-4

Fay Sudweeks and Celia T. Romm
(Eds)
Doing Business on the Internet
1-85233-030-9

Elayne Coakes, Dianne Willis and
Raymond Lloyd-Jones (Eds)
The New SocioTech
1-85233-040-6

Elizabeth F. Churchill,
David N. Snowdon and
Alan J. Munro (Eds)
Collaborative Virtual Environments
1-85233-244-1

Christine Steeples and Chris Jones
(Eds)
Networked Learning
1-85233-471-1

Barry Brown, Nicola Green and
Richard Harper (Eds)
Wireless World
1-85233-477-0

Reza Hazemi and
Stephen Hailes (Eds)
The Digital University
1-85233-478-9

Elayne Coakes, Dianne Willis and
Steve Clark (Eds)
Knowledge Management in the
SocioTechnical World
1-85233-441-X

Ralph Schroeder (Ed.)
The Social Life of Avatars
1-85233-461-4

Erik Andriessen
Working with Groupware
1-85233-603-X

Kristina Höök, Alan J. Munro and
David Benyon (Eds)
Designing Information Spaces
Technologies in Industry
1-85233-661-7

Bjørn Erik Munkvold
Implementing Collaboration
Technologies in Industry
1-85233-418-5

Paul Kirschner, Chad Carr and
Simon Buckingham Shum (Eds)
Visualising Argumentation
1-85233-664-1

A list of out of print titles is available at the end of the book

Christopher Lueg and Danyel Fisher (Eds)

From Usenet to CoWebs

Interacting with Social Information Spaces

With 55 Figures

Springer

Christopher Lueg, Dipl-Inform, Dr. sc. nat.
Department of Information Systems, Faculty of Information Technology, University of Technology Sydney, PO Box 123, Broadway NSW 2007, Sydney, Australia

Danyel Fisher, BS, BA, MS
Information and Computer Science, University of California Irvine, Irvine, CA 92697-3430, USA

Series Editors

Dan Diaper, PhD, MBCS
Professor of Systems, Science Engineering, School of Design, Engineering and Computing, Bournemouth University, Talbot Campus, Fern Barrow, Poole, Dorset BH12 5BB, UK

Colston Sanger
Shottersley Research Limited, Little Shottersley, Farnham Lane
Haslemere, Surrey GU27 1HA, UK

British Library Cataloguing in Publication Data
From Usenet to CoWebs : interacting with social information
    spaces. - (Computer supported cooperative work)
    1.Human-computer interaction 2.Usenet (Computer network)
    3.Teams in the workplace - Data processing 4.Distributed
    databases
    I.Lueg, Christopher II.Fisher, Danyel
    004'.019
    ISBN 1852335327

Library of Congress Cataloging-in-Publication Data
From Usenet to CoWebs: interacting with social information spaces/Christopher Lueg
and Danyel Fisher (eds.).
        p. cm. – (Computer supported cooperative work, ISSN 1431-1496)
    Includes bibliographical references and index.
    ISBN 1-5233-532-7 (alk. paper)
        1. Internet–Social aspects. 2. Electronic discussion groups–Social aspects. 3. Usenet
    (Computer network)–Social aspects. 4. Wikis (Computer science)–Social aspects. 5. Social
    interaction. I. Lueg, Christopher, 1966- II. Fisher, Danyel, 1975- III. Series.
    HM851 .F76 2002
    303.48'33–dc21   2002070843

CSCW ISSN 1431-1496
ISBN 1-85233-532-7 Springer-Verlag London Berlin Heidelberg
a member of BertelsmannSpringer Science+Business Media GmbH
http://www.springer.co.uk

Typesetting: Electronic text files prepared by Gray Publishing, Tunbridge Wells, UK
Printed and bound at the Athenæum Press Ltd., Gateshead, Tyne & Wear
34/3830-543210 Printed on acid-free paper SPIN 10842967

Contents

List of Contributors

Brian Amento is a Research Scientist at AT&T Labs – Research.

Erin Bradner, PhD is a researcher at the University of California, Irvine. In her work, she examines the interplay between interface design and social interaction as it is mediated by technology.

Lynn Cherny is an interaction designer who is currently Director of Research and Development at Axance.com, a usability consulting company in Paris, France. She is the author of *Conversation and Community: Chat in a Virtual World* (CSLI Press, 1999).

Andreas Dieberger is a Research Staff Member in the USER group at the IBM Almaden Research Center in San Jose, CA.

Danyel Fisher is a graduate student at the University of California, Irvine. His research centres on studies of online interaction and social network analysis.

Mark Guzdial is an Associate Professor in the College of Computing at Georgia Institute of Technology.

Will Hill researches novel human-interface technologies, particularly those involving collaborative filtering of information. He received his PhD from Northwestern University.

Joseph A. Konstan is Associate Professor of Computer Science at the University of Minnesota. His work focuses on human–computer interaction, broadly defined. Up-to-date information about his interests and activities can be found at www.konstan.org.

Christopher Lueg is a Senior Lecturer in Information Systems at the Faculty of Information Technology, University of Technology Sydney. His research interests are cross-disciplinary in the intersection of computer science, information science, and cognitive science.

Bradley N. Miller is a graduate student in Computer Science at the University of Minnesota. His research is focused on reducing information overload through the use of recommender systems on pocket-size devices.

Blair Nonnecke is a faculty member in the Department of Computing and Information Science at the University of Guelph, Ontario. He is interested in all forms of human–computer interaction and in particular, on online communities and lurkers.

Bryan Pfaffenberger, Associate Professor of Technology, Culture, and Communication at the University of Virginia, uses approaches drawn from Science and Technology Studies (STS), social anthropology, and legal scholarship to examine the crucial and conflicting issues raised by the rise of ubiquitous computing, including the nature of online social interaction, the changing role of intellectual property in digitized media, and the potential of the free software/open source software movement.

Jenny Preece is a professor and department chair of information systems at the University of Maryland, Baltimore County. Her research focuses on understanding social dynamics online and on developing interfaces to better support interaction in online communities.

John T. Riedl is Associate Professor of Computer Science and Engineering at the University of Minnesota. He is co-founder and co-director of the GroupLens Research project, which studies collaborative filtering in all of its aspects.

Warren Sack is a software designer and media theorist. Before joining the faculty at UC Berkeley, SIMS he was a research scientist at the MIT Media Laboratory and a research collaborator in the Interrogative Design Group at the MIT Center for Advanced Visual Studies.

Marc A. Smith is a sociologist at Microsoft Research. His work focuses on building tools to study the structure of social cyberspaces to generate maps and novel interfaces to these environments.

Loren Terveen is an Associate Professor at the University of Minnesota.

Steve Whittaker is a Senior Research Scientist at AT&T Labs – Research. He works on theory and tools for computer-supported collaborative work.

Part I
Introduction to Online Studies and Usenet

Chapter 1
Studying Social Information Spaces
Danyel Fisher

1.1 Social Spaces: Online and Offline Conversations

We live, work, and play in social spaces – both online and off. Our offline spaces are tremendously descriptive: they speak vividly to us as we interact within them. Imagine stumbling into a party at which you know virtually no one. Within moments of entering the room, you quickly determine how many people are present, and how actively they are engaged with each other. Is this a lively group, or a quiet one? Is it an office cocktail hour, a gathering of friends, or a wake? Is the room packed shoulder to shoulder, or is it so empty that people are clinging to the walls? Are people dancing, or nervously nursing their drinks?

People tend to be highly attuned to the spaces around them and to the social signals they send and receive from each other. The party is comprised of the cues and signals each individual broadcasts in order to share something about themselves with those around them. Goffman (1961) describes their actions as a "performance". Placing yourself back at the party, the impression you will form of that space is an interpretation of the combination of the other revellers' intentional acts and unintentional impressions. You quickly realize who seems to know each other how well, noting a few forced smiles where the conversation is not so comfortable. Given time, you may decode other subtle cues: who is not talking to whom, who is secretly admiring another, and which people are the most socially important to engage. Those observations – how you decode these cues – alter the way you interact at the party, and therefore the ways in which others react to you. They are crucial, if commonplace, social skills.

The online world can be far more muted. While some of the cues are there, to be sure – established social groups often have a rich shared history, and regular participants may be attuned to the feel of the group – they can be harder to find. In a Usenet newsgroup, for instance, you may not know who is around, although you can tell what is being said. Mood can be hard to judge – was that line spoken in jest, or seriously? Is the person speaking an authority, or a pretender? Is that question a novel one, or is it retreading old ground?

Online conversation moves more slowly than offline, so it can be harder to correct mistaken impressions or to establish a mood. Even for quick methods, like instant messaging, it takes longer to type a response than it might to speak a few words aloud. For slower media, such as email discussion lists, discussions can stretch out over weeks or months. A frequent contributor is one who says something hourly, or daily. Several conversations are usually going on at once, and they may have overlapping participants and ideas. Rather than the smiles and handshakes of the party, there is often only monochrome text – subtle nonverbal cues must be made explicit to be understood. There may be no way at all to know who might be listening in, or how much attention they are paying; there are almost never ways to learn the tone of a space except to immerse oneself in it. Although every word you hear comes from someone wearing a nametag, some are using false names.

There are more sophisticated signals that a reader can learn in time. Old hands in a Usenet newsgroup or an online system will eventually know something about their online space – that a group is helpful, or combative, or informative. There are, however, few signals to direct new readers to know what a group is like, and what constitutes their shared history. The wisdom of the old hands is valuable: they know what the crowd looks like, and remind us that these spaces can have an identity and a distinct feeling to them. They help carry on traditions, and enforce rules of acceptable behaviour.

This shared online identity can be expressed in a variety of ways: as favourite in-jokes and as topics of appropriate conversation. Groups may have an agreed-upon pace for contributions, and perhaps some degree of respect for old traditions. They have opinions on issues such as whether it is desirable to introduce new users immediately, or to have them observe quietly. Newcomers who violate the rules may be gently chastened, or violently flamed.

Although participating in a space for a long time may be a useful way to become an active member, it can be difficult to assess the value of a group during briefer visits. This is particularly a problem when a user prefers to find and share information – preferably, credible information – and move on. So while the group may delight in long, tangential discussions, the reader may not. Credibility, authority, relevance, and even friendliness – all these issues are compressed into a few brief words on the screen from an otherwise-anonymous group. It would be valuable to learn about both the social aspects of the groups, and the information that groups share. With that sense, the visiting user can evaluate whether a group is worth the time and energy it would take to search for useful information, and can decide whether it is worth more time and effort to become a regular participant in the group.

This volume explores ways to look at, and instrument, spaces for social awareness. We want to learn how to look at a space, and understand what is going on with the group that inhabits it. We want to come to a space to learn what it has to offer. We want to build new spaces that open themselves to productive exploration, both to researchers and to participants. These are tasks for statisticians and designers, sociologists, anthropologists, and technologists to work together to explore, characterize, and build these spaces.

A previous volume in this series (Munro et al, 1999) talked about ways to add cues to various types of spaces. "Social navigation" describes ways to add hints about location and context into information spaces, from chat-rooms to databases, by analogy with the real world – the cues we get from dog-eared books, lines in front of stores, and footprints on a trail (Dieberger et al, 2000). The essays in that volume outlined ways to add similar subtle cues to web pages and conversation areas, like adding tracks to web pages, and using shared navigation information to suggest directions for the next visitor to follow.

This volume complements many of those ideas. While we share interests in social spaces, social navigation looks specifically at facilities for enhancing those spaces. In contrast, we examine the online gathering spaces themselves, as well as the data that flows through them, in greater detail. Where social navigation specifically tries to highlight interaction through easily visible road signs, we both study and build on cues that already exist within the groups, searching for the signs that are already there, though hidden.

Through this book, we ask what aspects of an online group are important to its participants. What tools do we have to measure online groups, and what do those measurements mean? What are appropriate tools for the researcher to use to examine the group? What tools might be brought to the group to examine itself?

We also try to understand a second question: how can we take advantage of the specific characteristics of social information spaces to build new or enhance existing interfaces to these spaces? Different kinds of spaces have been built with different attributes: some are highly controlled spaces, carefully limiting what sorts of contributions can be made to the space, while others grant a high degree of freedom to their users. These technical attributes partially drive the social abilities of users. Because software can be used to restrict certain types of use, software drives the culture, norms, and understandings in the groups. Differences in user interfaces can be affect the participants' experience of the space – as well as the ability to study the groups, and the ability to collect data from them. These differences will delineate some of the abilities to measure and understand the spaces, and will shape the conversation happening within the spaces.

This tie between technical attributes and social behaviour is a common theme in computer-supported collaborative work (CSCW) as the social-technical design circle (O'Day et al, 1996). Conceptualized as a cycle, it reflects on the way that a project can improve incrementally: a version of software is deployed, and is used. After the software has been in use for a period of time, careful examination of the social structures that have arisen allow an improved version to be built. This does not necessarily require a CSCW researcher to accomplish: many spaces have evolved interesting mechanisms by common consensus in combination with participants' contributions.

We want to understand something about how information spaces have developed over time. Some of the techniques we examine are meant to help them move further through the cycle by providing feedback to designers and participants alike, allowing them to evaluate their spaces, and to re-design them incrementally.

1.2 Asynchronous Online Social Information Spaces

A common filament runs between a Usenet group and a conversation space attached to a web page; between email discussions, and the online user-modifiable web-page known as a "Wiki". We examine the shared attributes between these "asynchronous online social information spaces" – places where users can engage in conversation, make their presence known through contributions, and can share ideas. Each of these partially consists in what Harrison and Dourish (1996) call a space, raw digital functionalities that allow structured data to be added and shared with others. Users can reply to messages, systems archive old notes, and conversations progress. They develop a growing dimension of "place-ness" – that is, the participants gain a shared social knowledge that evolves it into a memorable, persistent online locale with its own social architecture: a place.

Many of the contexts we discuss are also referred to as persistent conversations, so-called because they tend to be archived, or at least can be archived. Unlike instant message systems, persistent conversations might be visible for an extended time on a server, and can be viewed by people who are not then online and in attendance. A new user coming into such a space, then, is confronted by both the historical messages, and the continuing conversation. Some recent works trying to analyse, implement, or visualize persistent conversations include papers by Erickson et al (1999), Churchill (2000), Jung and Lee (2000), and Smith and Fiore (2001).

To address these issues, we have collected a portion of the current research literature in these areas. The papers in this book are a mix of original works written for this occasion, and expansions or reprints of past texts. Our analytical method is a largely quantitative one; the research we highlight here takes advantage of statistical methods of analysis and measurement, as well as automated methods of feedback.

1.2.1 Analysis Techniques on Spaces

Researchers have enjoyed extensive access to social information spaces. Usenet is publicly accessible and discussion lists are often easy to join, so an anthropologist can lurk quietly, asking questions of a few key informants but remaining largely hidden. Online spaces have been a popular domain of study: a researcher of virtual worlds once commented half in jest, "every MUD [multi-user dimension] has its own ethnographer". The longer tradition of formal online research has been dominantly qualitative, as those public spaces allowed for close examination. From this tradition has emerged a rich variety of projects, from examinations of individuals and their social interaction, to larger-scale issues of group overload and crises of filtering.

The qualitative work has been rich and extensive, and branches into many fields. For example, the recent volume *Communities in Cyberspace*, edited by Smith and Kollock (1999) examines issues of identity, contribution to group dynamics, and other online issues of group interaction. Their volume fits into a larger history of online behaviour studies. Turkle's pioneering book *Life on the Screen* (1995) discusses how users manage multiple identities online as they move from email to chat-rooms. Baym (1993) has written about the development of a social community on a newsgroup, examining the in-jokes and customs that arise in a group of people dedicated to watching soap operas. Kiesler et al (1984) have examined flaming and other social interaction online, and discusses the social factors that seem to encourage hostile behaviour. Researchers have used a variety of tools for data analysis, including social networking (Wellman and Gulia, 1999) and ethnographic investigation to understand how users interact online.

Our emphasis in this volume, however, is on fine-grained, quantitative studies. Quantitative researchers take advantage of the fact that online spaces are easily amenable to computer analysis. Of course, some aspects of online interaction can be invisible to quantitative techniques. Although these types of studies may never fully convey the texture of a space, they can be powerful tools for describing many of the important group behaviours and attributes. They have the ability to process large amounts of data at once, allowing visualizations to interactively compare different data sets. Quantitative methods can therefore be very good at highlighting potentially interesting sites for closer future study.

Studying word frequency or participation patterns in offline meetings, as Gibson (1999) does, is a gruelling process of recording and transcription. It can be far easier to analyse the traces left behind by persistent conversation. Similarly, some analytical techniques developed for offline conversation can be used on the transcripts and logs that can be automatically generated from a virtual space. The data that is extracted from these spaces can even shed light on non-virtual conversation. Indeed, quantitative and qualitative analyses complement each other nicely; the results from one can often inform the other.

Visualization is a useful hybrid technique, allowing qualitative analysis to be performed over quantitative results. For example, Paolillo (2002) has recently used visualization to examine the process by which new Usenet groups are created. He compares the voting patterns for new newsgroups with certain offline voting mechanisms, and found – to his surprise – that the votes he saw online were not well-organized into interest groups and voting blocs, but rather that individuals tended to vote idiosyncratically, reflecting their own needs.

One of the largest-scale systems for collecting this sort of data is Microsoft's Netscan system. Netscan is a piece of software that collects Usenet message information – the author, date, and title of all messages posted to Usenet. Netscan allows interactive exploration of newsgroup usage statistics: how many users are participating, how much they say, and who responds to each other. Smith (this volume) discusses what Netscan is able to collect about Usenet. The chapter outlines some of his findings about who is contributing to groups, and what they talk about. His viewpoint is necessarily high-level, as the data he collects is truly massive. However, Netscan's data can be used as a jumping-off point for many other types of studies, through its Usenet "report cards" on groups as well as individual posts and threads.

Whittaker et al (1998 and this volume) examine a smaller slice of newsgroups, and collect a number of statistics on participation and population. They then test those statistics to determine whether the presence of a list of frequently asked questions (FAQ) is relevant to the conversational flow of a group. He also investigates how moderation of groups – examining those with someone with the ability to reject postings – affects conversation flow. In a related study, Jones et al (2002) cast an archaeological eye on newsgroups. They find that users cope with seeing too many messages simply by leaving – the higher the number of messages posted, the lower the long-term population of the group.

Sack (this volume) has developed the "Conversation Map", which allows readers to wander through newsgroups, following associations between messages, looking for word patterns in common, and trying to understand which posters are interacting frequently with each other. His system is an automated, interactive one that encourages exploration and discovery. Other important visualizations of conversations have included views of individual threads (Rohall, 2001), a treemap view of Usenet (Smith, 2001) and a colourful map of threads overlapping (Donath et al, 1999). The canonical collection of visual representations of online spaces is presented in Dodge and Kitchin (2001).

We, of course, do not claim that mass collection of user data and conversation is unproblematic. Several authors have pointed out the many privacy risks of doing this sort of work, calling attention to the important task of defining a research ethic for examining communities online. Any collection of large-scale data is potentially dangerous; data collected with the best of intentions can be found to be destructive. There are continuing challenges in defining even what data can ethically be used from publicly accessible spaces. Even though individual Usenet posts are public, for example, the massive collection of data associated with names may draw an all-too-accurate picture of a user's recreational habits, can be used to learn about current topics of professional interest, and might be used for other violations of online privacy. But with searchable Usenet archives available, does it do any good to disguise the names of users who are quoted?

In this volume, we emphasize the usefulness of these studies. This is not to claim that ethics are unimportant. Rather, we encourage researchers and developers to consider the ethical implications of their work carefully. Unlike a recorded conversation in which the participants know that they have been recorded, archived conversations are often undertaken without the realization that they might be studied later. The privacy of the users who contribute to them must be considered; the question of whether the writer might reasonably have expected individual posts to be analysed must also be considered. It is worth examining the formal statements of ethics by the American Anthropological Association, the American Sociological Association, and various codifications by researchers such as Sharf (1999). Despite the implicit ambiguities, respectful and ethical treatment is a crucial element of online studies.

In this chapter, we introduce the social spaces that will be examined later in the text, and consider how the disparate viewpoints fit together. We explore a range of spaces, starting from Usenet and discussion lists. We contrast Usenet with newer systems, such as Wiki webs (and their close cousin, CoWebs; Dieberger, this volume) and IBM's BABBLE (Erickson et al, 1999, and Bradner, this volume). These differ in structure, in organization, and in design methodologies; they provide a wide spectrum of design possibilities.

This introduction, then, provides a brief preamble to the different social spaces, and finds a common research direction in the many threads explored in the book. We describe some variations in the notion of a social space, and discuss what goes into making a space. We introduce relevant terminology that will help describe these social spaces, and discuss some important differences between types of spaces. We explore both the technical and social capabilities of the software that supports groups, and how those capabilities shape the spaces they produce. Last, we discuss some of the techniques for analysing and enhancing the spaces.

1.2.2 A Few Social Information Spaces

We begin with several spaces that are well-established, and have strong user bases. This allows us to examine both the factors behind the large user base, and the abilities that have come out of a large, dedicated group. Some of the technologies we discuss may appear to be low-tech: few of them have been around for less than 5 years, and all of them can be used on the most modest of home computers. But even as the net moves to high-bandwidth applications, some classic aspects remain constant. For example, the most popular spaces for net users to trade ideas and raise their voices are not interactive graphical worlds, but online textual discussions. Many companies and groups have started to add online bulletin boards or message spaces to their web pages. Slashdot (www.slashdot.org), for example, is a discussion board for news stories based on technology updates; Free Republic (www.freerepublic.org) is an online space for discussion of conservative American ideas. Some organizations, such as LiveJournal (www.livejournal.com), provide nothing but a large number of online shared spaces. These spaces need not be dedicated to the task of conversation alone: from comic strips (such as Dilbert), to magazines (such as Slate), to auction houses (such as eBay), online discussion groups have been an important part of the page. And when the conversation is well-integrated into a site that provides other services, the discussion and the content can build on each other.

One of the earliest online systems was Usenet news. Although the infrastructure has changed since the mid-1980s, the concept has remained the same: messages are organized into topics and shared between severs. The first few tentative groups of two decades ago have since expanded to tens of thousands, with millions of users. They have had two decades to evolve complex mechanisms for debate, for self-government, and for social awareness (Smith, this volume; Pfaffenberger, this volume). Since the mid-1980s, basic email protocols have also allowed users to send messages to a canned list of recipients all at once. Distributed in 1986, the LISTSERV system allowed automated maintenance of mailing lists – users could subscribe and remove themselves (Thomas, 1996). Before then, other manually maintained lists had been a staple of system administrators. With a mailing list, a message sent to a single address – distribution@site.com – would be propagated to dozens, or hundreds, of users. Before the growth of the modern web, Usenet and mailing lists were responsible both for a substantial part of the data flowing across the net, and for a significant part of the information that sites could share.

Pfaffenberger (this volume) expands this history of Usenet, illustrating how the network has grown. His chapter illustrates the way that Usenet has developed, as a series of tensions between different groups trying to control the distribution, growth, and discourse online. This growth is intimately linked to a rhetoric of unconstrained free speech on Usenet and the internet in general. His ideas are important, because every group on Usenet is shaped by its social context as much as the technical means that form it. Even the newest groups, created long after the relevant historical events have passed, are shaped as a result of earlier developments and the prevailing culture of Usenet.

1.2.3 Spaces and Places

For this volume, we discuss asynchronous social information spaces. The notions of "spaces" and "places" have been popular ones in computer design in the last few years. The terms work to help describe what factors change a stream of data into a social encounter that a number of people can share. The movement takes its inspiration from – among other sources – Kevin Lynch's *Image of the City* (1960). Lynch outlined some of the features that make cities memorable. Lynch found that that people remember their boundaries, landmarks, and open spaces. These features are used for wayfinding; for anchoring important events; and as gathering places. For example, there is a long tradition of travellers to New York meeting under the clock of Grand Central Station. The clock is a well-recognized location, and has certain strong associations as a good meeting place. In online spaces, however, there is less opportunity for architecture. Instead, the designers of online communities strive to build online spaces that can be memorable on the basis of their content. Spaces are potentials: open sites that allow future interaction, opportunities for users to contribute and interact.

A collection of information must have several properties in order to be called a space. These properties are borrowed from architecture, and described by Harrison and Dourish (1996). First, and simplest, a space must have some sort of outer border – there must be a way to tell where the space comes to an end. For example, we might count all the discussions on a web site as one space. We would, however, be loath to group together too many sites without a strong unifying theme.

Next, there must be a mechanism for participants to interact with each other. They must be able to leave some mark, to write down words and share them with others. The spaces we discuss do so by allowing participation in conversation. They must also be able to see interactions from others. For online participatory spaces, like multi-user dimensions (MUDs), the analogies are simple – users that are involved in the space can be seen to be there, in the room; they leave behind magic scrolls and notes stapled to the wall and footprints. In a Usenet newsgroup, the terms are subtler: the participants leave behind only messages with their names, which other participants can read.

The texts in this book also emphasize asynchronous sources. A synchronous conversation means that all participants are simultaneously online and in conversation with each other; conversely, an asynchronous space allows individuals to participate at different times, to come in later and see what has changed. Synchronous spaces often do not record their conversations, and can be quite informal. Recent studies (Grinter 2001) have discussed the social conventions that have arisen around these fast-paced spaces. In contrast, asynchronous conversations tend to allow a little more thought and contemplation, and so can be somewhat more formal. It is also hard to know who will see a message – there is no list on the side of current users – so the space may feel less protected. Furthermore, many asynchronous spaces will maintain an archive, so that participants can check in on the history of the recent conversation.

Thus, we limit our space to asynchronous, social information spaces. There is still much territory to explore in these spaces, though; so much so, that it is worth while breaking down some important distinctions between types of spaces.

1.2.4 Usenet News, CoWebs, and This Book

Two of the contemporary information spaces we examine are Usenet news and Wiki webs. They span a spectrum of technologies, and represent differing design philosophies. As such, they are put to different uses, and have different strengths and weaknesses. The former is an old system, and well developed. It has millions of users; its tentacles stretch across the net so that almost every net user can participate in the mass of the system. The latter is a private system, newly established at research and teaching sites. Although it is growing rapidly, it tends to be used for more specialized needs.

Here, we provide a brief overview of each system: who participates, and how; what measures they have of social control; and how those contribution patterns lead to the development of the group in general.

Usenet News

Usenet news, as discussed earlier, is a broadly distributed decentralized bulletin board system. Users can read the collections of existing messages that have made it to their local server, and can then post messages in response. Messages are clustered into newsgroups and are propagated around the world, server to server. There are few guarantees about how soon, if ever, a particular message will arrive at its destination. However, on the whole, the system seems to deliver most messages in a fairly timely way. Usenet has been used for hundreds of purposes: schools set up private newsgroups so students can communicate between classes, and developers share strategies for programming. There are newsgroups dedicated to every conceivable purpose, and each actively discusses a wide variety of topics.

Users who contribute to Usenet can see it from any number of user interfaces. They might log on to a textual interface from a UNIX system, or view it with a current graphical viewer (see Figure 1.1), or even read it from a web-based interface. The boundaries between groups are fairly well drawn: most user interfaces are coordinated toward reading a single group at a time. Because Usenet consists of so many groups, it can be difficult to find discussions of interest. Experienced Usenet users are usually subscribed to a small set of groups, which they check frequently. It is harder to say how new users find groups of interest. Many hear about

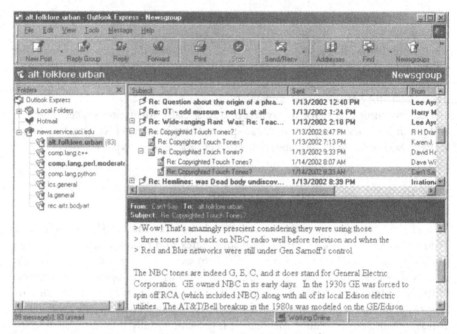

Figure 1.1 A screenshot from a popular Usenet client, Microsoft Outlook Express. Screen shot reprinted by permission from Microsoft Corporation.

groups from friends or web pages; others find their target by guessing names and digging around listings of groups, a strategy that is feasible so long as the user knows what they want to find.

For each group, a user sees a list of all the messages in groups. In most viewers, the messages are threaded: the user can see how a message relates to others with the same subject line. Some viewers also allow users to search groups for particular messages of interest, by keyword or by name. Messages are presented by their headers; the message itself is usually only shown once the user selects a particular message. Lueg (this volume) has a more thorough discussion of message headers.

Because Usenet is large, and well known, it has had to evolve a number of measures to help keep traffic flow from overwhelming groups. For example, some advertisers have found it to their advantage to "spam" newsgroups, i.e. to send identical advertising messages repeatedly to dozens or hundreds of groups. Group members who do not want their conversation interrupted by advertisements for irrelevant products found this practice undesirable. In response to their irritation, a mechanism known as the cancel message has arisen. Special-purpose scripts comb through the Usenet feed, looking for messages that are repeated too many times to be truly focused on any particular group. They then issue cancel messages, which cue servers to delete the message and its target, leaving the group unsullied. It is worth noting that this solution to the problem, like much of the rest of Usenet, is a decentralized one.

Many Usenet groups use a mechanism known as moderation to control the traffic of posts that can be sent to the group. Moderators are users authorized to approve posts – each message posted to the group must be reviewed before it can be seen by the public. Some studies, (including Whittaker, this volume) show that moderated groups tend to have fewer posts and less interaction, and as such are less prone to overload. On the other hand, the conversation is limited to the scope chosen by the moderator, and the speed of conversation is limited to the moderators' ability to deal with submissions.

Wiki Webs

Wiki webs, or CoWebs, are a newer development. They are an expansion of the tradition of web logs and guest book (illustrated in Figure 1.2). Where guest books allow users to append a few lines to the bottom of a page, Wiki webs offer users powerful control of web pages. Developed in 1994 (Cunningham, 2000), they use a simplified mark-up language that allows pages to be formatted quite easily. Unlike previous systems, they allow participants to create new pages on a web server by merely referring to the new pages; the reference creates the page to which it points. This means that users are not constrained to contributing to a single page; rather, participants have an opportunity to design the space that holds the information as they go. Each page maintains its own history: it tracks what users have created it, and which users have edited it. Using that information, the system is able to display a history of how a page has changed. Readers can review who else has written to a page, and can therefore learn about authors to the space. Wiki webs have proved popular in a number of contexts that call for more local use than Usenet news, and that want more integrated links, or more complex information structures.

Unlike many other spaces, Wiki webs are largely unstructured. There is no limitation to where a user can contribute a few lines, or a page; no structure is imposed merely by contributing earlier or in response to some message. Users choose, on their own, what page gets their contributions; participants are therefore rather free to structure information as they wish. They are unconstrained to a particular hierarchical or associational structure. Annotations can be placed wherever desired; a user can create a whole new web page to explore a related idea. Spaces structured this way also place a lot of responsibility on the contributors. The so-called "first

---

     view   edit attach history home changes search help

Swiki Swiki

Welcome to the Swiki Swiki Swiki Front Page

This is a place to talk about Swiki, also known as CoWeb (for Collaborative Website). Consider this a sandbox to play around with the ideas. You'll find people testing structures here that they use in other Swikis, discussing Swikis, and thinking about what to do with these things. Feel free to edit what you find here, to add to it, to make it useful. You will want to click the "help" button at the top of the page, to find out how to edit things here.

Swiki is a Squeak-based version (see http://squeak.cs.uiuc.edu for more on Squeak) of the WikiWikiWeb invented by Ward Cunningham. Swiki was originally built on top of PWS, the

Figure 1.2 A A page of a Swiki (CoWeb).

writer" problem arises: the first contributor to a conversation is responsible for placing information appropriately, and for organizing the information intuitively. If this is done poorly, there is a later and repeated cost for others to rearrange the space appropriately to reflect their developing needs.

Because users' poorly planned modification can be counterproductive, some Wikis have developed a variety of social controls to ensure that users contribute in an orderly way. A team collaboratively editing a report, for example, might find it useful for everyone to be able to modify the document; on the other hand, a group of readers recording their reviews for a new book, more likely, might not. Some webs, therefore, ask their users to append to the bottom of a page only: to contribute in a well-defined area, and to sign their changes. Others ask users to simply sign their updates at the bottom of the page.

In practice, though, contributors can both add and delete data from the system, providing a lot of leeway for any individual user to make substantial changes. Since each page stores its own history, it is impossible for a malevolent user to destroy old information. Still, future users need to know to go back and look to see what has been changed. Real systems have dealt with this problem in a number of ways. For example, one Wiki web, after an act of vandalism, had a volunteer go back through and restore all the pages that had been damaged.

This is a different sort of damage, not necessarily more or less destructive, than that which happens from pollution of a Usenet group. There are no reported incidents of Wiki spam, as yet, although there is no reason not to believe it will not come in time.

CoWebs are a modification of Wiki webs, re-implemented and enhanced slightly for educational use. One important addition to the original Wiki webs is that all links in a CoWeb document have a reciprocal backward link. These inverted links allow a stronger sense of organization than do traditional one-way hyperlinks. Dieberger (this volume) explores several case studies with CoWebs. The high degree of freedom with CoWebs means that errors can be fixed promptly, and new ideas can be contributed freely. CoWebs have been found to be useful in educational settings, as a place where classmates can share ideas; and in shared workgroups, as a place to gradually build up shared knowledge pools.

1.2.5 Studying Online Spaces, Improving Online Spaces

In tandem with examining spaces, we are also looking to both improve the spaces we have, and to create new spaces that can take these results into account. The remainder of the book examines techniques for allowing introspection and analysis on various levels.

The constraints of social control work somewhat differently for private spaces than they do for public ones. A corporate internal workgroup, for example, may have specialized internal tools for sharing data between group members, and may be more willing to share information about participants. In those groups, it is interesting to examine what factors lead to success for the group-work. For example, Ackerman and Palen (1996) examined the "Zephyr help instance" in a qualitative study of instance records. They investigated the uses that students found for a shared chat system. They found an extensive system of shared social capital and of voluntary contributions, and an awareness of the value of a system. That sort of unity might be more common across more tightly delimited spaces: either shared systems kept within the same organization, or newsgroups kept to a fairly specialized topic. Businesses also make good testbeds for technology: a small workgroup can choose to adopt a piece of software and try it for a limited period. Bradner (this volume) discusses the teamwork implications of BABBLE, a shared semi-synchronous space created and used at a research site. Unlike many of the other systems, BABBLE allows awareness of activity of others around them: users can not only learn who else is logged in, but can examine how active they have been. Bradner finds that the asynchronous aspects of this system allow users to log in periodically to watch activity without saying much; however, the properties of the interface make it clear who is logging in often.

One of the most direct forms of enhancement is to mine the information that is being shared in online groups. For example, a system might make recommendations based on existing articles. Amento et al (this volume) specifically start with recommendations for web pages that are found in social information spaces. Their system, PHOAKS, extracts links from messages in newsgroups, and tallies the recommendations. How many users have suggested a particular link? How recently has the link been referred to in a message? They use uses these minor artefacts, notes left behind by surfers for each other, to generate recommendations for future surfers.

Collaborative filtering is a tool from social navigation: it allows users to examine the reading preferences of other users, and to only read popular and well-liked articles. Miller et al (this volume) describe the GroupLens system, which allows a group to share information with each other on the larger mass of Usenet News. They take advantage of the fact that users like to exchange recommendations, and build a social system that takes advantage of those recommendations. Participants in the system can rate articles that they find of interest; other users get to use their rating information to choose further articles and exchange more recommendations.

Lueg (this volume) also enhances the space he works in. While Miller et al work to relate ratings between users, Lueg instead allows the user to consider knowledge that they have already provided to the system. His notion of "interactive filtering" takes into account ratings on individual articles on a thread when deciding what ranking to give the next article. He takes the opposite extreme of the spectrum with "personalized social navigation", allowing users to see their individual article choices, and to share information about their choices. Each participant in the group is able to see what others thought of this particular topic.

1.3 Important Attributes of Spaces

This discussion of collaboration in Wiki webs and conversations in Usenet news highlights some of the important distinctions between types of spaces. Although not all chapters make explicit reference to these properties, they shape a group in a variety of important ways. This section discusses some of those attributes, and attempts to illustrate how they can affect a group. The attributes we highlight here are:

- access control
- the ability to contribute anonymously
- the ability to connect to offline discussions
- the ability to thread and organize conversations
- the availability of archives.

Groups also seem to have a characteristic pace that shapes conversation. Some of these ideas are adapted from discussions in Preece's *Online Communities* (2000), which explores many of these issues.

The first attribute is access control, the ability to decide who can contribute to and read from a space. How, in other words, do messages make it into the space, and who can see them there? This has important implications for quality, for the freedom and openness of conversations, and for privacy. Most Usenet newsgroups allow anyone to post to the group although, as discussed earlier, a few have a moderation system requiring posts to be approved. Most Usenet groups allow anyone to read them; however, there are many local and regional groups that are not distributed out of their local region. Therefore, a reader needs to be logged into a machine in, say, Germany to read the local German de.* newsgroups. Many mailing lists have a subscription policy, limiting who can join the list; most then allow only participation from subscribers. On the other hand, some then archive their results to a web page, where anyone can read the old conversation.

A related issue is whether it is possible to be anonymous, either when contributing to the group or when reading its messages. Anonymity allows freedom to speak about anything, but also removes many of the inhibitions associated with accountable speech. The freedom to speak without consequences allows both whistle-blowing and slander. The web sites Fucked Company and The Vault, for example, have wrestled with this, as the free flowing conversation about the deaths of dot-coms has led to public releases of internal memos and trade secrets by disgruntled employees. Angered employers have attempted to force the online boards to release information about who leaked confidential memos; the boards have responded that they don't have any information about their contributors.

Reading anonymously is more common: it is difficult to monitor the readers of a newsgroup. Some discussion groups report the list of subscribed users; others don't even allow that. Preece and Nonnecke (this volume), discuss the presence of "lurkers" on discussion lists: these are users who read the list often, but do not contribute to the main conversation. These silent readers are important to the continuation of groups, by propagating ideas from the group to other contexts, and by communicating out of the group with members of the group. For the latter to happen, though, it must be possible to learn the source of a message so it can be the destination of a responding message. This is not possible in all online spaces; it is worth considering what it means for that quiet community to be unable to send their side-messages. Would the community lose the benefit of the lurkers' insights, or would more lurkers change into participants?

Threading is an attribute of both the user interface and the group. Threading – the ability to view messages segregated by discussion topic, organized as responses to each other – is a key step in organizing lists. It requires infrastructure on the part of the group's server to track responses; it is also an attribute of the user interface, as not all systems portray threaded conversation. In a threaded conversation, each message is seen as either the head of a tree, or is a continuation of a conversation. A threaded interface, then, allows users to see messages in context, knowing to which message each subsequent message is a response. For example, the screen shot in Figure 1.1 shows the headers of a conversation stretched out into a thread.

The ability to search current messages and archives in groups deserves special mention. Groups that are searchable allow a special degree of introspection: users can search through the archives to find out if a question has been asked before, and can avoid redundant discussions. They can also review a speaker's previous comments, and decide whether they trust that writer. On the other hand, archiving also places contributors into a fixed position in an inevitable history: an archived group cannot forget regrettable incidents and outbursts. Some groups are archived from the start and make themselves publicly open, but others only create archives later in their lifecycle. This "outing" can be shocking for participants who many not have expected to be public participants. In 1995, for example, Deja News made available a several-year archive of Usenet news messages, and allowed a wide-scale search of current messages. In 2001, Google completed the archive, and now provides access to messages as far back as 1981. Many posters were chagrined to discover messages they had written many years ago coming back to haunt them. Their formerly private space was now globally searchable through a convenient web interface.

The experience of entering a space that may be archived can be daunting for a new user. The user must face crowds with established protocols, knowing that their words may be searchable for all time. Even as some contributors may write (to their later regret), others will pause, and consider: is it worth contributing to an old conversation with a new idea? Will a note contributed to a new conversation be seen as interesting, or will it be an accidental retread of many years' writing? Many groups' FAQs ask new users to refrain from posting for a few weeks, until they have read some of the conversation and are familiar with the terms of debate. (One of the editors of this volume once observed a flame war – a heated exchange of insults – in a group, in which various members of the group tried to prove that they had waited the longest before posting for the first time.)

Many groups seem to have a characteristic pace that varies both with the group, and with the current conversational topics. Although there is little or no research into the speed of asynchronous conversations, pace is a relevant implicit aspect of groups. How often should a user be expected to check the web site, to read email, or to log into the newsgroup in order to keep up with the current discussions? Sometimes, of course, near-real-time discussions occur – such as groups discussing up-to-the-minute news reports, sometimes from on-sites; many others are far slower. Jones' work (Jones et al, 2002) has suggested that participation in a group is related to the number of participants and the number of messages that each participant contributes. It is plausible that the pace of conversations also affects the size of the group: a great many contributors may overwhelm a slow-paced group.

There are other attributes important to an online space, attributes of social convention as well as of technological design. Different degrees of introspection are available through visualization tools, and users may have varying degrees of privilege or ability to modify the group's conversation. This complex interplay of tools can change the feel of a group, and can profoundly affect the groups' interactions.

Any researcher hoping to approach these issues should have some understanding of how they play out technically: what mechanisms make them possible? How are messages stored, and propagated? What parts of a message are reliable, and what is easily forged? The appendix to this volume (Fisher and Lueg) walks through a brief introduction to the technical aspects of these social spaces.

1.4 Conclusion

Online social spaces are an increasingly interesting area to explore. They are active conversations in their own rights and in their connections to the outside world. There are real challenges to decoding the subtle social signals in online information spaces. Without message threads – a basic tool common to newsreaders, but still unusual in mail tools (Smith, 2000) – it can be hard determine what a message is responding to, much less to understand the pattern of communication.

A variety of tools, both quantitative and qualitative, are being developed to understand who is participating in groups and sharing information. Through this volume, we hope to introduce and explore some ideas for examining and studying Usenet groups, and their successor technologies. Our contributors show a variety of perspectives into the ways that groups can be examined and enhanced, and pave the way for many future studies. Our hope is that we can learn to understand more about both online conversation, and its live counterparts

Acknowledgements

I am grateful for the extensive comments, revisions, and encouragement from Paul Dourish, Dan Glaser, Christopher Lueg, Katy Farber, Nora Williams and Michelle Moore.

References

Ackerman, M. and Palen, L. (1996) The Zephyr Help Instance: Promoting Ongoing Activity in a CSCW System. Proceedings of ACM CHI 96 Conference on Human Factors in Computing Systems v.1 p.268–275.

Alexander, C., Ishikawa, S., Silverstein, M., Jacobson, M., Fiksdahl-King, I. and Angel S., A Pattern Language. Oxford University Press, 1977.

Baym, N. Interpreting Soap Operas and Creating Community: Inside a Computer-Mediated Fan Culture. Journal of Folklore Research, 30, 143–176, 1993.

Churchill, E. , Trevor, J., Bly, S., Nelson, L., and Cubranic, D,. Anchored conversations. Proceedings of the CHI 2000 conference on Human factors in computing systems April 2000.

Cunningham, W. (1998). The wiki wiki web. Viewed online at http://c2.com/ cgi/wiki?WikiWikiWeb.

Dodge, M. and Kitchin, R. (2001).Mapping Cyberspace. Routledge: New York.

Donath, J., Karahalios, K., and Viégas, F (1999). "Visualizing Conversation." Paper presented at the Hawaii International Conference on Systems Science, HICSS-32, January 1999, Hawaii.

Erickson, T., Smith, D., Kellogg, W., Laff, M., Richards, J., Bradner, E. (1999). Socially Translucent Systems. Proceeding of the CHI 99 Conference on Human Factors in Computing Systems. v.1 p.72–79.

Gibson, D.R. (1999) Taking Turns and Talking Ties: Conversational Sequences in Business Meetings. PhD thesis, Sociology Department, Columbia University, New York.

Goffman, E. (1961). The Presentation of Self in Everyday Life. New York: Anchor-Doubleday.

Harrison, S. and Dourish, P. (1996). Re-Place-ing Space: The Roles of Place and Space in Collaborative Systems. Proceedings of ACM CSCW'96 Conference on Computer-Supported Cooperative Work p.67–76.

Kiesler, S, Siegel, J. and McGuire, T. (1984). Social psychological aspects of computer-mediated communication. American Psychologist, 39 (10): 1123–1134.

Jones, Q., Ravid, G., and Rafaeli, S. (2002) An Empirical Exploration of Mass Interaction System Dynamics: Individual Information Overload and Usenet Discourse. Paper presented at the Hawaii International Conference on Systems Science, HICSS-35, January 2002, Hawaii.

Thomas, E. (1996) "The History of LISTSERV." Retrieved December, 2001 from http://www.lsoft.com/products/listserv-history.asp.

Jung, Y., Lee, A. (2000). Design of a social interaction environment for electronic marketplaces. Proceedings of DIS'00: Designing Interactive Systems: Processes, Practices, Methods, and Techniques 2000 p.129–136.

Lynch, K. (1960) "The Image of the City." MIT Press: Cambridge, Mass.

Munro, Alan J.; Kristina Hook, David Benyon, ed (1999). Social navigation of information space. London: Springer.

O'Day, V. Bobrow, D., and Shirley, M. The social-technical design circle. Proceedings of ACM CSCW'96 Conference on Computer-Supported Cooperative Work p.160–169.

Paolillo, J. (2002). Democratic Participation in the Discursive Management of Usenet. Paper presented at the Hawaii International Conference on Systems Science, HICSS-35, January 2002, Hawaii.

Preece, J (2000). "Online Communities: Designing Usability, Supporting Sociability." London: Wiley.

Rohall, S., Gruen, D., Moody, P., and Kellerman, S. Email Visualizations to Aid Communications. IEEE Symposium on Information Visualization. San Diego, California.

Sharf, B. (1999) "Beyond Netiquette: The Ethics of Doing Naturalistic Discourse Research on the Internet" in Steve Jones, editor, Doing Internet Research: Critical Issues and Methods for Examining the Net. London: Sage, 1999.

Smith, M., Fiore, A. (2001). Visualization components for persistent conversations. Proceedings of ACM CHI 2001 Conference on Human Factors in Computing Systems 2001 p.136–143.

Smith, M and Kollock, P. (Eds) (1999). "Communities in Cyberspace." London: Routledge.

Turkle, S. (1995). "Life on the Screen". New York: Simon and Schuster.

Wellman, B., and Gulia, M. (1999). Net surfers don't ride alone: Virtual communities as communities. In M.A. Smith and P. Kollock (Eds.), Communities in cyberspace (pp. 167–194). London: Routledge.

Chapter 2

"A Standing Wave in the Web of Our Communications": Usenet and the Socio-Technical Construction of Cyberspace Values

Bryan Pfaffenberger

Author's note: This essay is dedicated to the memory of Usenet pioneer Jim Ellis, who passed away in June 2001 after a battle with non-Hodgkin's lymphoma.

2.1 Introduction

Of all Internet services, Usenet (Salzberg, 1998; Spencer, 1998) is probably the least understood and – arguably – the most intriguing. Often confused or conflated with the Internet and predating the Web by more than a decade, Usenet is a logical network that employs the Internet and other physical networks as transport mechanisms. The network is internally structured into tens of thousands of topically organized forums, called newsgroups. Like electronic mail, Usenet is asynchronous; messages and replies to messages do not appear immediately. Usenet is designed so that a message, once posted to a local service, propagates through the network so that all or most servers soon contain a copy, but this process may take several hours to complete. The result is an active deliberative system of global reach and undeniable importance. Usenet cannot be ignored by anyone attempting to understand the nature of social information spaces.

Still, comparatively few scholars have grappled with Usenet. In retrospect, this fact is hardly surprising; the network's diversity defies generalization, and the huge amounts of data generated daily – as much as 100 gigabytes – make the network exceptionally difficult to study. One gets the feeling, as Usenet participants themselves say, that any assertion made concerning Usenet is bound to be proven false – including, they add, the one just made. Typically, observers tend to study just one or two newsgroups rather than taking on the whole network. Nevertheless, scholars and participants often observe that Usenet, though it is riven with disagreement on virtually everything else, possesses its own, unique political culture. This political culture is evident from semi-official documents, online and written commentaries by Usenet veterans, and the informal social controls that characterize thriving newsgroups. It can be defined as a set of core propositions:

- Usenet cannot be regulated by governmental power. Thanks to Usenet's distributed, anonymous technology and multinational presence, governments will find it difficult, or impossible, to regulate Usenet.
- Usenet can successfully self-regulate. To the extent that Usenet needs control, it must be grounded in consensus and sanctions that punish only those actions that threaten the network's ability to function as a forum for deliberative debate. Government intervention should be fiercely resisted, lest it prevent this experiment in self-regulation from evolving to its logical conclusion.
- Usenet is dying (or dead). Although continued efforts to save and defend Usenet are valuable, the quality of today's discussion is but a pale reminder of a past Golden Age.

The fact that these propositions are internally self-contradictory is of little consequence to Usenet aficionados; for example, if Usenet is unregulable, why should the network need protection from regulation? If Usenet is dying, why should it be protected so that it can evolve? These propositions more closely resemble myths than logical propositions; myths, after all, are retained even if they are obviously contradicted by facts or internal inconsistencies.

Where did these propositions come from? Clearly, some of these propositions stem from the Libertarianism that has long typified Usenet participants, but others – "Usenet is unregulable" and "Usenet is dying" – cannot be so easily attributed to external influences. The origin of these propositions is best found, it appears, in Usenet itself.

Recent scholarship provides valuable clues pointing to Usenet's capacity to repeatedly generate its own, distinctive culture, one that emerges from patterned, online interaction. Because newsgroups cannot function unless new participants are socialized to conform to the rules of proper online comportment, called netiquette (Shea, 1994; Templeton, 1995), individual participants must reshape their identities and learn new interactive strategies, including selecting the appropriate degree of self-disclosure (Pritchard, 1999) and learning how to convey group-specific, highly codified cues (Baym, 1998). To provide an effective forum for deliberative debate, the newsgroup must collectively adapt to the specific challenges posed by the nature of its topic (Baym, 1995), define boundaries (David, 1996), and sanction disruptive participants (Gardinali, 1996). The result is that individual newsgroups generate both the overall contours of Usenet political culture and also cultural themes that are newsgroup-specific (Baym, 1995, 1996, 1998).

These studies have made an important contribution to the understanding of Usenet's political culture, but they omit an important but hidden component: the small percentage of Usenet participants who are capable of using technical measures to accomplish their goals, whether they be despotic or benign. Included in this category are Usenet's system administrators. Usenet is not an ethereal vibration that emanates from the void; physically, it consists of tens of thousands of servers as well as the network protocols (communication standards) that enable these servers to communicate with each other and propagate messages throughout the network. Each of these servers is managed by a person, most likely an employee of an Internet service provider, a university, or some other organization. Within their domains, they can do whatever they wish, including deleting unwanted news-groups; moreover, they can and do communicate with one another to deal with Usenet's crises and formulate general principles of administrative policy. Also included are hackers, the more knowledgeable of whom quickly learn how to issue the administrative commands that system administrators use.

As this chapter will illustrate, much of Usenet's political culture – the mythic propositions that form a "standing wave in the web of our communications", as John Perry Barlowe put it so poetically – makes sense only when placed into a broader context than most sociologists and psychologists envision. In this broader context, which takes technological modes of agency into account rather than viewing technology as a passive vehicle through which social relations occur, people are seen to appropriate, modify, and deploy technological measures as well as opinion and argument in support of their goals (Bijker, Hughes et al, 1987; Latour, 1987). For Usenet, what this perspective reveals is a long, passionate strug-gle, one that is far from concluded, concerning who will control Usenet, and how such control will be achieved.

2.2 Usenet Origins

Usenet dates to the 1979 insights of two Duke University graduate students, Tom Truscott and Jim Ellis (Hauben, Hauben et al, 1998; Abbate, 1999). In those days, UNIX users faced the often monumental task of installing, configuring, and main-taining the complex UNIX operating system all on their own, because AT&T – kept out of the computer business by an Federal court's antitrust ruling – did not doc-ument or support the software. Universities with Department of Defense contracts could share information about UNIX by means of the fledgling ARPANET, the ancestor of today's Internet, but access to ARPANET was denied to schools that did not have DoD contracts.

It was in this context that Truscott, Ellis, or one of their assistants experienced a flash of insight (none of the participants recalls who thought of it first). Various ele-ments of the UNIX system, already in existence, could be cobbled together to create a totally new kind of information system. These elements included the following:

- **Shell scripts:** A means of creating a program using simple text instructions. One of the great virtues of UNIX is its many software tools, which can be linked by scripts to perform processing tasks.
- **UNIX-to-UNIX Copy Program (UUCP):** A program that enabled UNIX users to exchange files by means of modems and telephone connections.
- **Find command:** A UNIX file-locating program that is capable of retrieving only those files created or modified after a specified date.
- **Autodial modems:** A serial communication device that enables computers to exchange data over the telephone, and dials a telephone number under the direction of a computer program.

- **Computer-based discussion groups:** Housed on a single computer, these consist of a series of electronic mail messages that are all focused on a single topic.

Gregory G. Woodbury, a Duke University computer science graduate student who joined the development team subsequently, notes that "The 'genius' of netnews was to see that the shell, the find command, and UUCP would allow categorized news discussions to be shared between machines that were only connected by a serial line".

The netnews software, as it was called in Usenet's early years, works in the following way. Under the script's direction, one computer calls a second computer, and a portion of the script called checknews examines the second computer's file directories to see whether they contain any new or newly updated files. If so, these are downloaded so that they are copied to the first computer's file directories. As additional computers join the network and employ the checknews program on the nearest computer's file directories, copies of all new or newly updated files will eventually propagate throughout the network, so that a copy of each file is present on each computer. This is what is meant by calling Usenet a distributed bulletin board system: it distributes copies of each new contribution throughout the network. In contrast to a local bulletin board system, each non-local discussion group would consist of messages and replies that originate from here and there throughout the entire network.

Recognizing that the potential adopters of Usenet would need to migrate from the known to the unknown, Truscott and Ellis decided that the Usenet software would enable local discussion groups as well as non-local ones. There was some debate among the development team, which by 1981 included a University of North Carolina programmer named Steve Bellovin, about the number of non-local groups that would be required. Bellovin thought that most users would prefer the local groups, and that only one non-local group, called net.general, would suffice. Ellis urged the team to see that the system's true innovation was the non-local groups, and that once they caught on, a means for categorizing them by subject would be needed (Bellovin, 1990). Still, Ellis recognized that local groups would be necessary to handle information that was of only local interest, as was proven decisively by a famous mid-1980s post, originating in New Jersey and titled "Dinette Set for Sale", which appeared as far away as Australia.

The Usenet pioneers first conceptualized Usenet as a UNIX user's network, a supra-local colloquium for "UNIX wizards", which would provide a forum for sharing hard-to-get information regarding the installation, configuration, and maintenance of UNIX. According to a January 1980 presentation at Usenix, a UNIX users and administrators' conference (recounted in Hauben, 1993), the network would consist of several "rapid access newsletters", organized by topic. Truscott and Ellis thought that the first newsgroups would be concerned with UNIX "bug fixes, trouble fixes, and general cries for help", but that additional newsgroups would surely be created to handle new categories of information (such as "have/want" articles). In addition to posting articles, the newsletter software also provided a means for newsgroup participants to reply to posted articles, either by posting a follow-up message, in which the original post's text was echoed, or by sending private electronic mail to the person who wrote the original post.

Truscott and Ellis' presentation of Usenet at the 1980 Usenix conference caused a sensation. They had made 80 copies of their text-based handout describing Usenet, but 400 people showed up to their session. Radically rejecting the committee mentality of academic organizations, Truscott and Ellis urged their audience to get hooked up to the network first and argue about it later. In truth, the code was not fully debugged.

2.3 The Poor Man's ARPANET

In its beginnings, Usenet's creators saw the network as a bottom-up proposition, a bid by the computer have-nots to remedy the inequities in the distribution of computer tools and resources. At the summer 1980 Usenix conference held in Delaware, Truscott and Daniel distributed tapes of the A News software. In announcing the software's availability, Daniel, then a graduate student, described Usenet as a "poor man's ARPANET", a phrase that, Daniel recalls,

> explained exactly what was going on. We (or at least I) had little idea what was really going on the ARPANET, but we knew we were excluded. Even if we had been allowed to join, there was no way of coming up with the money. It was commonly accepted at the time that to join the ARPANET took political connections and $100,000. I don't know if that assumption was true, but we were so far from having either connections or money that we didn't even try. The "poor man's ARPANET" was our way of joining the computer science community, and we made a deliberate attempt to extend it to other not-well-endowed members of the community (Daniel, 1993)

The sense of bottom-up democracy was built into the software, as Daniel (1993) recalls. "Usenet was organized around netnews, where the receiver controls what is received". To put this another way, from a technical point of view Usenet encourages everybody to say anything, and it's up to the reader to screen out unwanted material.

Usenet grew slowly at first, a fact that Truscott and Ellis attributed to the limited availability and high cost of autodial modems. They themselves built a home-brewed modem for the first successful iteration of the net, which linked a computer at Duke to one at nearby University of North Carolina – significantly, a local phone call away. But it was soon found that the growing net could be funded surreptitiously by including the distribution calls as a normal item in departmental telephone budgets. An early Usenet participant named Mark Horton recalls,

> There was a strong mentality that the main cost was the phone bills, and since nobody saw the phone bills, it was free. In the early days the net was kept alive by a few SA's [system administrators] who followed Grace Murray Hopper's immortal words: "It's much easier to get forgiveness than permission" and just did it (Horton, 1990).

As inexpensive modems became widely available and the knowledge of this funding mechanism became widely known, the network began to grow rapidly – and in an unexpected way. Truscott and Ellis thought that there would be not one but many Usenets, each linking a number of contiguous sites within a local or regional dialling area. As more and more sites were able to sneak the costs of Usenet into departmental telephone accounts, a single, transcontinental network quickly emerged. An early Usenet system administrator, Greg Woodbury, recalls how this development shocked everyone involved:

> I do not recall that anyone was quite expecting the explosion that followed. What developed took everybody by surprise. When the direction of evolution took an unexpected turn, and a continental network emerged ... from California to North Carolina, and Toronto to San Diego, it was sort of a shock to realize what had happened" (Woodbury, 1991).

By 1984, nearly 1000 sites were participating in the rapidly growing network, and it was clear that Truscott, Ellis, and their co-workers had effectively launched an entirely new kind of human communication system.

2.4 "Usenet Is Dying"

With Usenet's rapid, unplanned expansion came a bewildering assortment of scale-up problems, difficulties that were never anticipated when the network served only two or three sites in North Carolina. For example, anticipating only a handful of messages per day, for the system's creators did not foresee the problems that would arise when a daily news feed brought in 15 megabytes of new articles. Disk drives were far more expensive in those days, and this figure seemed likely to bring Usenet under unwelcome scrutiny at sites short on disk space. At many sites, the only way this gargantuan influx could be accommodated was by deleting articles more than a few days old, thus making space for new ones. No one had ever intended Usenet posts to last for ever; the earliest software permitted the user to select an expiration date some weeks or months away, on which systems would erase the post. To cope with the huge influx of postings, though, system administrators were forced to advance expiration dates so that, in some cases, messages would stick around for only a day or two before disappearing into the void: if you didn't read today's news, you might miss the action. It is hardly surprising that one Usenet participant found it apposite to quote Job's lament (9:25): "Now my days are swifter than a post; they flee away, they see no good" (Murakami, 1989)

But there were even more serious problems. From the standpoint of Usenet system administrators, the network's congenial egalitarianism had scaled up to anarchy; for example, sites ran various incompatible versions of the netnews software, causing problems for newsgroup distribution and naming. Was Usenet growing itself to death, like a weed sprayed with 2,4–D? Opening a 1985 mailing list devoted to discussion of Usenet's scale-up problems, Gene Spafford summed up the situation in the following dire terms:

> Basically, the Usenet is dying. It has a had a long and fruitful life, especially considering how it came about and grew to its present form (not bad for some former shell files, eh?), but its lifetime is limited. Maybe Usenet has another year of functionality left. Maybe two at the outside (Spafford, 1985).

Spafford's assertion was by no means the first in a long series of predictions of Usenet's impending demise, but the network has outlived such predictions and proceeded to grow and, in some areas, to thrive. Irony born of these frequently refuted assertions of impending death lead Usenet regulars to sum up the entire matter with a sarcastic phrase: "Usenet is dead; film at 11".

Spafford was quite convinced, however, that the network's death was near. One of the most serious problems, Spafford argued, was the lack of control in the newsgroup-creation process. From a technical standpoint, any site administrator – or, indeed, any technically knowledgeable UNIX user – could create a new newsgroup by issuing the appropriate UNIX control command – but there was no guarantee that other sites would carry the group. In the same way, newsgroups could be removed from a site by issuing another control command. In the days when a handful of sites were involved, the newsgroup creation and removal process was a matter of congenial cooperation, but by 1985 those days were gone. In its place, Spafford lamented, there was now a pattern of "strife and hostility" (Spafford, 1985). Some of the strife arose from the growing volume of newsgroups, which forced some site administrators to delete newsgroups unilaterally.

In an attempt to rein in the newsgroup creation process, Spafford had voluntarily begun the arduous task of publishing a monthly list of "officially recognized" newsgroups, a task he continue until 1993. The list, not an official document but rather a kind of advisory newsletter, listed only those groups that had been created by orthodox methods and contained appropriate content.

Newsgroups were not only breeding promiscuously; even worse, they were straying from the network's original intention – namely, to provide support for UNIX system users. Many of the newer groups had nothing to do with UNIX, nor even with computers, but concerned themselves with hobbies, games, recreation, entertainment, sports, and literature. Such a development was not so surprising; after all, one of the most popular of ARPANET's mailing lists was concerned with science fiction. Remembering Hopper's "immortal words", system administrators allowed such groups to flourish, but they worried. After all, the machines on which Usenet depended were owned by corporations and universities, not by Usenet participants. In virtually all cases, the use of such machines is governed by regulations that restrict usage to tasks connected with the organization's mission, which presumably does not include storing several thousand messages about the television series *Star Trek*.

It was not long before proposals surfaced to create newsgroups pertaining to topics far more controversial than mountain climbing or science fiction. In 1982, an online argument – mild by contemporary standards – broke out in net.singles regarding same-sex dating, so a proposal was brought forward for a new newsgroup to be called net.gay. Such proposals placed system administrators in an awkward position; on the one hand, they sympathized with the need for reasoned public discourse on such issues, but on the other, they feared that management might pull the plug if it was learned how the organization's computer resources were being utilized. Spafford recalls, "Many people could just imagine: 'Searching for new groups. Add net.gay? [yn]' popping up on their manager's screen" (Spafford, 1990). If a crucial, centrally located site were to be shut down, it could kill the whole network. The compromise reached was to call the group net.motss, after the U.S. Census Bureau's euphemistic "members of the same sex" designation on 1980 Census returns. People on the net would know what "motss" meant, but outsiders wouldn't have a clue (Horton, 1990).

From the standpoint of system administrators, Usenet's worst problem lay in the attitudes of users themselves, who seemed to regard the network as a right rather than a privilege. System administrators knew only too well that Usenet used computers and telephones owned by corporations and universities; there is no constitutional right to free speech using someone else's printing press (or computer). From the user's standpoint, this was a mere technicality to be dismissed with a wave of the hand; what was emerging was a global medium for totally free expression. Epitomizing their attitude is the following quotation from Jake Zeitlin, published – appropriately enough – in a recent Usenet document entitled "How to Receive Banned Newsgroups":

> I cannot convince myself that there is anyone so wise, so universally comprehensive in his judgment, that he can be trusted with the power to tell others: "You shall not express yourself thus, you shall not describe your own experiences; or depict the fantasies which your mind has created; or laugh at what others set up as respectable; or question old beliefs; or contradict the dogmas of the church, of our society, our economic systems, and our political orthodoxy" (Gebis, 1994).

Increasingly, free-speech-minded users saw Usenet as a right, not a privilege, and deeply resented any attempt by system administrators to impose order on the network's growing anarchy. The mentality, as one system administrator described it, was, "If I want it it's okay" (Von Rospach, 1990).

The more aggressive adherents of this position were determined to force the issue, posting whatever they pleased, with no regard for the problems they were causing for system administrators. But system administrators feared that the ethnic and racist jokes, foul obscenities, and controversial topics could sink the network; already, in 1983 or 1984, as one long-time Usenet participant recollected, a major West Coast oil firm had dropped its Usenet feed "because some joke with racial content was posted, and someone internal to the company filed an affirmative action complaint about it"(Spafford, 1993).

Not only did technically knowledgeable users create new, controversial newsgroups willy nilly, they also freely indulged themselves in provocative speech, obscenities, and name-calling, causing too many newsgroups to degenerate into the entirely undesirable phenomenon that came to be known as a flame war (Dery, 1993; Simpson and Stoner, 1997). A good, solid flame war could consume an entire newsgroup's postings for a period of months or more, generating much more heat than light. A flame war often began with flame bait, a post that seems deliberately designed to engender hysterical reactions A choice example, from a notorious (male) poster:

> It is important to recognize that the undiminished pronouns males have historically attempted to reserve exclusively to themselves, are connected, in the minds of many men, to the pronouns they used to refer to their male deities. Even when not capitalized, many men believe that an undiminished pronoun is not merely a

title of honour and respect, but actually a term of deification... It was not respect for American women that had male doctors strapping women to stretchers on their backs with their legs spread and their hands tied down. It was to slow the birth process, make it more difficult and painful, and give the doctor more ability to schedule it so as not to interfere with his golf game. And to anyone who is about to flame me for offending men in this group by expressing my anger, go right ahead. Somebody has to defend the rapists, incestuous fathers, abandoners, batterers, non-payers of child support, discriminatory employers, harassing co-workers, and other bums, why not you?

For Usenet "old-timers" – we're only talking about 5 years here – the licentious behaviour of the new wave of hot-tempered users stood in sad contrast to the resource sharing, congeniality, and mutual support that marked the network's early days.

Anyone trying to impose order on Usenet quickly learned that there was a stiff price involved: vicious opposition, manifesting in a mailbox full of angry and even threatening email as well as vilifying personal attacks in Usenet newsgroups. In 1983, for example, Chuq Von Rospach expressed the opinion that net.wobegon, a newsgroup founded to discuss Garrison Keiler's *Prairie Home Companion*, should be removed because it had been inactive for some time. Von Rospach still feels the flames:

> The net.wobegon people were vicious. Absolutely and totally nasty. One of their arguments, which echoes stuff you still hear today, was they didn't need to use the group, they just wanted it to exist so they knew they were important. Man, no asbestos in the world could have saved me from this flame war. I was crisped, and to this day I still cringe when I think of it. I don't think I've ever seen a flamefest quite that nasty – and I've been part of many of the worst (Von Rospach, 1991).

In his call for change, Spafford lamented, "Posters are becoming ruder, maliciousness abounds, and the general response to everything is "just try to make me do it" (Spafford, 1985). By 1985 there were even threats of what amounts to electronic terrorism. For example, Spafford started a private mailing list concerning a successor network called Usenet II that would (among other things) provide for better centralized control, but within days of its inception word leaked out. Lauren Weinstein, a Usenet system administrator and one of the recipients of the list, warned darkly, "I've gotten messages from people who have threatened to do everything in their power to WRECK both Usenet and the mail network if restrictions are put in" (Weinstein, 1985).

2.5 The "Backbone Cabal"

At the same time that Usenet users ferociously asserted their perceived right to do whatever they wished on the network, system administrators came to understand that the network's technical evolution had given them the means to impose order and discipline. To understand the power they possessed, recall how Usenet works with UUCP dialup transfers: to get the news, a given computer calls the nearest computer that belongs to the net, and receives the news (this is called a news feed).

That second computer has obtained the news from another nearby computer, and so on. But what happens if a system administrator somewhere along the way doesn't like one of the newsgroups, and refuses to make it available? Any computer getting its feed from this machine will find that that it has experienced a form of censorship by default. In short, it soon became apparent that downstream sites – sites positioned at or near the end of the chain of feeds – were inherently less privileged than upstream sites. Accentuating the upstream/downstream inequity was the emergence of well-funded sites providing feeds to multiple downstream sites, which would have no other way of obtaining the news.

In an attempt to conceptualize the hierarchical structure that was emerging, Usenet system administrators employed the term "backbone site". Such a site provided feeds for two or more downstream sites (in other words, it functioned as a hub), or served as a single point of entry for a series of sites in a defined geographical area (such as Australia).

By 1984, then, an essentially hierarchical structure had been grafted to an egalitarian information system, creating the type of contradiction that sorely tempts one to start quoting Marx. For Usenet, though, history was going backwards: the system's initial democracy and egalitarianism had been replaced by a feudal structure, in which system administrators deliberately, if self-mockingly, referred to themselves as "barons" (and to users as "serfs"). The barons, lords of the large UNIX backbone systems, knew that they could do whatever they pleased, and nobody at any other site, and certainly no user, could force them to alter their decisions. They could carry newsgroups, or not carry them; they could give you a UNIX account, or take it away; they could delete controversial newsgroups in favour of just the ones carrying UNIX-related information. Becoming conscious of themselves as a class, the system administrators of the key backbone sites began working closely together, reaching consensus on the key issues confronting the network. This group, later to be known derisively as the "Backbone Cabal", chose to flex its muscles in a now-mythic political implosion called "The Great Renaming" (Bumgarner, 1995).

2.6 The "Great Renaming"

By 1985, system administrators became increasingly concerned about the proliferation of newsgroups; predictions had been rife about the "imminent death of the Net" by self-strangulation. The proximate problem was the "flat" newsgroup naming system. With all the newsgroups beginning with the single prefix net, the system of Usenet nomenclature could not handle a burgeoning Usenet with thousands of newsgroups. Various proposals had been made to use a hierarchical naming system with additional naming levels, which would both organize newsgroup categories and enable the proliferation of additional newsgroups: in place of net.culture, one could have net.culture.greek, net.culture.japanese, net.culture.celtic, and so on. In other words, newsgroups could be classified into categories called hierarchies, within which their names could be organized in a logical way. At a 1986 meeting of Usenet system administrators held at Usenix, all but three of those in attendance agreed that a new newsgroup naming system was needed (Adams, 1987).

Obvious to almost any Usenet participant was the fact that change was needed. What began to disturb many users, however, was the apparent desire by the Backbone Cabal to relegate all the controversial newsgroups to a hierarchy called net.flame – and for obvious reasons. In UNIX, you can delete a whole hierarchy of newsgroups immediately simply by issuing a command that includes a wildcard symbol; users feared that system administrators would not tarry long to use the rmgroup net.flame.* command, which would consign the controversial newsgroups to oblivion (Bellovin, 1990). Such fears launched a struggle to keep certain groups out of the flame category (subsequently talk), because everyone knew that these groups – dubbed "pariah groups" by one system administrator (Von Rospach, 1991) – would be the first to go. The resulting flame wars consumed a great deal of Usenet's bandwidth, but by 1987 the renaming had taken place. The result was the creation of the standard newsgroup hierarchies: comp, misc, news, rec, sci, soc, and talk. Predictably, many sites – particularly corporate sites – dropped the talk hierarchy.

As the renaming took place, it became apparent that there was a need for a better system to control the creation and naming of newsgroups. As system administrators had learned only too well, however, any hint of the imposition of central control was likely to be greeted by user hysteria, flames, and sabotage threats; no system administrator wanted to wind up on the wrong end of a flame war such as the net.wobegon controversy. The solution was elegant, if somewhat disingenuous: a voting procedure, which would provide at least some appearance of democratic participation, even though most system administrators had no intention of considering its votes to be binding. In this procedure, still in place, the creation of a new newsgroup required an orderly procedure of discussion and voting; a person who wished to create a new standard newsgroup posts a request for discussion in a newsgroup devoted to this purpose. In the discussion, users and system administrators debate the need for the newsgroup, and the logic of its name in relation to other, existing newsgroups. At the end of the discussion period, the proposal might be withdrawn, or put to a vote. To be created, the new group would have to receive at least 100 positive votes, but just as significantly, no more than 100 negative votes. The latter measure was obviously designed to permit system administrators, numbering far in excess of 100, to exercise veto power. As one system administrator was to recall, the voting procedure was deliberately designed to obstruct the creation of unwanted newsgroups in such a way that system administrators wouldn't have to take the heat:

> The function of the group voting process is to PREVENT the formation of newsgroups – newsgroups with poorly chosen names, newsgroups that won't be read at most sites, newsgroups with that are for some reason inappropriate ... If the [vote] is "no", then the news administrator can simply tell users, "sorry, it didn't pass, you're out of luck, it's not my fault" (Mack, 1991)

Notwithstanding the apparent intent to obstruct the creation of unwanted newsgroups, the advocates of "anything goes" managed to get two "undesirable" newsgroups past the voting procedure: rec.sex and comp.protocols.tcp-ip.eniac. (Eniac, built in 1947, did not support network protocols such as TCP-IP – a joke that would be familiar to most system administrators, if confusing to users). In both cases, the voting procedures for rec.sex were carried out to perfection. But the proponents of these groups were in for a surprise: system administrators flatly refused to carry them (Salzenberg, 1991). The flame war that resulted was prodigious and bitter, and with it came a forthright statement that system administrators did not consider themselves to be bound by the voting procedure's outcome. In a 1988 post, Gene Spafford stated flatly,

> There is "NOTHING" that anyone can do to force a site to carry a group. If 500 people or 50000 people send in votes for a group, that doesn't mean it will be carried by a majority of sites. Thus, groups like "soc.sex" and "net.rec.drugs" that could cause difficulties will likely not be carried by many major sites because their admins don't believe them appropriate (Spafford, 1988).

Spafford continued by pointing out that he would use his list of official newsgroups as a means of enforcing discipline on the network:

> If a [voted-in] group is not going to be carried by a significant percentage of sites, I don't include it in my list-of-lists because that is misleading to people at sites where the group is not received. The backbone is a representative group of experienced system admins and what they carry and their concerns serve as a good indicator of the likelihood of a group being carried. 3/4 of the backbone won't ever carry anything like soc.sex, no matter what the vote, so it will not be in the list-of-lists (Spafford, 1988).

Spafford was later to recant these strong words, admitting that during the heyday and aftermath of the Backbone Cabal he was under the "delusion" that his list was official. He later described his list as an advisory newsletter. But this is perhaps disingenuous; the list was more than a newsletter. A program called check-groups checks the current newsgroup list against the "official" list – the "advisory list", if you prefer – and determines whether a given newsgroup is properly sanctioned or "bogus" (not on the list). Most newsreaders, as well as site administration software, automatically detects and provides the option to delete bogus newsgroups.

There were two outcomes of the soc.sex flame wars: the rapid growth of the alt hierarchy and the abdication of the Backbone Cabal, who had grown weary of being on the wrong end of flames and mailbombs. Not part of the standard newsgroup hierarchies, the alt newsgroup hierarchy, created in 1986, was developed by Usenet participants who felt that the standard hierarchies were too constrained. Within the alt hierarchy, anyone who knows how to issue the make-group command can create a newsgroup, but there is no assurance that sites will carry it. soc.sex found life as alt.sex, and it quickly became the most popular newsgroup in those sites that carry the alt hierarchy.

The demise of the Backbone Cabal was joined by the demise of the backbone itself. Responsible for this change was the gradual migration of Usenet from UUCP dial-up exchanges to the Internet, thanks to the creation in the mid-1980s of the Network News Transport Protocol (NNTP), which was developed in 1984–85 by Phil Lapsley, Erik Fair, Seven Grady, Mike Meyer, and other Berkeley graduate students (Moraes, 1995). A version of the C news software, which supports NNTP, was released in 1987. NNTP not only transported the news more quickly and more cheaply, but it also made it possible for many sites to obtain feeds from virtually anywhere they liked. A given system administrator might choose to remove certain groups, or even an entire category of groups, but this decision would not affect anyone else; a system administrator could always obtain an NNTP feed elsewhere that stocked the full list of standard and alternative newsgroups.

By late 1987, the backbone had all but disintegrated from a technical angle. In a famous post the same year, the Backbone Cabal "abdicated" power – not because it was forced out, but rather because its members had grown tired of the vociferous opposition they encountered every time they tried to do something good for the network.

2.7 "Usenet Is Not a Democracy"

It was in the foregoing context, then, that Usenet participants debated the meaning of "democracy" as it applied to the complex world of Usenet. In 1991, a system administrator called Chip Salzenberg drafted a document titled "What is Usenet" (Salzenberg, 1991), which was intended to benefit new Usenet users. Salzenberg chose to begin by defining Usenet negatively, and one of his assertions was that "Usenet is not a democracy":

> Usenet has no central authority … In fact it has no central anything … A democracy can be loosely defined as "government of the people, by the people, for the people". However… , Usenet is not an organization, and only an organization can be run as a democracy. Even a democracy must be organized, for if it lacks a means of enforcing the people's wishes, then it may as well not exist. Some people wish that Usenet were a democracy. Many people pretend that it is. Both groups are sadly deluded.

Arguably, Salzenberg's definition of democracy was influenced by the lingering authoritarianism of the Backbone Cabal's reign; perhaps that is why, on publication, it set off a flame war of prodigious dimensions. Salzenberg's chief opponent was Albert Langer, of the Computer Services Centre of Australian National University in Canberra, Australia.

Voicing the perspective of many Usenet users who distrusted the motives of the Backbone Cabal, Langer replied, "I always get suspicious when somebody says 'there are no authorities here'. My suspicion is that there is indeed an authority, but it does not welcome scrutiny". Langer countered Salzenberg's linkage of democracy and coercive force by pointing out the consensus-based governance of voluntary associations, which are democratic but do not (and probably cannot) employ coercive force without seriously alienating the membership. Continuing this line of argument, Langer concluded that Usenet closely resembles a democratic voluntary association, with the exception of the power wielded by an unelected coterie of "volunteers" – largely composed of former Backbone Cabal members – who published the official list of newsgroups. Langer went on to insist that a democratic revolution had occurred, in which a binding newsgroup creation process had effectively countered the Backbone Cabal's power.

In reply to Langer's post, Dave Mack, a system administrator and former member of the Backbone Cabal, posted the following remarkable notice:

> Albert Langer, you have been tried in absentia by the Usenet High Council and have been found guilty of heresy, to whit the referenced article disputing the validity of the Writings of St. Spaf the Omniscient. This Council hereby decrees that, on or as soon as practicable after the day of your arrest, you shall be taken to the Place of Punishment and there you shall be buried alive beneath alt.flame articles and that you shall remain interred there until you are dead and for thirty-six days after the day of your death, after which time your family, if they so choose, may claim your rotting corpse for burial in unhallowed ground.
>
> May Uunet <BLESSED BE THE NAME> have mercy upon your soul.
>
> So shall all be treated who attempt through profane word or thought to defile the Pure and Holy Writ of Usenet.
>
> The Usenet High Council hath spoken. So shall it be. Amen.
>
> Cardinal Mack
> Principle Inquisitor for the Usenet High Council

This is the type of self-parody for which Usenet humour is justly famous, but one has to wonder whether, in some sense, Mack was serious in his accusation of heresy. But Langer was soon to receive more damaging criticism. Several posters pointed out that, contrary to Langer's assertion that the voting procedure was binding, several newsgroups had been properly voted into existence, and thereafter ignored by system administrators. A case in point was comp.protocols.tcp-ip.eniac – obviously a joke. The demise of rec.sex provided another and more convincing example.

In response, Langer argued that democracy requires time to strike root:

> Let it take six months or a year, or two years to acknowledge. As long as voting results are being announced and acted on EVERY MONTH democracy is becoming more deeply entrenched and the power of feudal barons is diminishing – whether they choose to admit it or prefer to console themselves with diatribes about the delusions of upstart serfs (Langer, 1991).

Langer later noted that the reluctance of former Backbone Cabal members to acknowledge the network's growing democracy stemmed from "not wanting to face up to the transfer of power that has occurred and a preference for maintaining a fictional belief that system administrators still have the dominance over Usenet that they used to have" (Langer, 1991)

In reply, several system administrators told Langer that he was living in a dream world. Dave Mack, the author of the Inquisition letter cited above, wrote:

> I administer two sites on Usenet, neither of them terribly important. There is nothing that the rest of the sites on Usenet can do to remove me from the net, force me to stay on the net, keep me from issuing a newgroup control message, force me to honour one, or prevent me from posting anything I damn well please... . You can call Usenet a democracy if you want to. You can call it a totalitarian dictatorship run by space aliens and the ghost of Elvis. It doesn't matter either way (Mack, 1991)

A Usenet pioneer, Gregory G. Woodbury, concurred:

> No matter what the current fad is in describing Usenet, there will still be the hard
> reality that for the machines under my control, the current guidelines are simply
> advisory. I can (and do) ignore certain aspects of the guidelines as I see fit
> (Woodbury, 1991).

What system administrators failed to grasp, or even acknowledge, was a
cornerstone of Langer's argument, namely, that the power of system administrators would be steadily undermined by technological change. Langer noted the
following:

> There are of course rumours of conspiracies among the proles. Some say it is pos-
> sible to receive any newsgroup whatever through email, whether one's "system
> administrator" approves or not, and that one can post to any newsgroup through
> mail gateways established for that purpose... Like the consequences of the steam
> engine and electric telegraphs, the consequences of such developments are too
> frightening for some to contemplate. Let's just get used to the idea of democracy
> for now, huh? (Langer, 1991)

System administrators, Langer concluded, were content to delude themselves
that they are all still lords of their domains, while meanwhile the former serfs "have
set up a Republic and do not recognize feudal authority".

In retrospect, it turns out that there is considerable justification for Langer's
view that technology is eroding the power of system administrators. The years
since the "What is Usenet" flame war have witnessed the democratization of the
technical means to create one's own Usenet site – in effect, to become one's own
system administrator – with the development of the freeware Linux operating
system, a UNIX clone, for x86-based PCs. In addition, the very fact that Usenet
sites are connected to the Internet gives users myriad means to access information
that may have been banned by a local system administrator, but is nonetheless
available to them through other means. "Usenet", remarked Electronic Frontier
Foundation (EFF) co-founder John Gilmore, "interprets censorship as damage and
routes around it" (Gebis, 1994).

Precisely how Usenet routes around censorship was known only to the user
cognoscenti until 1994, when Joseph Gebis, a computer science graduate student at
the University of Illinois, posted "How To Receive Banned Newsgroups" (Gebis,
1994), now an automatic, periodic posting to a number of newsgroups concerned
with free speech and censorship on Usenet. The document lists a number of strategies that enable any Usenet user to access banned newsgroups.

More significantly, "How To Receive Banned Newsgroups" offers a coherent and
persuasive argument that Usenet should be conceptualized as a library. If a library
is to fulfil its function in a democracy, Gebis argues, it is essential that it function
in a manner that is neutral to document content. Viewpoint-based discrimination
has no place in a library, the primary function of which is precisely to make all
viewpoints accessible. It follows, argues Gebis, that system administrators should
view their role as librarians: they should make all of Usenet available, without
regard to the content of Usenet documents.

2.8 A Democratic Network

The "What is Usenet" flame war, long and vituperative, ended in characteristic Usenet style: a consensus emerged and a long-time volunteer quit in disgust. A patient and even-handed observer of the dispute, Ed Vielmetti, contributed an alternative version of Salzenberg's "What is Usenet" article, which still appears along with Salbenberg's in automatic monthly postings to the news.newusers.questions and news.announce.newusers newsgroups. In response to Salzenberg's assertion that Usenet is not a democracy, Vielmetti wrote:

> Usenet has some very "democratic" sorts of traditions. Traffic is ultimately gener-
> ated by readers, and people who read news ultimately control what will and will
> not be discussed on the net. While the details of any individual person's news
> reading system may limit or constrain what is easy or convenient for them to do
> right now, in the long haul the decisions on what is or is not happening rests with
> the people. On the other hand, there have been (and always will be) people who
> have been on the net longer than you or I have been, and who have a strong sense
> of tradition and the way things are normally done. There are certain things which
> are simply "not done". Any sort of decision that involves counting the number of
> people yes or no on a particular vote has to cope with the entrenched interests
> who aren't about to change their habits, their posting software, or the formatting
> of their headers just to satisfy a new idea (Vielmetti, 1991).

Not long after the "What is Usenet?" flame war ended, Usenet witnessed the latest in a long series of conspicuous departures of net.gods, individuals who had long played important roles in shaping and guiding the network's evolution. In conspicuously posed "Farewell" message, Gene Spafford announced his "retire- ment" from Usenet. The status of Spafford, the maintainer of the "official" or "advi- sory" newsgroup list, had been at the centre of this and many other flame wars, and eventually Spafford decided that enough was enough. Passing the responsibility of maintaining the lists to system administrator Mark Moraes, Spafford declared that

> Usenet is like a herd of performing elephants with diarrhoea – massive, difficult
> to redirect, awe-inspiring, entertaining, and a source of mind-boggling amounts
> of excrement when you least expect it (Spafford, 1993).

2.9 Rise of the Cancelbots

The Backbone Cabal hoped to use technical measures to rein in what they saw as Usenet's less desirable phenomena. Users developed their own means: cancelbots. A cancelbot is not an automated program, as the name suggests, but rather a forged cancellation message that appears to the system software as if it originated from a message's author. Usenet software permits authors to cancel their own messages; third-party cancellations, although strongly discouraged, are nonetheless relatively easy to perform.

This point was proved in 1993 when a microbiology professor named Richard DePew began a one-man war against anonymous postings in science newsgroups.

DePew's commands went awry, and drew widespread criticism; for his efforts, he was rewarded with a satirical newsgroup named alt.fan.dick-depew. DePew retired from his censorship role, but – as the following sections make clear – this technical measure was to take on increasing importance in Usenet's evolution.

2.10 The Scientology War

The Backbone Cabal's retreat and retirement freed Usenet from the threat of internal control, but the medium was to face increasing hostility from the outside world. Lying in wait was a prodigious external force: spam (unwanted commercial posts). Although unwanted commercial messages had been posted to Usenet before, nothing like the famous Green Card spam of 12 April 1994 had ever been witnessed, and it caused an uproar that caused national media to take notice (Campbell, 1994; Siegel, 1998).

The Green Card spam originated from two Arizona lawyers who specialized (they claimed) in immigration law. The post was advertising of the most egregious sort: the attorneys offered assistance, for a fee, to would-be participants in a U.S.-administered immigration rally; what they didn't mention is that the forms could be obtained by calling the U.S. Immigration and Naturalization Service (INS) and required no expertise to fill out. Within minutes after their post, the attorneys' service provider was overwhelmed with emails voicing complaints, causing the service provider's systems to crash.

The message's content was not the sole reason for the widespread outrage. To carry out the massive cross-posting, the attorneys had hired a programmer to create a script that went down the list of newsgroups and bombarded each one with the same, unwanted message. The spam was not only offensive; it was also omnipresent. Once again, Usenet regulars began to speculate that the much-predicted death of Usenet was finally at hand; how could the network defend itself against spam of this magnitude? As the Green Card attorneys pointed out, there was no law in existence at that time that prevented them from posting a commercial message to every newsgroup in existence.

Initially, the solution chosen by Usenet's defenders was a reply of the Green Card offensive's opening day: flooding the attorneys' service provider with complaints and voluminous email, which invariably resulted in the service provider kicking the attorneys off of their systems. But they'd be back on line the next day.

Soon, a solution emerged. Richard DePew had already demonstrated the utility of cancelbots. An anonymous figure named Cancelmoose, whose identity was concealed through the use of the famed Finnish pseudoanonymous remailer anon.penet.fi, wrote scripts that sought out the Green Card attorneys' posts and automatically forged cancellation messages wherever they appeared.

Many Usenet participants were troubled by the cancellations. What would happen to the network, they asked, if anyone who disliked a particular message used a cancelbot to eliminate it? Still, the lingering rage over "Green Card" spam helped to sway opinion, if not entirely in favour of third-party cancellations, then at least in favour of Cancelmoose. The community's assessment was captured in the alt.net-abuse FAQ, which noted that the Cancelmoose "has behaved altogether admirably – fair, even-handed, and quick to respond to comments and criticism, all without self-aggrandisement or martyrdom" (Southwick, 1998).

2.11 "The First Internet War"

Among the forces arrayed against Usenet was a formidable enemy indeed: the Church of Scientology (Post, 1996). Whatever the merits of scientology as a religion, one point is quite clear: those who would revile the church are as persistent and dogmatic as those who would defend it, such that there are few Usenet newsgroups with a level of passionate ferocity exceeding alt.religion.scientology. Soon after its 1991 founding, the newsgroup exploded with passionate debate, most of it on the anti-scientology side; some postings included what were described as "secret" internal documents known as "The Advanced Technology". Church defenders bemoaned the publication of these documents, insisting that the knowledge they contained could be extremely dangerous if wielded by the untrained; the church's critics replied that the public could not assess the church's validity unless these writings were made public.

Angered by the publication of these documents, the Church of Scientology filed lawsuits in three U.S. states as well as Amsterdam, seeking to reveal and punish those responsible for posting the material, which the Church described as copyrighted material containing valuable trade secrets. Some of the people who posted this material had affixed their names and email addresses to the messages, so they were easily located. But much of the material originated from anon.penet.fi, located in Finland. Pressured to conform to an increasingly rigid U.S. intellectual property regime, Finnish police seized the remailer's computer and discovered the identity of those who had posted the material, leading the remailer's system adminstrator to shut down the system (Newman, 1995). At this point, one would think that Usenet's ability to "route around censorship" had been proved illusory – but this isn't the end of the story.

The attack on anon.penet.fi convinced hackers that pseudoanonymous remailers, even if located outside U.S. jurisdictions, could not be safeguarded from external legal assault; the fact that all the messages had to travel through a single system, where the message originators' true identities (or at least their true email addresses) were stored, made the system too vulnerable. The solution lay, they came to agree, in a distributed solution; namely, a network of anonymous remailers, which function so that investigators cannot trace a given message to any single remailer; moreover, the remailer network assures true anonymity in that no permanent record is made of a message sender's true identity. Impossible to attack without unplugging much of the Internet, anonymous remailer networks enabled scientology's critics to restore the church's documents to the network.

Yet these documents were soon to disappear, replaced by a message stating that they had been removed "due to copyright violations". It appears that someone – perhaps someone inside the Church of Scientology, but this has never been proved – learned the Cancelmoose trick; messages containing scientology documents mysteriously disappeared, to be replaced by a message claiming that the message had been removed "for copyright reasons". But this strategy, if it was indeed a church strategy, was doomed to fail. Soon, the cancelled messages reappeared, restored to the newsgroups by an unknown figure who signed his messages "Lazarus". Today, the documents can be found in many places on the Internet; scientology was able to harass and to silence many individual contributors, but they failed to stop the propagation of internal documents through the network.

2.12 "Usenet Cannot Be Regulated"

The development of NNTP support for Usenet served not only to undermine the power of the "Backbone Cabal"; it also made the network significantly less amenable to external regulation. As Post (1996) explains,

> Alt.religion.scientology is not like, say, a bookstore or some similar physical "place" that can be located, boarded up, and its operators hauled into court; like the Internet itself, it has no owner, no operator, no central computer on which it "lives". Usenet groups like alt.religion.scientology come into existence when someone (like Scott Goehring) sends a proposal to establish the group to the specific newsgroup (named "alt.config") set up for receiving such proposals. The operators of each of the thousands of computer networks hooked up to the Internet are then free to carry, or to ignore, the proposed group. If a network chooses to carry the newsgroup, its computers will be instructed to make the alt.religion.scientology "feed", i.e. the stream of messages posted to alt.religion.scientology arriving from other participating networks, accessible to its users, who can read – and, if they wish, add to – this stream before it is passed along to the next network in the worldwide chain. It's a completely decentralized organism – in technical terms, a "distributed database" – whose content is constantly changing as it moves silently around the globe from network to network and machine to machine, never settling down in any one legal jurisdiction, or on any one computer?. Trying to stop a Usenet group this way is punching a paper bag; there's no forum in which to make these arguments other than Usenet itself, no central decision maker that can evaluate the validity of those claims and decide whether or not alt.religion.scientology should survive. That decision is entirely in the hands of the owners of each of those thousands of computers, most of whom, in this case, simply chose to ignore the request to delete the alt.religion.scientology group.

Usenet's capacity to resist censorship was put to the test in 1993, when a Canadian woman named Karla Homolka was tried for her role in a series of bizarre sexually related murders. Owing to the probability that the trial would become a media spectacle, the Canadian judge closed the trial to the media. Canadian newspapers honoured the ban, but American newspapers carried the story. Angered by the hush order, two University of Waterloo students created a new newsgroup, called (with irony) alt.fan.karla-homolka. When Canadian backbone managers learned of the new newsgroup, most of them stopped carrying it. But new newsgroups appeared immediately, including alt.pub-ban.homolka, alt.censorship.Canada.dumb, and many more. As administrators scrambled to drop the groups, discussion travelled to groups with no obvious connection with the trial, including alt.true-crime. Ultimately, Canadian backbone administrators were faced with the choice of remaining connected to Usenet or pulling the plug on the entire network; they chose the former (Wisebrod, 1995).

2.13 The Breidbart Index

Cancelmoose's intervention was hailed by many Usenet participants, but some warned darkly that the Usenet equivalent of a nuclear weapon – the third-party cancel command – could be used by those intent on removing unwanted content from the network; they were subsequently proved correct by the scientology fracas. Faced with a dilemma, the Usenet community was forced to come to terms with its own self-regulatory structure, in which the phenomenon of third-party cancellation amounted to a self-regulatory black hole.

Prevailing Usenet policies stated plainly that "only the author of a message or the local news administrator [presumably on the author's behalf] is allowed to send" a cancellation message; other, slightly less official documents conceded, however, that third party cancelling was indeed possible, but "frowned upon". But mere frowning doesn't amount to a coherent policy. If Usenet's self-styled defenders used third-party cancelling to remove unwanted content, their actions would destroy the very rationale for the medium's existence. As many of Usenet's free-speech advocates pointed out, commercial messages – however unethical or offensive they might be – are protected speech under the U.S. Constitution; as much as Usenet participants detested the growing tide of commercial spam, some were mindful of the deeper issues at stake.

In the end, the Usenet community arrived at a solution expressive of its congealed techno-societal values, so aptly expressed by David Clark: "We believe in rough consensus and running code". The "rough consensus", in this case, was a prevailing (but far from unanimous) view that messages cannot be excluded based on content-including commercial content. On the contrary, third-party cancellation may be legitimately used only when a given message exceeds the Breidbart Index (BI), named after its originator, Seth Breidbart. Here is the formula:

$$BI = \sqrt{x_1} + \sqrt{x_2} + \ldots + \sqrt{x_n}$$

where x is the number of newsgroups spammed with the nth copy of a given posting. If two copies of a message are made, and one is posted to 9 newsgroups while the second is posted to 16, the Breidbart Index is 7.

Currently, the threshold for the cancellation of excessively cross-posted (ECP) and excessively multi-posted (EMP) messages is a Breidbart Index of 20 over a 45–day period, conceptualized as a sliding time window; once a given message reaches a BI of 20 within any given 45–day window, it is cancelled. Such cancellations, the policy notes,

> have nothing whatsoever to do with the contents of the message. It doesn't matter
> if it's an advertisement, it doesn't matter if it's abusive, it doesn't matter whether
> it's on- topic in the groups it was posted in, it doesn't matter whether the posting

is for a "good cause" or not – spam is cancelled regardless, based on how many times it was said and not what was said.

In this formal statement of policy, Usenet administrators affirmed not only a core Usenet value, but what is more, a compelling rationale and a technology for self-regulation, one that has worked reasonably well. (It should be noted that this policy applies only to newsgroups within the standard newsgroup hierarchies; no attempt is made to regulate the alt.binaries.* groups, where user-posted porn has given way to advertisements for commercial web sites as well as an unholy crop of swindles, scams, and nefarious schemes.)

2.14 Conclusion: Assessing Usenet

As this chapter has shown, Usenet's distinct political culture arose in a long and sometimes painful debate over Usenet's internal governance, a debate that was carried out partly in verbal argument and partly by means of technical measures. What is more, Usenet's culture seems to be highly replicative; newcomers are socialized into a newsgroup's modes of self-regulation. When they encounter spam and abusive postings designed to interfere with the group's conversation, they must face the crucial moral questions concerning the use of third-party cancellations. In time, they come to share the deeply held belief that today's Usenet is but a pale shadow of its glorious past (which most of today's participants, it should be noted, did not directly experience).

A review of the scholarship concerning Usenet suggests that observers, perhaps without their fully realizing what was happening, have also been caught up in Usenet's mythic narratives. For some, the network – despite flame wars, spam, cancelbots, and all the other ills and apparent ills of Usenet today – is an invaluable experiment that is worth defending – particularly from government regulation, no matter how well intentioned. They take Langer's view, applauding the efforts of Usenet's newsgroups to resist despotic rule and establish their own republics, which are democratically constituted. They point out to a variety of positive impacts, including the network's ability to foster discussion on topics that are verboten in everyday life (Plymire and Forman 2000) and its capacity to foster flourishing support communities (Stoney, 1998; Walstrom 2000; White and Dorman 2000). More importantly of all, Usenet – despite its faults – is seen to hold out the promise of reenergizing a public sphere (Benson, 1996; Schneider, 1996; Hauben, Hauben et al, 1998; Tsagarousianou, 1998; Pritchard, 1999; Slevin 2000; Gaiser 2001), that – in the U.S. – is shrinking to levels associated with political dysfunctional societies (Putnam, 1996; Dahlgren, 2000); cf. Etzioni (2001).

Other scholars take Spaffordian view, namely, that the network, formerly a positive medium for deliberative debate, has been overcome by rowdy, obnoxious intruders. These scholars bemoan the dominant role played by aggressive white males, predominantly conservative or Libertarian, who have little tolerance for other viewpoints (Watson, 1997; Herring, 1999; Quinby, 1999; Uslaner, 2000). Their adversarial, offensive style drives women and more thoughtful men away from Usenet and toward more hospitable discussion environments, such as Web-based chat and weblogs (Baker, 2001; Foreman, 2001). What remains of Usenet discussion, these scholars say, tends to promote racism, gender discrimination, the commoditization of women, non-consensual sexual violence, and global economic inequality (Cushing, 1996; Sardar, 1996; Streck, 1997; Winner, 1997; Damphousse and Smith, 1998; Kim and Kim, 1998; Durkin and Bryant, 1999; Sharpe, 1999; Barron, 2000; Cunneen and Stubbs, 2000; Engelen-Eigles, 2001; Herring, 2001).

Which is the real Usenet? The answer cannot be known without performing long-term ethnographic studies of tens of thousands of newsgroups, which isn't likely to happen. Broad-based content analyses could provide an automated approach; indeed, such techniques have already been used to analyse individual newsgroups (Harmon and Boeringer, 1997). But the most compelling answer to this question, in my view, is that it does not matter, and indeed, that asking the question in this way only serves to disguise what is truly significant about Usenet: its development of a unique political culture into which users are socialized, both deliberately and by means of unintended consequence, and its achievement of a world of deeply internalized meanings that seems to have taken scholarly observers as well as participants into its fold.

References

Abbate, J. (1999). Inventing the Internet. Cambridge, Mass, MIT Press.

Adams, R. (1987). Communication posted to backbone mailing list (February 18, 1987).

Baker, P. (2001). "Moral Panic and Alternative Identity Construction in Usenet." Journal of Computer-Mediated Communication 7: n.p.

Barron, M. and M. Kimmel (2000). "Sexual Violence in Three Pornographic Media: Toward a Sociological Explanation." Journal of Sex Research 37: 161–167.

Baym, N.K. (1995). "From Practice to Culture on Usenet." Sociological Review Monograph 29(52).

Baym, N.K. (1996). "Agreements and Disagreements in a Computer-Mediated Discussion." Research on Language and Social Interaction: 315–345.

Baym, N.K. (1998). The emergence of on-line community.

Bellovin, S. (1990). Communication posted to usenet.history mailing list (October 10, 1990).

Benson, T.W. (1996). "Rhetoric, Civility, and Community: Political Debate on Computer Bulletin Boards." Communication Quarterly 44(3): summer.

Bijker, W.E., T.P. Hughes, et al. (1987). The Social construction of technological systems : new directions in the sociology and history of technology. Cambridge, Mass., MIT Press.

Bumgarner, L. (1995). The Great Renaming: 1985–1988. 2002.

Campbell, K.K. (1994). "A Net Conspiracy So Immense": Chatting with Martha Siegel.

Cunneen, C. and J. Stubbs (2000). "Male Violence, Male Fantasy and the Commodification of Women through the Internet." International Review of Victimology 7: 5–28.

Cushing, P.J. (1996). "Gendered Conversational Rituals on the Internet: An Effective Voice Is Based on More than Simply What One Is Saying." Anthropologica. 38(1): 47–80.

Dahlgren, P. (2000). Media, Citizenship and Civic Culture. Mass Media and Society. J. Curran, and Gurevitch, Michael. London, Arnold: 310–328.

Damphousse, K.R. and B.L. Smith (1998). The Internet: A Terrorist Medium for the 21st Century. The Future of Terrorism: Violence in the New Millennium. Thousand Oaks, CA, Sage. Harvey W. Ed: 208–224.

Daniel, S. (1993). Communication posted to usenet.history mailing list (January 25, 1993).

David, J.P. (1996). "Defending the Boundaries: Identifying and Countering Threats in a Usenet Newsgroup." The Information Society 12(1): 39.

Dery, M. (1993). Flame wars : the discourse of cyberculture. Durham, NC, Duke University Press.

Durkin, K.F. and C.D. Bryant (1999). "Propagandizing Pederasty: A Thematic Analysis of the On-Line Exculpatory Accounts of Unrepentant Pedophiles." Deviant Behavior 20(2): Apr-June.

Engelen-Eigles, D.A. (2001). "White Racial Formation on Usenet." Dissertation Abstracts International 61(11): May.

Foreman, M. (2001). Offensive Intruder Poisons Chat Lines.

Gaiser, T.J. (2001). "An Evaluation of the Emerging Social Forms in Cyberspace." Dissertation Abstracts International 61(7): Jan.

Gardinali, P.A. (1996). Cybervillains and Vigilantes: The Construction of Social Order on Usenet. American Sociological Association, 1996.

Gebis, J. (1994). How to Receive Banned Newsgroups. 2002.

Harmon, D. and S.B. Boeringer (1997). "A Content Analysis of Internet-Accessible Written Pornographic Depictions." Electronic Journal of Sociology 3(1): Sept.

Hauben, M., R. Hauben, et al. (1998). "Netizens: On the History and Impact of Usenet and the Internet." Journal of the American Society for Information Science 49(11): 1.

Herring, S.C. (1999). "The Rhetorical Dynamics of Gender Harassment On-Line." Information Society 15(3): July-Sept.

Herring, S.C. (2001). "The Rhetorical Dynamics of Gender Harassment Online." Information Society 15(3): 151–167.

Horton, M. (1990). "Communication posted to usenet.hist mailing list (November 13, 1990).".

Horton, M. (1990). Message posted to usenet.hist (October 20, 1990).

Kim, J.-K. and S.-J. Kim (1998). "Prospects of Organizing Communities in Usenet Newsgroups: Analyzing the Expansion Process of Han.* Newsgroups." Han'guk Sahoehak/Korean Journal of Sociology 32(2): summer.

Langer, A. (1991). "Communication posted to news.admin (June 5, 1991).".

Langer, A. (1991). Communication posted to news.admin (May 26, 1991).

Langer, A. (1991). "Communication posted to news.admin (May 30, 1991).".

Latour, B. (1987). Science in Action: How to Follow Scientists and Engineers through Society, viii+274, CI, Cambridge, MA: Harvard U Press viii+274, CI, Cambridge, MA: Harvard U Press.

Mack, D. (1991). Communication posted to news.admin (June 9, 1991).

Mack, D. (1991). "Communication posted to news.admin (June 22, 1991).".

Moraes, M. (1995). Usenet Software: History and Sources. 2002.

Murakami, G. (1989). Communication posted to usenet.his (June 30, 1989).

Newman, R. (1995). "Church of Scientolgy vs. anon.penet.fi.".

Plymire, D.C. and P.J. Forman (2000). "Breaking the Silence: Lesbian Fans, the Internet, and the Sexual Politics of Women's Sport." International Journal of Sexuality and Gender Studies 5(2): Apr.

Post, D.G. (1996). "The State of Nature and the First Internet War: Scientology, Its Critics, Anarchy, and Law in Cyberspace." Reason.

Pritchard, G.S. (1999). Placeless Publics: Identity, Community, and Activity in the Usenet's Media. American Sociological Association, 1999.

Putnam, R.D. (1996). "The Strange Disappearance of Civic America." American Prospect 24: 34–48.

Quinby, L. (1999). "Virile-Reality: From Armaggedon to Viagra." Signs 24(4): summer.

Salzberg, C. (1998). What is Usenet?.

Salzenberg, C. (1991). Communication posted to news.admin (July 1, 1991).

Sardar, Z. (1996). alt.civilizations.faq: Cyberspace as the Darker Side of the West. Cyberfutures: Culture and Politics on the Information Superhighway. Z. a. R. Sardar, Jerome R. Washington Square, NY, New York University Press: 14–41.

Schneider, S.M. (1996). "Creating a Democratic Public Sphere through a Political Discussion: A Case Study of Abortion Conversation on the Internet." Social Science Computer Review 14(4): winter.

Sharpe, C.E. (1999). "Racialized Fantasies on the Internet." Signs 24(4): summer.

Shea, V. (1994). Netiquette. San Rafael, CA, Albion Press.

Siegel, C.D. (1998). "Rule Formation in Non-Hierarchical Systems." Temple Environmental Law and Technology Journal 16.

Simpson, K. and M. Stoner (1997). "The Dark Side of the Internet: From free speech fights to e-mail flame wars, journeys into cyberspace can bring you as many problems as solutions Here's how to cope." Currents 23(7): 24.

Slevin, J. (2000). The Internet and Society. Cambridge, Polity Press.

Southwick, S. and J.D. Falk. (1998). net.abuse Frequently Asked Questions.

Spafford, G. (1985). Communication posted to usenet-2 mailing list (November 10, 1985).

Spafford, G. (1988). Communication posted to news.admin (April 18, 1988).

Spafford, G. (1990). Communication posted to usenet.hist mailing list (November 10, 1990).

Spafford, G. (1993). Communication posted to news.misc, news.admin.misc, and soc.net-people (April 29, 1993).

Spafford, G. (1993). Communication posted to usenet.hist mailing list (January 25, 1993).

Spencer, H. (1998). Managing Usenet. Petaluma, CA, O'Reilly & Associates.

Stoney, G. (1998). Suicide prevention on the Internet. Suicide prevention: The global context. R.J. Kosky and H.S. Eshkevari. New York, NY, US, Plenum Press: 237–244.

Streck, J.M. (1997). "Pulling the Plug on Electronic Town Meetings: Participatory Democracy and the Reality of the Usenet." New Political Science: 17–46.

Templeton, B. (1995). Emily Postnews Answers Your Questions on Netiquette. 2002.

Tsagarousianou, R. (1998). Electronic Democracy and the Public Sphere: Opportunities and Challenges. Cyberdemocracy: Technology, Cities, and Civic Networks. R. Tsagarousianou, Tambini, D., and Bryan, C. London, Routledge.

Uslaner, E. (2000). Trust, Civic Engagement, and the Internet. European Consortium for Political Research, Workshop on Electronic Democracy, Univ. of Grenoble, April 2000.

Vielmetti, E. (1991). Communication posted to news.admin (December 26, 1991).

Von Rospach, C. (1990). Communication posted to usenet.hist mailing list (October 26, 1990).

Von Rospach, C. (1991). Communication posted to usenet.hist mailing list (October 12, 1990).

Walstrom, M.K. (2000). ""You know, who's the thinnest?": Combating surveillance and creating safety in coping with eating disorders online." Cyberpsychology and Behavior 3(5) Oct 2000: Inc.

Watson, N. (1997). Why We Argue About Virtual Community: A Case Study of the phish.net Fan Community. Virtual Culture: Identity and Communication in Cybersociety. S.G. Jones. London, Sage: 102–132.

Weinstein, L. (1985). "Communication posted to usenet-2 mailing list (November 16, 1985).".

White, M.H. and S.M. Dorman (2000). "Online Support for Caregivers: Analysis of an Internet Alzheimer Mailgroup – Potential advantages of online communication as adjunct to traditional support." Computers in nursing 18(4): 9.

Winner, L. (1997). "Technology Today: Utopia or Dystopia?" Social Research 64(3): fall.

Wisebrod, D. (1995). "Controlling the Uncontrollable: Regulating the Internet." Media and Communications Law Review 33(1).

Woodbury, G.G. (1991). Communication posted to news.admin (June 6, 1991).

Part II
Studying Spaces

Chapter 3
Measures and Maps of Usenet
Marc A. Smith

3.1 Introduction

This is a study of Usenet, a collection of social cyberspaces in which people gather, interact, and exchange digital objects. Digital objects include a range of media and data structures not limited to lines or pages of text, complex formatted documents, sound, still images and videos, 3D geometry, programs, and databases. Hundreds of millions of people are already engaged in interactions in social cyberspaces, and the number is likely to grow into the billions as networked computers become as widespread as radios or light bulbs. Over the next few years, the Internet will become a popular medium of a scale that dwarfs and subsumes earlier communication media including telephone, radio, and television. In the process, the net is creating new forms of social space, new kinds of publics, in which there are rare but remarkable examples of collective action.

Data mining can be used to create novel interfaces to social cyberspaces. The data that results from analysis of social cyberspaces can be voluminous; the gigabytes of data describing myriad dimensions of these spaces that result from data mining pose real challenges to comprehension and manipulation. The collective result of millions of people interacting through Usenet is a tangled territory of thousands of interlinked groups and messages. In the endless stream of individual messages it is easy to lose sight of emergent patterns and connections. Reading these groups assiduously for months will still leave vast areas of these systems unexplored and much of the patterns of activity and internal structure only dimly visible. Even the metadata created by data mining these spaces is itself vast. How can these complex terrains be grasped and visualized?

The problem is essentially an issue of tools. Interfaces to social cyberspaces, such as discussion boards, email lists, and chat-rooms, present limited if any information about the social context of the interactions they host. Basic social cues about the size, activity, and demographics of groups are missing. Although people can eventually develop a refined sense of the rhythms, leaders, and fools of a particular social cyberspace, the information does not come easily or easily transfer to other spaces. With little sense of the presence of other people, individuals have a hard time forming cooperative relationships.

For example, Figure 3.1 shows a common view of Usenet that is intended as the primary way to select a newsgroup to explore. Other than an alphabetical sort, the

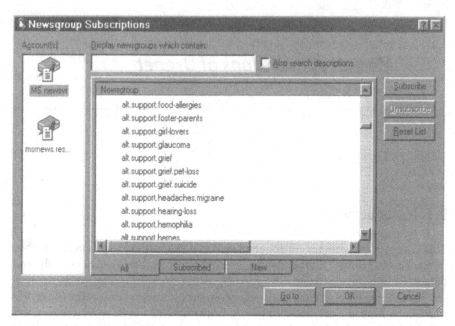

Figure 3.1 A common newsgroup selection interface – Microsoft Outlook Express. Screen shot reprinted by permission from Microsoft Corporation.

40,000+ item list contains only the name of the newsgroup, which can be fairly informative, but lacks much of the core information that presence in a physical social space provides: extensive information about the number of people around, the relative size of groupings, and their composition both in terms of demographics and activity. Interfaces to discussion spaces like Usenet lack any indication of the size, activity, or connections between people or groups present. Histories of participants in newsgroups are difficult to construct, undermining the best method people have of assessing one another, developing trust, and cultivating collective contributions to common goals. This blackout of social context may be responsible for what is widely viewed as a tragic pollution and over-consumption of the commons of human attention created through Usenet.

3.1.1 Alternate Approach: Data Mining Social Cyberspaces

The following is a description of the evolution of interfaces to the Netscan datasets created from analysis of Usenet. The primary goal of this project is to construct a range of basic measurements of Usenet as a whole from multiple perspectives, dimensions, and scales and use that data to help visualize these social spaces. The following describes the methods used in the Netscan system to gather, analyse and publicly report data from Usenet. Netscan is a database system that models and accumulates a range of measures about Usenet. It is possible to generate detailed information about the nature of social cyberspaces by data mining log files of the message bases created through such systems. Data mining involves the analysis of extensive databases with the goal of extracting patterns and information that cannot be seen within the isolated details of the constituent elements. Netscan has collected details from each message exchanged through Usenet for several years, starting at the end of 1999 and continuing to the present.

Interfaces to this data attempt to illustrate patterns present in the data generated by the data mining process that are difficult to perceive in raw form. In addition, the goal was to deliver these tools to anyone interested in accessing the data. This is both to support the research community interested in the study of social cyberspaces and to begin to address the need for enhanced interfaces to social cyberspaces for their participants. The ultimate goal is to explore the ways access to metadata about newsgroups changes the behaviour of the people who use the tools.

Social accounting data have applications in user interfaces that could provide researchers and general users with an improved sense of the social context of Usenet as a whole and of individual newsgroups in particular. Documenting the patterns of interaction in each newsgroup will allow a picture to emerge that will convey their range of diversity and offer guideposts for navigation within these spaces. Many group social processes rely on information about the various levels of contributions members provide to group projects in order to succeed – for example, an awareness of the size of the group, its central members, and the relationship of the group in terms of others (Ostrom, 1990). Introducing such information about groups in social cyberspaces may help orient participants within each group and support self-regulation and boundary maintenance activity that could improve content quality and user satisfaction (Donath, 1995; Sack, this volume).

3.1.2 Community User Tasks

The measures generated by Netscan can be used to support four major tasks people engage in when coming to a social cyberspace: discovery, selection, evaluation, and motivation. Discovery is the process of locating appropriate discussion spaces of interest. This is currently a challenge with many interfaces to Usenet and other social cyberspaces because such systems do not separate active groups from dormant or dead ones, or distinguish discussion groups from job posting and other non-interactive group types. By defining the signature ranges for a variety of major types of groups, interfaces can be constructed that enhance the discovery of discussions of interest and awareness of the dynamics of groups already monitored.

The data created by Netscan can address a range of questions people often ask themselves about social cyberspaces, including:

- In which groups can I talk about a particular topic?
- Which of those groups are for what I want to do: ask a question, discuss a topic, post announcements, post software or files?
- Which groups are active?
- Which subjects generate lots of interest from other participants in the newsgroup?
- Which participants are influential here?

Once an appropriate social cyberspace is identified the next task, selection, becomes dominant. Selection is the process of identifying the subset of content that is worth reading. Given that many newsgroups receive many thousands of messages a month, and any particular person may be interested in monitoring several newsgroups, the challenge of sifting through the ever-expanding mountain of content is daunting. The problem is made more difficult by the prevalence of off-topic or otherwise low-quality material that obscures the fraction of content with high value. Like trying to drink from a polluted fire hose, the experience often overwhelms people, driving them away from otherwise valuable content and interactions. To support selection processes, interfaces can more directly address the implicit questions many participants have as they interact with any newsgroup:

- Did someone I think is important post?
- Did someone who has a history of behaving in ways that I find interesting post?
- Did someone respond to my post?
- Does anyone think I am important here?
- Are there questions I could answer here?
- What's the hot topic today?
- What are people talking about recently?
- How are different subjects and people related to each other?

Once a particular piece of content is selected, the next task is evaluation, the process of determining the value or merit of a message. In many contexts the consequences of selecting low-quality content is simply wasting time, but in some discussions the topics can be critical and the information exchanged potentially dangerous. Many people seeking advice on medical, legal, and technical issues are turning to online discussions that are now common sources of information and guidance. Following bad information in these spaces can have dire consequences. For example, although several professional associations have warned that the quality of health information on the web can be highly variable, social cyberspaces continue to teem with such conversations. Content evaluation is a complex issue even for people outside computer-mediated spaces. Computers can do more to assist in this process in social cyberspaces by offering information about the behavioural histories of the authors of each message answering questions such as:

- How often does this person come to this newsgroup?
- How long has this person been contributing to this newsgroup?
- What other newsgroups does this person participate in?
- Is this a person other people pay attention to (as shown by response patterns)?
- Who are the core people in this newsgroup? Is this person one of them?
- How often do core people interact with each other?

The final task social interfaces must support is motivation. Interfaces need to answer questions like "why should I contribute here?" by displaying the ways prior contributors of material the assembled group has valued are highlighted and granted differential attention. Contributors to social cyberspaces have many motivations but most are related to the opportunity to gain the attention, and potentially respect, of a large and widely distributed peer group.

The existing Netscan interfaces fall short of addressing each of these questions but they are designed with these tasks in mind. In addition to the goals of any interested participant in a newsgroup, Netscan interfaces were also designed with the goals of a social scientist in mind. As a sociologist, my goals are to capture and convey the macro and microstructure of Usenet. I want to grasp it in ways that capture its total shape and structure, like the ways satellite photographs illuminate a patterns of habitation and terrain. At the other end of the scale I want to illustrate the smallest structures in Usenet, the details of turns and responses in individual conversation threads in a way analogous to the way electron microscopes illustrate patterns of connection at the molecular scale.

3.2 Usenet Has Many Dimensions and Can Be Seen at Multiple Scales

Using a combination of tools, including news servers, dedicated news browsers, web browsers, email clients, and others, a daily flood of messages are sorted and organized into tens of thousands of "newsgroups" where they are structured into strings of turns and responses. Usenet is composed of several major subcomponents with complex relationships to one another.

Usenet newsgroups are organized in terms of a naming hierarchy that can go as deep as dozens of levels but are usually three or four terms long (Figure 3.2). Data

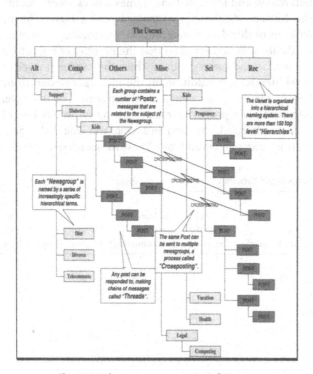

Figure 3.2 Schematic representation of Usenet.

could be aggregated at each and every level of this naming structure, however, in the data presented here, data were aggregated at selected levels of the naming hierarchy starting with Usenet as a whole: first, second, third name segments, all leaf node levels (i.e. the complete newsgroup name). In other words a newsgroup such as microsoft.public.vb.general.discussion has its measures aggregated with other newsgroups at higher levels of its hierarchy. For example, metrics for all the newsgroups that start with the name microsoft.public.vb are aggregated together then further rolled up with all the microsoft.public newsgroups, all the microsoft ones and finally all newsgroups throughout the entire Usenet. Data are aggregated for multiple time slices, periods of time useful for analysis. Data were aggregated for each day, week, month, and the complete year 2000. The authors of messages are another dimension of Usenet. Authors are identified by information on the From: line of the message header.

Authors, the people who actually write the messages that appear in newsgroups, are identified by an email address, which has a structure such as masmith@microsoft.com. Data about authors can be aggregated to develop measures across each of the different top-level domains, such as com, edu, and uk. These domains offer limited information about the geographic location of the author. The second part of the email address, the qualified domain, such as aol.com or ucla.edu, identifies specific computers and offers some information about the commercial organization, service provider, or institution with which the author is associated.

As seen in Table 3.1, major elements of this structure are: authors and domains; posts, threads, and cross-posts; "leaf" newsgroups, first, second, and third level newsgroup hierarchies; and multiple time frames – days, weeks, months, quarters, and years. The Netscan database is organized into a matrix formed by three primary dimensions of this data: newsgroup/hierarchy, author/domain, and time.

The Netscan database is organized so that the number of posts from a particular author is counted in each newsgroup in which they appear as well as counted in each higher-level hierarchy. In addition all the messages posted from all authors from each domain hierarchy are counted in aggregate. For example, a message from masmith@microsoft.com posted in comp.lang.perl.misc would be tallied in that group, as well as comp.lang.perl, comp.lang and comp, and would also be added to the tally of authors from microsoft.com and com. These measures were generated for each

Table 3.1 Dimensions of the Netscan Usenet analysis database

	All newsgroups	1st level hierarchy (e.g. comp)	2nd level hierarchy (e.g. comp.lang)	3rd level hierarchy (e.g. comp.lang.perl)	"Leaf" newsgroup (e.g. comp. lang.perl.misc)
All authors					
Top level domain (e.g. .com, .edu)					
Qualified domain (e.g. aol.com, hotmail.com)					
Email address (e.g. x@y.com)					

day, week, month, and the entire year 2000, which can be imagined as a third dimension of the data, making this into a data cube. Within each intersection is a collection of measures of various aspects of newsgroups: the messages they contain, the threads they link into, and the people who create them.

3.2.1 All Newsgroups, All Year, All Authors Measures

Netscan has collected data since September 1996. However, the format of the data has shifted over time as the collection system has changed. As a result, only data since September 1999 is published. In the year 2000 the Netscan system received 151,655,377 posts created by 7,927,452 unique poster identities sorted into 103,000 newsgroups. It is difficult to determine conclusively how many distinct newsgroups exist worldwide. This measure here may be inflated by messages that are cross-posted to groups with incorrectly spelled names. Of these messages, 82,365,296 (54%) were replies to other messages. The messages were linked together into 14,974,772 threads, which combined accounted for 97,340,068 messages or 64% of the total. An additional 54,315,309 messages (36%) were "barren", and received no replies at all.

Of the participants, 3,170,209 (40%) started a new thread by posting a message that was not a reply to any other. Less than half (43%) 3,418,605 of these participants replied to another poster's message.

On an average day in the year 2000, 120,338 posters (as shown in Figure 3.3) posted 417,281 messages or posts. On its peak day, 5 December, 1,023,397 messages were created by 264,337 posters.

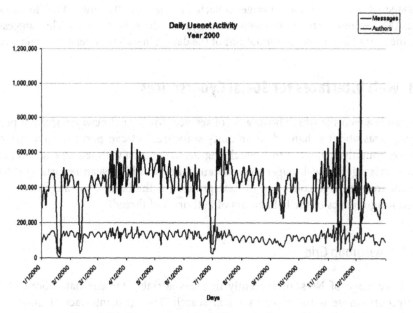

Figure 3.3 Daily messages and participants in Usenet, year 2000.

Messages were not contributed at a steady rate throughout the week. Many Usenet newsgroups have a weekly cycle of activity that builds during the workweek and falls off over the weekends, suggesting that many people access Usenet from their workplace. As this pattern holds for both work-driven and socially oriented groups, this may challenge the belief that recent network growth has been predominantly driven by home use.

On its peak day on 8 January 2000, a total of 31,011 unique newsgroups received at least a single message. On an average day, 19,565 newsgroups received at least a single message; at its lowest point on 20 January, only 5,208 newsgroups were seen active, which is very likely an artefact of our data collection. The real minimum is more likely to be around 15,000 active newsgroups.

It is likely that the results reported here are systematically lower than the actual figures. First, there is no guarantee that the news server we collected data from received all the messages available to all other news servers: the newsgroups, and messages, available vary by location and by upstream feed. Second, the data collection software was prone to crashes and was all-consuming in its demand for computational resources. An example of such a crash was the period in early July and the prolonged under-collection during August.

However, there are some offsetting qualities to the data that suggests that they are not too skewed or partial. First, in many cases the data collector was able to fill in the missed messages by pulling them again from the news server. However, the news server stored messages in different hierarchies for different periods of time before deleting the message to make room for incoming new messages. Another check on the integrity of the data is the fact that lost messages were often "referred to" by other messages that were collected. In other words, a reply to a message that never arrived or was deleted before collection provides an indication of the existence of the missing message. Of the 151 million messages collected in the year 2000 only 14 million messages (8%) were referred to but were missing from the collected data. This suggests that the overall impact of the limitations of the data collected were relatively minimal.

3.3 Web Interfaces for Social Cyberspaces

Netscan is a web site which hosts a set of services for Usenet newsgroups that prototype ideas about enhanced community software. Netscan performs a series of services roughly analogous to a search engine. In contrast with search engines that return messages or web pages that contain a key word, Netscan reports selected content from a large collection of newsgroups on the basis of a range of social accounting metrics of the behaviours of authors and threads.

3.3.1 Newsgroup Grid

The front page of Netscan currently displays sortable tabular data about each newsgroup whose name matches a text search. This grid interface (Figure 3.4) dominates the most recent version of the system.

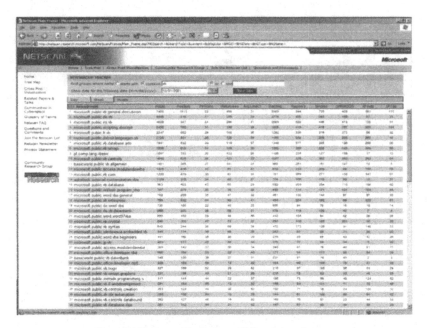

Figure 3.4 Netscan with the latest XML web interface.

The Netscan site provides researchers and interested users with a range of reports about public Usenet newsgroups. Netscan now offers reports for each day, week, and month since September 1999 on a collection of 93,000 active Usenet newsgroups. From the main Netscan page users can request a report on any Usenet newsgroup or group of newsgroups. Measures of the number of posts, posters, posters returning from the prior month, average message length, posters who posted replies, reply messages, messages that are never replied to, one-time-only posters, cross-posted messages, and cross-posted newsgroups are displayed for all the newsgroups in the selected set. Each newsgroup name is a hyperlink to a more focused "report card" page containing a more detailed report for that individual newsgroup. The next steps for this part of the Netscan interface focus on better mechanisms for newsgroup discovery and selection, the addition of more flexible charting tools, and user registration so that requested reports can be tracked for easy retrieval.

Netscan presents data on both the web site and in an Extensible Markup Language (XML) format. XML is an emerging technology for representing data in ways that facilitate machine analysis and manipulation. The resulting data files are far simpler for computers to parse and act on than free text, allowing Netscan data to be pulled more easily into spreadsheet and statistical analysis tools for further exploration.

3.3.2 Newsgroup "Report Cards"

The newsgroup report card (see Figure 3.5) focuses on a specific target newsgroup in a given time period and contains a chart of daily activity of a selectable set of

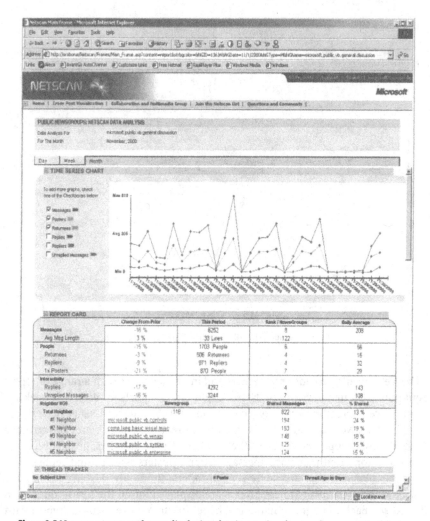

Figure 3.5 Netscan report card page displaying the time series chart and core metrics block.

six measures; the numbers of posts, posters, returning posters, reply posts, reply-ing posters, and unreplied-to messages. Below the time series chart a report of the percentage change over the previous month and daily average measures for many of the measures displayed in the newsgroup table on the prior page. In addition, the top five "neighbour newsgroups" are listed along with the percentage and raw shared message count for each group.

These components of the Netscan system provide access to a range of social accounting metrics but include nothing that describes the actual content of news-groups. The next stage in the development of these interfaces was the creation of an extension to the report card page that provided information about the size and activity of conversations (known as "threads") within each newsgroup along with information about the most frequently active participants ("authors").

3.3.3 Thread and Message Browsing Interfaces

Threads are an important structure in Usenet discussions that are created when messages reply to one another. Threads support turn-taking organization in a way that chat-rooms and even many email systems do not encourage or allow. Responses to earlier messages link together to make chains or trees of related postings.

Each newsgroup contains a collection of posts that are organized into threads – chains of messages linked like paper clips to one another. Any post can have one or more responses. Messages are connected to their parents to create trees of conversations, like the discussion seen in Figure 3.6, which visualizes the ninth largest thread in January 2001 in the comp.sys.ibm.pc.games.action group. The thread had a subject line that read "Please help me decide Cable or ADSL".

Threads are not contained within newsgroups; it is more precise to imagine threads floating above a layer defined by the newsgroups. Posts within threads can target a changing collection of multiple newsgroups, potentially moving the thread in and out of newsgroups from post to post.

In almost all news browsing tools messages are "threaded" into branching outline-like structures. As shown in Figure 3.7, selecting a particular message in a thread causes its contents to be displayed in the pane below.

The replies to initial messages are indicated by a plus sign, which opens up the chain of replies. As shown in Figure 3.7, many of these initial turns start with a subject that contains "Re:" a convention indicating that the message itself is, in fact,

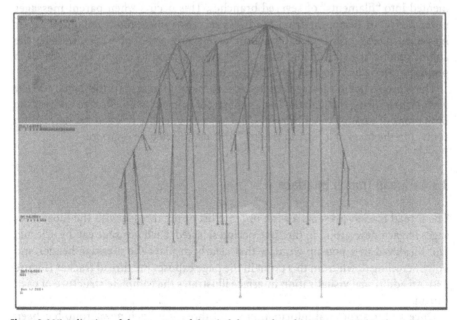

Figure 3.6 Visualization of the structure of the ninth largest thread in January 2001 in the newsgroup comp.sys.ibm.pc.games.action, with the subject line "Please help me decide Cable or ADSL". Time progresses downward; a small block represents a message. A message connected to a previous message indicates a response.

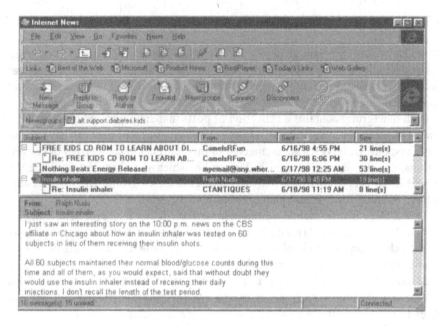

Figure 3.7 A common newsgroup thread and message display interface. Screen shot reprinted by permission of Microsoft Corporation.

a reply. This means that most news browsers display message threads that are fragmented into "filaments" of severed branches. This occurs when parent messages never arrive, or disappear from the news server to make room for other, newer messages. These browsers expose only a few properties of each message, the author's name, the subject and date of the message, and its size in kilobytes. Each property can be used to sort and sift the content.

These properties of messages fail to capture many other aspects that could be very useful when sifting through the large volumes of content. In an effort to address the limitations of existing news browsers, the Netscan interface reorganizes newsgroup content in the form of a "thread tracker" for each selected newsgroup.

3.3.4 Thread Tracker Interface

The thread tracker presents a rank ordered list of the threads with the most messages in each newsgroup in the time period selected. Each message can be selected and displayed in a pop-up window that clearly displays the message header and body. Scrolling down from this point in the page exposes the thread tracker (Figure 3.8). An additional visualization interface illustrates the complete structure of each thread.

Once all the structural information about threads in each newsgroup has been reconstructed it is possible to select threads on the basis of a range of dimensions. The tree structures created by message threads have properties such as the total number of messages in the thread, the depth and breadth of the thread, and the

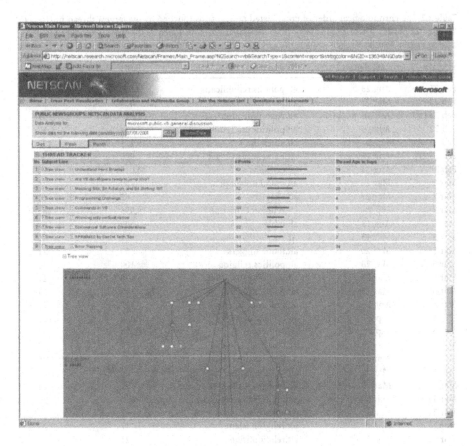

Figure 3.8 Netscan Thread Tracker.

number of newsgroups that the thread spans. Each measure captures a particular dimension of a thread, some of which may be useful for identifying content of particular value. For example, very long threads are likely to indicate an extended discussion, and shorter threads with many replies to a single message may indicate a particularly contentious point in the conversation.

Netscan thread trees present a novel way to browse message threads and understand their structure. In a thread tree, the message that begins a thread appears as the root of the tree, from which successive replies branch down. Square glyphs – small, graphical units – represent the messages. The vertical space of the tree view is divided into grey bands that represent calendar days on which messages are posted during the thread's lifetime. The size of each band is proportional to the number of generations of messages exchanged on that day; days on which no messages were posted do not appear at all but are suggested by a more dramatic shift in shading in the succeeding band. Because the sizes of the day bands vary, the vertical scale cannot be used linearly to infer time differences between messages.

Thread trees reveal information about message sequencing and ancestry that is difficult or impossible to gather from traditional news-browsing interfaces, espe-

Table 3.2 The chronological order of crossposted newsgroups touched by the largest thread in Usenet, "Bigots for Bush". These groups vary from serious discussion (such as alt.atheism) to jokes (such as alt.alien.vampire.flonk.flonk.flonk); while some groups adopted the discussion, others did not

First day	Last day	Newsgroup	Posts	Days
Feb 21	Aug 23	alt.politics.republicans	3,650	185
Feb 22	Mar 25	alt.politics.elections	439	33
Feb 22	Apr 18	alt.rush-limbaugh	2,887	57
Feb 22	Apr 18	alt.politics.usa.republican	3,334	57
Feb 23	Sep 2	alt.atheism	19,121	193
Feb 26	Apr 15	alt.flame.jesus.Christ	966	50
Feb 27	Aug 24	talk.origins	4,015	180
Mar 1	Mar 24	alt.rush.Limbaugh	39	24
Mar 2	Mar 21	sci.skeptic	62	20
Mar 2	Sep 2	alt.religion.Christian	10,993	185
Mar 3	Aug 18	alt.bible	509	169
Mar 5	Mar 15	Al	15	11
Mar 5	Mar 25	alt.flame.niggers	39	21
Mar 5	Mar 28	alt.politics.religion	100	24
Mar 5	Mar 25	alt.politics.radical-left	128	21
Mar 5	Mar 28	alt.politics.liberalism	141	24
Mar 5	Apr 1	alt.politics.white-power	187	28
Mar 5	Sep 2	alt.bible.prophecy	7,034	182
Mar 5	Sep 2	talk.atheism	13,124	182
Mar 7	Mar 28	alt.christnet.religion	11	22
Mar 7	Mar 29	alt.politics.libertarian	47	23
Mar 7	Mar 29	alt.politics.homosexuality	54	23
Mar 11	Mar 30	alt.politics.white-power.com	25	20
Mar 11	Mar 30	alt.politics.usa.republican.	25	20
Mar 11	Apr 5	Atheism	42	26
Mar 12	Apr 5	uk.religion.islam	17	25
Mar 12	Apr 5	alt.religion.islam	21	25
Mar 12	Apr 10	alt.politics.democrats.d	39	30
Mar 12	Apr 10	alt.fan.rush-limbaugh	39	30
Mar 12	Apr 10	alt.politics.bush	39	30
Mar 12	May 7	alt.religion.christian.roman-catholic	56	57
Mar 13	Apr 23	alt.atheism.satire	227	42
Mar 16	Apr 10	alt.religion.Gnostic	8	26
Mar 16	Apr 10	alt.christnet.philosophy	46	26
Mar 16	Jul 11	alt.christnet	91	118
Mar 20	Apr 10	lt.bible.prophecy	12	22
Mar 20	Apr 10	alt.atheism.alt.atheism.satire	24	22
Mar 24	May 20	alt.stupidity	38	58
Apr 4	Apr 23	alk.atheism	24	20
Apr 6	Apr 23	alt.abortion	36	18
Apr 10	Jul 2	de.test	67	84
Apr 24	Jun 30	alt.flame	11	68
Apr 24	Jun 30	alt.troll	11	68
Apr 24	Jun 30	alt.fan.Madonna	25	68
May 2	Jul 11	talk.religion.misc	34	71
May 3	Jun 13	alt.alien.vampire.flonk.flonk.flonk	14	42
May 3	Jun 13	alt.fan.karl-malden.nose	14	42
May 3	Jul 2	alt.religion.apologetics	28	61

Table 3.3 Top 20 threads by number of unique authors, year 2000

Rank	Thread subject	Posts	Posters	Max depth	Max breadth	Duration	First day seen	Last day seen	Cross-post targets
1	And they still expected a tip ...	5,269	710	85	340	138	2000.08.15	2000.12.30	2
2	Neu-Ankündigung!	4,021	692	94	156	198	2000.02.07	2000.08.22	1
3	Bigots for Bush	19,377	688	277	240	195	2000.02.21	2000.09.02	48
4	The End of the Affair	1,367	611	26	209	80	2000.05.30	2000.08.17	216
5	Does Anyone Care About Elian?	2,844	561	51	155	108	2000.03.30	2000.07.15	121
6	I salute this *m*f* fellow and his long story to Chinese voters	3,862	544	36	705	435	1999.11.25	2001.02.01	30
7	OnlIneAnonymity Resources	7,970	517	73	389	441	1999.11.19	2001.02.01	440
8	Who Made God?	2,193	495	54	93	378	2000.01.05	2001.01.16	30
9	Women and childrend are still in poverty	6,178	482	133	191	441	1999.10.11	2000.12.24	85
10	ali intelligent	1,399	478	20	350	432	1999.09.15	2000.11.19	147
11	Recovery on a Monday... I think....	5,873	465	132	184	165	1999.09.21	2000.03.03	1
12	Are Catholics Christians?	5,247	425	129	91	241	1999.11.15	2000.07.12	37
13	THE 2000 WAREZ LIST IS COMING!	616	417	24	48	104	1999.12.20	2000.04.01	23
14	SAFE and happy BRITON laughs at VIOLENT American SAVAGES [x11]	3,849	395	145	140	141	1999.12.03	2000.04.21	52
15	The sweet syrupy love of WOF	13,026	391	171	258	101	2000.10.24	2001.02.01	34
16	Gas: Prices getting worse!	3,992	371	125	92	130	2000.02.17	2000.06.25	25
17	THE 2000 WAREZ LIST IS COMING! HURRY !!!!	542	371	22	59	238	1999.12.20	2000.08.13	38
18	The List of Character Survival Techniques	2,042	363	77	59	109	1999.10.22	2000.02.07	7
19	Puns of the Weak 6-9-00	3,835	357	25	1,015	428	1999.11.02	2001.01.02	26
20	Y2Luser PHB's	1,843	355	52	114	69	1999.12.20	2000.02.26	2

Table 3.4 Top 20 deepest threads, year 2000

Rank	Thread subject	Posts	Posters	Max depth	Max breadth	Duration	First day seen	Last day seen	Cross-post targets
1	Frage an alle	1,318	23	402	15	430	1999.11.26	2001.01.28	1
2	IHR SEID VERRUECKT!!!! :-)))	510	8	401	3	466	1999.10.21	2001.01.28	1
3	Achtung! Wichtige Mitteilung an ALLE Dummschwätzer	1,063	21	362	10	501	1999.09.18	2001.01.30	1
4	Ich bin mal wieder da...........	428	6	349	4	485	1999.10.02	2001.01.28	1
5	Babsi outet sich!	655	13	329	4	257	1999.10.14	2000.06.26	1
6	25 Jahre Ikea!	15,967	189	322	135	506	1999.09.15	2001.02.01	11
7	Knuddelorgie fuer Danny!!!!!	1,555	26	308	19	368	2000.01.27	2001.01.28	1
8	Ich bin mal wieder da........	307	5	307	1	505	1999.09.12	2001.01.28	1
9	I c h l e b e n o c h....!!!!!	524	8	306	6	300	1999.10.21	2000.08.15	1
10	In "de.alt.admin" tut sich was!!!	441	9	300	6	500	1999.09.21	2001.02.01	1
11	Pause..	299	5	299	1	485	1999.10.02	2001.01.28	1
12	English for Runaways?	337	10	298	2	251	1999.10.14	2000.06.20	1
13	A N D R E A...!!!	651	10	296	45	505	1999.09.12	2001.01.28	1
14	Where can I buy a hacker t-shirt?	2,062	146	295	21	417	1999.10.05	2000.11.24	2
15	Download site	297	11	288	2	358	2000.02.08	2001.01.30	1
16	The Queen Is Dead voted best album of all time	6,306	233	287	92	146	2000.01.06	2000.05.30	71
17	Hochzeit im d.a.d.!	1,181	18	282	19	470	1999.10.17	2001.01.28	1
18	Homepage	967	23	278	6	373	2000.01.09	2001.01.15	1
19	Bigots for Bush	19,377	688	277	240	195	2000.02.21	2000.09.02	48
20	Antrag auf Umschreibung.........	405	8	277	4	469	1999.10.18	2001.01.28	1

cially when threads split into several sub-threads as time passes. The separate, parallel development of sub-threads is essentially invisible in any other view.

Threads develop over several days and in some cases live on for many months. Thread size and structure varies from newsgroup to newsgroup. For example, threads in the comp.sys.ibm.pc.games.action newsgroup tend to be short. Nearly a quarter of all messages posted to the newsgroup, 1061 posts, were barren (i.e. were never replied to). Of those that grew longer, attracting a chain of replies and replies to replies, the average thread contained 13 messages and grew four generations deep (a reply to a reply to a reply to an initial turn or "thread head"). The biggest thread in this newsgroup in this month grew to 64 generations deep and was 150 messages "wide" at its widest point (150 messages replying to the same message).

Threads have a pattern of diffusion through newsgroups. Table 3.2 lists the newsgroups in which the thread "Bigots for Bush" was posted. This thread touched 48 different newsgroups, but nearly all of the messages in the thread were sent to the newsgroup alt.atheism. This is despite the fact that the thread began in the newsgroup alt.politics.republicans, as indicated by the date it was first posted. This thread is also one of the most long-lived, starting on 21 February 2000 and continuing until 2 September 2000. The thread jumped to additional newsgroups within a day, expanding to an additional newsgroup or two almost each additional day for a month. It takes almost another week before the thread touches the newsgroups alt.bible.prophesy and talk.atheism, the last newsgroups to be added to the thread that will attract a significant portion of the posts. Throughout the rest of March 2000 the thread touches a range of newsgroups related to religion and politics. By May, the thread touches no additional newsgroups.

Reading down the list of newsgroups displays a pattern of diffusion in which one after another newsgroup is touched by the thread but only a few give the thread a home. In many cases the thread exists for only a few dozen messages within a particular newsgroup. The effective end of the thread's diffusion occurs when it touches the newsgroups alt.alien.vampire.flonk.flonk.flonk, alt.fan.karl-malden.nose, and alt.religion.apologetics, suggesting the outer limit of the spaces interested in the topic.

Threads also vary in terms of the number of authors they attract (Tables 3.3 and 3.4). The largest threads attracted about 700 unique posters, while the most common thread has just 2 posters and 2 posts, a question and a reply.

3.3.5 Author-to-thread Report

The ability to present the largest threads in a newsgroup is useful, as large threads are likely to be about topics of broad and active interest. However, this view into a newsgroup clearly misses smaller threads that may be of high value. An alternative way to sift content in newsgroups is to follow the participation of the authors most likely to have the highest value. There are no doubt a variety of ways to conceive of "value", but one metric from the Netscan analysis of authors – the number of different days the author has been active in the month – stands out as a way to predict commitment to a newsgroup. In the "author-to-thread" report (Figure 3.9), the top 40 most frequently active authors are sorted and displayed with a number of mea-

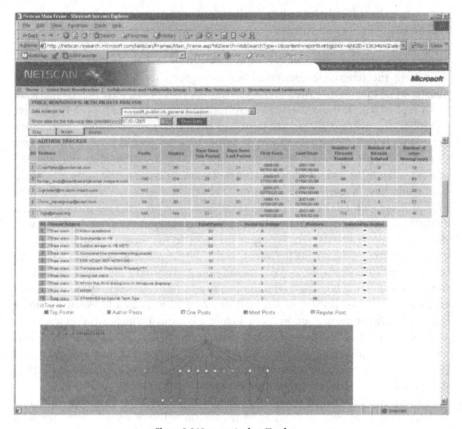

Figure 3.9 Netscan Author Tracker.

sures describing their recent activity. For each author, the top 10 threads they contributed to, sorted by the number of posts they sent to each thread, is displayed. Each thread can then be opened and displayed either as a traditional outline display or as a thread-tree visualization. From that level individual messages can be selected and read.

A next step would be to re-rank threads by taking into consideration the behavioural histories of the posters, granting more weight to posters who are more regular and long-term participants who also respond predominantly (but not only) to a wide range of others.

3.3.6 Author Profile

The author profile provides a unified summary of each participant's activity across Usenet for the period studied.

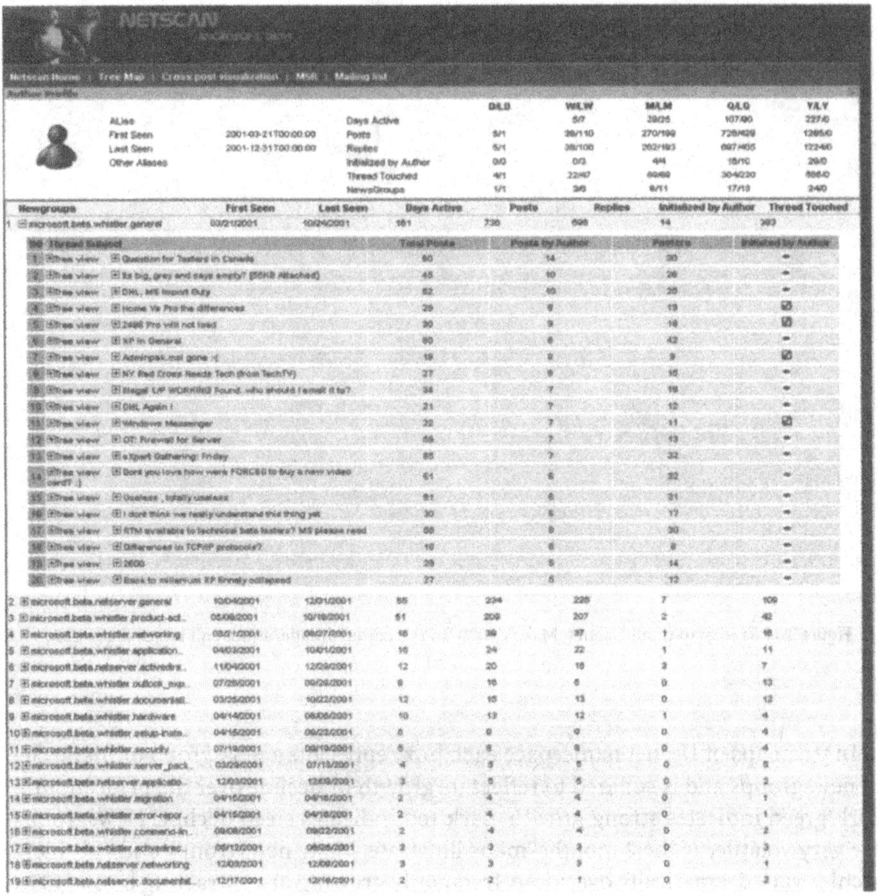

Figure 3.10 Netscan author profile report page.

3.3.7 Treemaps of Usenet

There is a level of organization in Usenet that exists above the newsgroup level. Newsgroup hierarchies create a meta-structure for newsgroups. Treemaps are an effective way to grasp the vast amount of data generated by the Netscan analysis of Usenet. On the basis of work inspired by Ben Shneiderman (Shneiderman, no date), treemaps have been increasingly used to visually present multiple dimensions of information about hierarchical structures (Figure 3.11). Other examples include Micrologic's DriveMap product and SmartMoney.com's Map of the Market. Treemaps make use of area to convey one dimension of a data set, and of location and nesting to indicate hierarchical location. They work at multiple scales, offering a straightforward zoom in/zoom out model. By zooming into increasingly focused points in the treemap, even the smallest details can be seen.

Figure 3.11 Tree map of all Usenet, March 2000. In the colour image, almost all boxes are green.

In treemaps of Usenet namespace each box represents a newsgroup or hierarchy of newsgroups and is collared to reflect its growth or decline over the prior month; dark green indicates strong growth, dark red indicates steep decline. Newsgroups are very volatile, as the 2 months' maps illustrate. Many newsgroups and sub-hierarchies vary dramatically over time, frequently growing or contracting by 30–40%.

Figure 3.12 gives a clear image of the rec.pets hierarchy. The group rec.pets.cats is located in the box labelled "pets" found within the larger box labelled "rec" along with the other 24 neighbouring newsgroups that share the hierarchy.

With such a map the relative proportions of the various hierarchies becomes immediately apparent. Looking back at the Usenet treemaps (Figure 3.11) it is clear that the alt hierarchy looms over the rest, a massive continent of loosely related newsgroups making up 36% of all newsgroups and receiving 43% of all messages. The size of alt is related to the less restrictive newsgroup creation process, created as an alternative to the more formalized major hierarchies. This means that the most active area of Usenet is not covered by the same political regime that rules the others. It does not mean that this activity equates to quality, value, or user satisfaction, but it does suggest that the difference in social regulation plays a role in the difference in activity.

Although the major sub-hierarchies of alt are comparable to the major non-alt hierarchies, alt.binaries looms over all else in the Usenet landscape. Making up about 25% of all Usenet message traffic and composed of newsgroups dedicated to the exchange of digital objects, images, software, sounds, and videos, alt.binaries is further subdivided, with alt.binaries.pictures alone larger than any other first-level hierarchy.

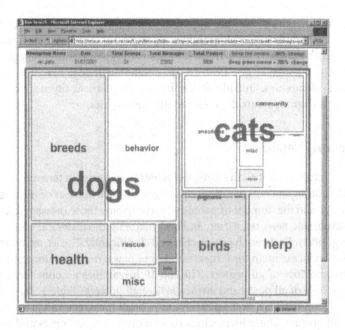

Figure 3.12 Tree map zoomed view of rec.pets, January 2001. In the colour display, cats.community is reddish, all other dark sections are green

Within alt.binaries.pictures, the alt.binaries.pictures.erotica hierarchy is the largest. Outside alt.binaries.pictures, alt.binaries.sounds.mp3 trails closely. Within alt, but outside the massive subcontinent of alt.binaries, a cluster of major sub-hierarchies are dedicated to fandom, music, sex, games, social support, television, religion, sports, and politics.

The treemap visualizations offer a number of benefits over tabular representations of the same data. In this view, the structure of the various sub-hierarchies becomes apparent. In many ways the treemap resembles a land use map, with some areas seemingly more rural than others. This analogy is tempting but flawed. The parts of the Usenet map with large, non-divided areas represent vast super-newsgroups with tens of thousands of messages per month. Still, the rural/urban distinction does convey the way in which some hierarchies vary in terms of the extent to which they are subdivided. Some seem highly refined, with sub-sub categories defining very specific topics, such as microsoft.public.windows.inetexplorer.ie55.programming.dhtml.authoring. Sub-hierarchies such as alt.music and soc.culture have fairly flat structures, with few further sub-divisions below the third level. In contrast, hierarchies such as microsoft.public and comp have high levels of sub-division.

A common pattern in these treemaps is the way many of the language-bounded sub-hierarchies, for example tw.bbs (Taiwan), it (Italian), de (German), uk (British), fr (French), pl (Polish), and nl (Netherlands), share a common quality. Each contains a fairly similar balance and division of its sub-hierarchies, with "recreational" groups largest in the German, British, French, and Polish hierarchies. Computer-related discussion commonly take the second position in all but the Italian newsgroups, where they dominate over the others.

Areas of strong growth are very apparent in this form of the treemap. alt.binaries, tw.bbs, and clari, it, and microsoft hierarchies all stand out, growing nearly 300% over the prior month in March 2000. In alt, it looks as though declining newsgroups are found mostly outside larger newsgroup neighbourhoods, like the alt.fan and alt.support subhierarchies. Outside alt, declining groups are again more common in the smaller newsgroups outside the large sub-hierarchies.

3.3.8 Top-level hierarchies

Usenet hierarchies are not all the same. Each hierarchy varies in terms of a variety of attributes including the number of groups it contains, the number of messages those groups receive and the number of people who contribute those messages. A group of eight (alt, comp, misc, news, rec, sci, soc, and talk) made up the historical core of Usenet (Salzenberg, 1992). That core has now changed significantly. The alt, rec, tw, comp, and microsoft hierarchies contain the largest number of newsgroups; alt alone attracts 61% of all posts and 50% of all posters. The top 10 hierarchies account for 44% of all newsgroups, 81% of all posts, and attract 96% of all posters (Table 3.5).

The top 10 top-level hierarchies receive 80% of all messages and attract as much as 96% of all posters. These hierarchies cover a diverse set of topics and languages with a clear bias towards technical discussions.

Each hierarchy can be measured along multiple dimensions. Table 3.6 shows the count of unique posters in each hierarchy, the number of those posters who were seen posting at least once in the preceding year, the total number of messages sent to each, and the average length of those messages. In addition, the number of messages that were replies to any prior message along with the count of all posters who posted a reply is displayed. "Starts" are the number of messages that were initial turns that eventually received replies. This measure could also be thought of as the thread count, the total number of threads. The number of initiators is the count of posters who posted at least one message that started a thread (which can have as few as just one additional message). "Singles" are messages that were posted by authors who posted just that message and no other in that hierarchy. "Barrens" are initial messages that were never replied to. "Cross-posts" are messages sent to more than a single newsgroup. "Newsgroups" is the number of newsgroups active (i.e. they received at least one message) in that hierarchy in the time period.

3.3.9 Second-level hierarchies

Second-level hierarchies offer a more refined view of the topical focus of Usenet. The largest sub-hierarchy is alt.binaries, which holds newsgroups devoted to the exchange of multimedia objects, pictures, videos, music, and software.

The top 10 second-level hierarchies account for 13.9% of all newsgroups, 57% of all posts, and 48.7% of all posters. These indicators offer an initial guide to discovering "where the action is" in these spaces. Note the dramatic difference in the average length of messages exchanged in alt.binaries and all other second-level hierarchies. Binary files tend to be long, so this is a strong indicator that most of the

Table 3.5 Top 30 Usenet hierarchies sorted by posters, year 2000

Rank	Hierarchy name	Posters	Returnees	Posts	Average line count	Replies	Repliers	Newsgroups
1	Alt	3,543,190	781,373	71,308,840	2,275	31,043,911	1,444,754	93,117
2	Rec	809,716	427,693	12,476,839	31	9,551,281	509,802	26,670
3	Tw	731,891	72,089	4,922,738	28	257,600	35,063	9,842
4	Comp	714,439	323,712	5,517,379	34	3,737,989	377,366	22,957
5	Microsoft	713,187	211,125	5,508,025	57	3,542,007	346,131	19,260
6	It	281,236	54,073	5,936,217	37	4,405,374	160,784	10,864
7	De	239,345	96,223	4,680,557	53	3,846,098	149,147	16,123
8	Fr	220,748	61,553	3,416,956	24	2,517,452	120,377	9,273
9	Uk	216,538	143,006	3,121,298	26	2,467,472	139,501	16,756
10	Soc	167,927	130,702	2,862,908	50	2,218,930	111,216	16,098
11	Misc	149,330	127,586	2,009,527	33	1,118,987	72,163	13,014
12	Pl	143,359	31,628	3,491,027	21	2,650,284	91,721	4,256
13	Sci	116,521	111,874	1,151,634	39	942,179	75,780	9,238
14	Es	114,337	22,829	1,390,075	1,369	771,513	64,602	8,255
15	Fido7	106,936	40,050	4,655,047	26	2,953,222	77,203	6,198
16	Nl	103,423	45,233	1,798,635	26	1,446,507	66,961	7,407
17	Han	89,586	10,079	278,783	351	57,678	21,398	3,369
18	Aus	76,116	64,287	1,003,131	33	805,860	46,899	10,464
19	macromedia	69,065	18,144	576,687	19	383,476	34,514	1,231
20	Clari	64,103	6,196	1,057,465	75	4,809	848	2,913

Table 3.6 Top 20 second-level Usenet hierarchies sorted by posters, year 2000

Rank	Hierarchy	Posters	Returnees	Posts	Average line count	Replies	Repliers	Newsgroups
1	alt.binaries	1,247,518	51,322	30,962,613	5,056	3,202,184	282,253	32,939
2	tw.bbs	730,165	52,707	4,907,386	28	256,673	34,750	9,283
3	microsoft.public	703,655	64,613	5,469,873	57	3,534,822	343,405	19,093
4	alt.sex	347,897	7,061	1,690,052	305	151,258	32,591	14,084
5	alt.music	224,287	27,219	2,816,178	52	2,107,278	134,007	17,605
6	alt.fan	211,020	22,564	3,639,166	366	2,740,187	136,107	26,077
7	alt.comp	197,106	14,665	1,190,215	30	854,710	120,109	9,052
8	comp.sys	190,140	23,519	1,620,633	27	1,244,199	114,020	8,059
9	alt.games	169,675	16,610	2,119,611	35	1,740,447	106,955	12,746
10	rec.music	144,930	21,132	1,693,989	33	1,254,685	73,658	7,656
11	comp.os	142,554	12,694	797,170	31	550,613	76,541	7,056
12	comp.lang	137,043	12,622	952,022	33	688,682	73,246	4,658
13	rec.arts	112,895	18,894	2,032,206	31	1,679,819	78,813	8,837
14	Soc.culture	109,289	13,011	2,013,227	54	1,549,916	76,300	12,672
15	alt.tv	107,812	12,796	1,734,323	37	1,460,166	74,255	10,412
16	alt.support	101,358	11,110	2,003,085	34	1,675,799	69,233	7,918
17	it.comp	97,921	11,555	1,209,780	20	857,930	54,448	3,986
18	fr.rec	92,104	10,935	1,214,369	23	937,145	54,747	4,096
19	alt.autos	85,314	8,708	559,569	45	401,746	48,432	4,575
20	alt.sports	79,189	11,677	1,629,878	28	1,309,958	53,692	7,068

binary traffic is confined to the alt.binaries hierarchy, which suggests that the coordination of behaviour in Usenet around posting large files is fairly successful. It also highlights the fact that although alt.binaries attracts about 16% of all posters, the remaining 19 of the top 20 hierarchies, by evidence of their average line counts, are likely to primarily host the exchange of human-readable text. These newsgroup hierarchies attract 50% of the overall Usenet posting population.

3.4 Network Analysis of Usenet Cross-posting Patterns

There is an underlying structure to Usenet that is very distinct from the hierarchical structure imposed by its naming convention. Newsgroups are highly cross-posted to one another, the same messages are shared between multiple newsgroups, and in some cases many hundreds of groups are densely interwoven into meta-clusters. The treemap, rooted in the naming hierarchy, ignores the ways newsgroups can actually be much closer to others in distant hierarchies than to those within their own hierarchy.

There are visualization techniques that can represent this structure. Network maps represent newsgroups and their interconnections in the form of graphs with nodes and edges. These maps represent newsgroups again as boxes but break each individual newsgroup out of its hierarchy space and link it to other newsgroups with which it shares any messages.

Network maps have limitations, however. In particular, they have difficulty clearly displaying information about large numbers of nodes. Without a hierarchical structure to guide the layout of the display, the layout of network maps becomes a difficult mathematical problem with no simple method for finding the optimum layout that balances every newsgroup's ties and thus location in relation to all others. In conditions with massive amounts of ties between nodes, as is found in the structure of Usenet, displays can be rendered into muddy smears. Careful reduction of the data can, however, be effective.

Using cross-posting records, it is possible generate network maps of the interconnections between Usenet newsgroups. Cross-posting patterns can be intuitively represented as a network map (Krackhart et al, 1994; Becker et al, 1995; Cox and Eick, 1995; Krebs, 1996). The patterns of its connections to others may indicate a great deal about the newsgroup (Rice, 1995).

These techniques can be used to illustrate neighbouring newsgroups. Network diagrams can be drawn that overlay information about the size and interaction style of each group. In these network diagrams groups are presented as blocks that are sized in proportion to the number of messages they contain, their colour is an indicator of their poster-to-post ratio (the darker they are, the less interactive they are likely to be).

Newsgroups are not islands. Through cross-posting, as shown in Figure 3.13, they aggregate into clusters that form meta-groups with significant overlap. Through the practice of cross-posting, newsgroups are densely interconnected with one another, forming large neighbourhoods of interrelated topics. Because the data included in each message's header does not identify from which group a post originates, all connections between newsgroups are bidirectional. No data is available to determine if a group exports more messages than it imports.

The high rate of interconnection through cross-posting means that there are fewer newsgroups than there are newsgroup names. The majority of newsgroups cross-post more than 50% of their messages, making them interconnected to the point that they agglomerate into larger meta-clusters. The highly interconnected nature of Usenet may be the quality that accounts for its extraordinary robustness.

3.4.1 Patterns of Interconnection

The newsgroup comp.sys.ibm.pc.games.action touched 489 other newsgroups through cross-posting but was linked most strongly with comp.sys.ibm.pc.games.strategic, sharing 619 of its messages (24%) with this newsgroup in January 2001. As seen in

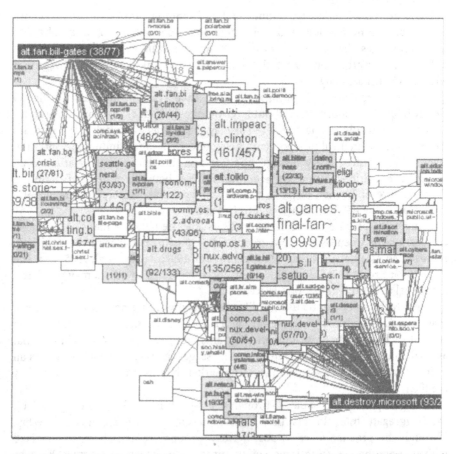

Figure 3.13 Network diagram of the newsgroups neighbouring and linking alt.fan.bill-gates and alt.destroy.Microsoft.

Figure 3.14, this pattern can be visualized as a network structure, which from the standpoint of a single newsgroup and looking out one degree (the newsgroups directly connected to it) is a hub and spoke structure.

Newsgroup connections can be measured in two ways. First, each is connected to a certain number of other newsgroups. This is the count of cross-post targets (Table 3.7). A related but separate measure is the cross-post volume, which is the count of the number of posts the groups share through cross-posting with other newsgroups. A newsgroup could be connected to many other groups but share only a small portion of its messages with them, or could be connected to only a few other newsgroups but share many of its messages.

Most Usenet interfaces present each newsgroup as if it were distinct and isolated. But very few newsgroups are in fact islands; only 1,222 (4%) non-empty active newsgroups are not connected to any other groups at all. Most newsgroups are connected to on average 162 other newsgroups, and they are often directly connected to one of the core newsgroups. A core newsgroup is one to which most other newsgroups are connected. Because of the presence of these core groups, no newsgroup is more than a few "steps" apart from any other. At the top end of the spectrum, 7423 (22%) are connected to more than 200 other newsgroups. Although only 1.5% of all groups are connected to more than 1,000 other groups through cross-posting, these massively cross-posted newsgroups are the core of Usenet, containing 20% of all the messages posted during the study.

This dense level of interconnection could give Usenet the ability to act as a powerful social information switch. Questions that appear in one newsgroup are likely to be seen by someone who has a connection with a more appropriate newsgroup, who then

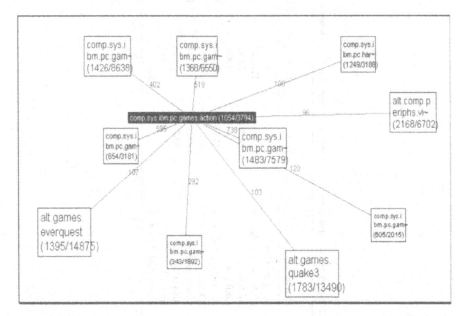

Figure 3.14 Visualization of the crossposting relationships between the newsgroup comp.sys.ibm.pc.games.action with its immediate neighbours.

Table 3.7 Top 10 newsgroups in terms of cross-post targets for all of Usenet, year 2000

	Newsgroup	Posts	Replies	Posters	Repliers	Returnees	% Returnees	Average line count	Cross-post targets
1	Alt.usenet.kooks	174,108	146,382	13,677	9,286	496	3.63%	46	5,227
2	Alt.fan.karl-malden.nose	122,864	117,413	7,410	7,077	475	6.41%	65	4,715
3	Alt.test	178,370	18,095	54,016	8,097	742	1.37%	557	4,594
4	Alt.flame	77,645	71,858	6,688	6,008	384	5.74%	43	3,922
5	Alt.hackers.malicious	131,731	100,246	10,637	6,851	243	2.28%	49	3,680
6	Alt.alien.vampire.flonk....	83,237	78,127	5,150	4,543	322	6.25%	61	3,104
7	Soc.culture.usa	120,507	93,047	13,325	11,865	1,253	9.40%	65	3,092
8	Alt.sex	49,206	3,414	15,304	1,460	281	1.84%	108	3,057
9	Alt.troll	57,438	49,474	6,902	6,114	168	2.43%	50	3,030
10	Alt.fan.rush-limbaugh	333,113	302,167	14,293	12,833	1,322	9.25%	47	2,597

forwards the message or redirects the questioner to a more appropriate newsgroup. In practice, however, high levels of cross-posting may indicate a lack of topical focus.

The top 20 most cross-posted newsgroups are not necessarily the most active or populous newsgroups, but their high levels of interconnection make these groups the Usenet dumping grounds. High levels of cross-posting are indications that a newsgroup lacks a clear boundary, possibly indicating the lack of focused content and a stable population. More distinct boundaries may be necessary for the emergence of social ties that characterize groups that are closer to what is commonly understood to be a "community". Many of these newsgroups advertise their desire to contain random content that fosters conflict; newsgroups like alt.flame are devoted to battles and insults. An indicator of a more topically focused newsgroup is a cross-post percentage closer to 10–15% linking only to topically related newsgroups and then only moderately.

In practice, when posters cross-post many messages to another newsgroup they can effectively merge into the same group. Readers and participants in each closely cross-posted newsgroup are effectively members of a single larger meta-newsgroup. There is good reason to believe that there are far fewer meta-groups than distinctly named newsgroups since 34% of newsgroups cross-post more than 50% of the messages they contain. In 4% of all newsgroups more than 90% of the messages are cross-posted to (or from) other groups.

3.5 Conclusion: The Benefits of Awareness of Social Context and History

Ostrom (1990) studied a wide variety of communities in order to determine what features of a group contribute to its success or failure in managing collective goods. She studied communities that had a long history of successfully producing and maintaining collective goods. She also studied a number of communities that had failed partially or completely in meeting this challenge. The set of cases she examined include common forest and grazing grounds in Swiss and Japanese villages, fisheries in Canada and Sri Lanka, and irrigation systems in Spain and the Philippines. She identified a set of design principles that are features of communities which have successfully met the challenge of producing and maintaining collective goods despite the temptation of free-riding and without recourse to an external authority.

3.5.1 Mutual Awareness Is the Foundation of Self-regulation

Effective self-regulation relies on sanctioning, which in turn relies on monitoring. If it is difficult to identify either the largest contributors or the most egregious free-riders, sanctioning, whether in the form of reward or punishment, cannot function effectively. In the physical world, monitoring occurs in many ways. The mutual awareness of co-workers around common coffee-pot chores or neighbours around maintaining common spaces is often constructed through casual interaction and fairly cheap monitoring and record-keeping. But without the background of a social network of general awareness among neighbours, most neighbourhoods become more dangerous and shabby. The widespread use of wireless digital devices means that monitoring the contributions and consumption of a common resource by potentially vast groups can be made fairly cheap and fluid.

In the physical world, sanctions can range from a quiet comment to banishment, physical containment, or violence (Festinger, 1950). But successfully cooperative communities in Ostrom's (1990) study employed a graduated system of sanctions. Sanctions could be as severe as banishment from the group, but the initial sanction for breaking a rule was often very mild. Community members realized that even a well-intentioned person might break the rules when facing an unusual situation or extreme hardship. Severely punishing such a person might alienate him or her from the community, causing greater problems. Reputation services offer an almost infinitely fine-grained system of reward and punishment.

The most interesting implications are the ways these tools can allow loosely related people to cooperate and collectively create a range of services that are otherwise costly or impractical. These tools allow groups of unrelated people to cooperate with one another by providing a framework for possible sanctions for misconduct and assurances of prior cooperation. As a result, matchmaking services supported by reputation services may be the one of the most central applications. If people who can provide one another with a needed good or service can easily find one another and get assurances and recourse so that they can trust one another, a wealth of pent-up value can be released.

3.5.2 Reputation and Behavioural Histories

The emergence of cooperation in any social group depends on a number of factors. When interactions and transactions are risky or costly, people rely on trusted partners who have developed reputations and stable identities. In online environments this information is often missing; in physical environments it is often limited and costly to verify. To address this void, Web services such as eBay (Kollock, 1999) and epinions have created systems that track the reputation and history of all participants by encouraging transaction partners to review one another and then publishing the resulting dossier through a link from every reference to the participant's name in their system. Epinions goes further, tracking the amount of attention each person receives as well as the web of endorsements and denouncements that people make about one another.

Google (http://groups.google.com) (formerly Deja.com) provides reports on the histories of individuals in newsgroups. The system allows users to enter a person's name or email address and get a list of all the messages that person has contributed to all Usenet newsgroups since the service started collecting data in March 1996 (access to earlier content is continually added over time). The discussion search feature went a step further, explicitly offering a "poster profile" report, a feature continued in the revised version created when Deja was purchased by Google in 2001. The report lists the number of times the person selected posted to Usenet over a period of time.

The Netscan service (http://netscan.research.microsoft.com) builds on this concept, providing aggregated meta-data about the pattern of behaviour each author displays; for example, the percentage of postings that were responded to as well as a breakdown of each newsgroup the person posted to and the number of messages the person posted there.

These forms of reputation and behaviour tracking systems can track the state of social relationships between potentially billions of people in real time. We already have this in the form of the global credit card network and its supporting credit history databases. The next step is the extension of Internet reputation services into the realm of face-to-face interaction. Wireless hand-helds will encourage the penetration of online reputation and personal information systems, from eBay to the more traditional credit, medical, military, educational, and property and tax record systems, into what Erving Goffman referred to as the "Interaction Order", the space of direct association and communication created between people.

3.5.3 Emerging Social Accounting Services

Social accounting is a form of record-keeping that tracks interactions as well as transactions between groups of people. This means that almost any set of interactions or transactions including the give and take of conversation, of questions asked and answered, can be tracked, as can exchanges of goods and services. This allows groups to develop reputations with one another (and potentially publish those reputations before a public or select global audience).

By agreeing to participate in interactions and transactions in an environment watched by social accounting systems, participants have the opportunity to benefit both by receiving good information about other participants and by gaining a way to build a reputation of their own which, if it is good enough, will make the participant's own material stand out. If data is not only collected but also made publicly and globally accessible, the nature of disclosure and surveillance change in interesting ways. As David Brin (1998) has argued in *Transparent Society*, universal disclosure can have unexpectedly positive results. Groups may find that there are benefits to operating within such an environment by helping them see themselves better.

Social accounting data shows several practical applications and is likely to grow in quantity and availability as more of the details of social life are computer mediated and thus immediately trackable and aggregatable.

Acknowledgements

Netscan has been developed with the generous support of the Microsoft Corporation since 1996 and it is where I have been employed since 1998. Duncan Davenport created the final version of the Netscan database engine used in this study. Dany Rouhana gave Netscan its public face, building the complex web interfaces with skill. Andrew Fiore, as my summer intern in 2000, realized the designs for the thread visualization and box plot maps of Usenet. Eugene Asahara contributed the lion's share of the technical design and implementation of the first version of Netscan on the Windows platform. Key members of the early Netscan development team include Gunnar Einarsson (who also interned with me in the summer of 1999), Alex Brown got the first versions of Netscan up on the Web, Rebecca Xiong developed the network visualization interface, David Faraldo rewrote the first versions of Netscan into a working system, Joni Chu, and Han Liang helped build out the first Netscan web site in the summer of 1996.

References

Brewer, R. and Johnson, P. 1996. "Collaborative Classification and Evaluation of Usenet." Unpublished manuscript.

Donath, J. 1995. "Visual who: animating the affinities and activities of an electronic community." in Proceedings of ACM Multimedia '95. ACM Press.

Festinger, L., S. Schachter and K. Back. 1950. Social pressures in informal groups. New York: Harper.

Hardin, G. 1968/1977. "The Tragedy of the Commons." Science 162:1243–48. Pp. 16–30 in Managing the Commons, edited by Garrett Hardin and John Baden. San Francisco: Freeman.

Hardin, Garrett. 1974/1977. "Living on a Lifeboat." BioScience 24. Pp. 261–79 in Managing the Commons, edited by Garrett Hardin and John Baden. San Francisco: Freeman.

Ostrom, E. 1990. Governing the Commons: The Evolution of Institutions for Collective Action. New York: Cambridge University Press.

Raymond, E, editor. 1993. "The On-Line Hacker Jargon File" (ver. 3.0.0). Electronic document: (FTP: rtfm.mit.edu). Also published as "The New Hacker's Dictionary." Second edition. Cambridge, MA: MIT Press.

RFC 977: Network News Transfer Protocol (NNTP), http://www.w3.org/Protocols/rfc977/rfc977.html.

RFC 1036: Standard for Interchange of USENET Messages http://www.w3.org/Protocols/rfc1036/rfc1036.html.

Shneiderman, B. (no date) "Treemaps for space-constrained visualization of hierarchies." Available at: http://www.cs.umd.edu/hcil/treemaps/.

Chapter 4
The Dynamics of Mass Interaction

Steve Whittaker, Loen Terveen, Will Hill and Lynn Cherny

4.1 Introduction

Usenet may be regarded as the world's largest and fastest growing conversational application. In 1988 there were fewer than 500 newsgroups. Current estimates vary, but at the time of our data collection in December 1996, there were over 17,000 newsgroups, with approximately 3 million users worldwide (Harrison, 1994). This growth has been achieved without any centralized organization or governing body (King, 1997). The ubiquity of Usenet, and the fact that it supports conversations between hundreds or even thousands of participants, provides the opportunity to study what we term mass interaction. However, we currently lack basic data about Usenet interactions. The current paper analyses over 2.15 million messages produced by 659,450 people in 500 representative newsgroups collected over 6 months. We provide descriptive data about newsgroup demographics, communication strategies, and interactivity. We then derive predictions from the common ground model of communication to test predictions about how these parameters interact.

Previous research on Usenet has tended to carry out small-scale qualitative studies of specific newsgroups, their culture and their conversation (Baym, 1993; Sutton, 1994). Although these studies have drawn attention to important phenomena, their specific focus means they cannot address general questions that are central to mass interaction such as the levels of communication between different newsgroups. They also cannot easily examine the effects on interaction of different demographic variables or communication strategies, in order to test specific communication models.

The current study attempts to redress the balance. We first present basic information from the 500 newsgroups about mass interaction addressing the following questions. What are the demographics of a typical newsgroup: how many people contribute and how often do they do so? Is participation roughly equal, or are groups dominated by a few verbose individuals? A second set of questions concern conversational strategies. Do participants restrict their interactions to the current newsgroup or do they broadcast them widely to multiple groups (a phenomenon

Originally published in *ACM Conference on Computer-Supported Cooperative Work – 1998* (CSCW'98), pp. 257–264. © 1998 ACM Inc. Reprinted by permission.

known as cross-posting)? How long is a typical message? Do most newsgroups have FAQs (lists of frequently asked questions) and how often do they post them? Finally, we can ask questions about interactivity: how deep is a typical conversational thread, and how often are attempts to initiate conversation successful?

We also tested how well the common ground communication theory (Clark, 1992) explains mass interaction. The scale of mass interaction, and the huge numbers of messages and participants, gives rise to two novel communication problems. The first of these concern how participants establish common ground in mass interaction. Common ground is a key principle of face-to-face conversation, and refers to the fact that participants must establish a degree of mutual knowledge for their conversational contributions to be understood (Clark, 1992). Face-to-face conversations generally take place between dyads or small groups, so how can common ground be established when there is a huge set of conversational participants with potentially diverse perspectives? There are also issues concerning the stability of the newsgroup population. In some newsgroups, there is a core set of participants who repeatedly converse, allowing participants to become familiar with one another. This familiarity supports common ground, but how do conversations fare in newsgroups where the participants are constantly changing? Some newsgroups employ a strategy of moderation to address the problem of common ground. In a moderated group, all interactions are filtered by a small set of moderators who are knowledgeable about the goals and history of the newsgroup. Only messages that are relevant to the newsgroup's goals are allowed to appear. Our first set of hypotheses concern how the three demographic factors of newsgroup size, the familiarity of participants, and the effects of moderation affect common ground. We also investigate how these same factors affect interactivity. One measure of conversational interactivity is the extent to which a given conversational contribution depends on prior context (Clark, 1992; O'Conaill, 1994). By this definition, deeply threaded conversations are indicators of interactivity. We therefore looked at how demographic factors affect threading.

The second major communication problem arises directly from the difficulty of establishing common ground. Lack of common ground may mean that participants are inundated with postings that are redundant or irrelevant. For example, new participants who are ignorant of a newsgroup's goals or conversational history may post questions that have been discussed before, or are largely irrelevant to the group's interests. We therefore investigated a second set of factors concerning people's conversational strategies in addressing redundancy and irrelevance. We tested the effects of three conversational strategies on interactivity:

- FAQ production
- long messages
- low levels of cross-posting.

These strategies are all derived from the notion of common ground. FAQs exemplify common ground by summarizing prior discussions and providing information about newsgroup culture; cross-posting can be seen as a failure of common ground, representing participants' need to go outside the newsgroup for conversation; long messages can be taken as evidence for substantive discussions and hence established common ground. The common ground model would therefore predict that FAQ production, decreased cross-posting, and greater message length should all increase interactivity. A second set of partially overlapping predictions about the effects of conversational strategy on interactivity, can be derived from the Netiquette guidelines (news.announce.newusers and news.answers). These are a set of prescriptive guidelines about effective communication strategies (Horton, 1993; Kollock and Smith, 1996). They tell users to be succinct ("avoid long postings"), avoid redundant or repeat postings ("read the FAQ"), and to avoid widespread posting of messages of only marginal relevance ("don't cross-post"). With the exception of succinctness, the Netiquette guidelines and common ground model make identical predictions about the effects of conversational strategies on interactivity.

To summarize, the paper first presents basic descriptive statistics for newsgroups:

- demographics – size, familiarity and moderation
- conversation strategies – FAQ production, message length, and cross-posting
- interactivity – the extent of conversational threading.

We then use predictions derived from the common ground model to test three further questions:

- how the three demographic variables affect conversational strategy
- how demographic variables affects interactivity
- how conversational strategy affects interactivity.

We conclude with a general characterization of mass interaction and a discussion of how well the common ground model applies to mass interaction.

4.2 Usenet Organization, Distribution, and Interaction

There are several levels of structure in Usenet. Collections of messages are clustered into newsgroups, and newsgroups themselves are organized into hierarchies. Each hierarchy is intended to address different conversational topics. There are over a hundred different hierarchies but the majority of newsgroups belong to one of eight main hierarchies ("the big eight"). These eight are:

- alt for alternative topics
- comp for computer issues
- humanities
- misc for miscellaneous discussions
- news for discussions about Usenet
- rec for recreational topics; soc for social issues
- talk for general conversations.

Each hierarchy is then subdivided into more specific sub-hierarchies. The name of each newsgroup begins with the relevant main hierarchy, and terms of increasing specificity are added to this. Typical newsgroup names are rec.music.dylan and rec.music.beatles, where both newsgroups are part of the music sub-hierarchy within rec. Twelve percent of newsgroups are moderated, and moderation is reflected in

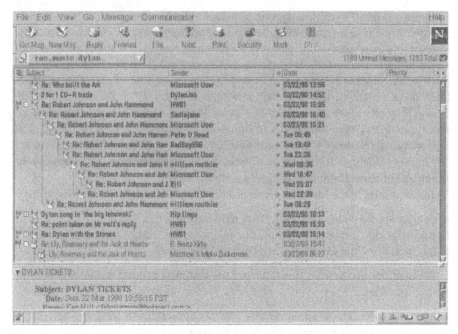

Figure 4.1 Interaction and threading in rec.music.dylan

the newsgroup name, e.g. soc.russian.culture.moderated. Newsgroup distribution also varies from site to site. Newsgroups are distributed through an informal network of servers, with the specific set of groups available at a given site being dependent on the administration policy of that particular site.

A third level of structure within newsgroups is achieved by a mechanism that tracks conversational threads (see Figure 4.1). A conversation begins with an initiating post about a new issue or question ("Re: Robert Johnson and Don Hammond", posted by HW61) and any messages responding to the new posting will be linked to the message to which they respond. This is a conversational thread, i.e. a conversation consists of an initiating post along with various responses (if the posting elicits responses). There are also multiple levels of threading, so responding to an initial post is different from responding to a response to the initial post. For example, Figure 4.1 shows that the final message in the "Robert Johnson" thread (from william routhier) was actually a response to the second posting in that thread (from Sadiejane), as revealed by the line joining them. Most newsreading software organizes messages according to threads, so users can view conversations in terms of the initiating post. They can also view the thread depth of a given message, i.e. whether it is an initiating post (depth of 0) a response an initiating post (depth of 1), and so on. Finally, cross-posting a message to multiple newsgroups is done by entering the names of additional newsgroups in the newsgroups field when composing a message.

4.3 Data Collection and Sampling

We sampled from 26 different top-level categories, including 7 of the "big 8" categories. We excluded various newsgroups for different reasons. We first excluded alt groups. Many server administrators have a policy of not distributing alt groups because of the tone and subject matter of many alt discussions. This makes alt groups less ubiquitous in terms of their distribution. The alt groups also differ from all other groups in their approval and creation process. We also excluded humanities groups because there are only a few of them (fewer than 10 worldwide that we have been able to find). We did not collect data for any binaries groups. These messages contain computer programs or images and we were only interested in textual messages, since we are studying conversation. For the same reason, we excluded news, *biz*, and *jobs* groups, because these groups are places for general announcements and advertisements, not conversation. We excluded regional groups, as our focus was on groups with global distribution.

This left us considering groups from the categories comp, misc, rec, sci, soc, and talk. From our news feed, we selected a stratified random sample of 500 newsgroups from these groups in proportion to their global occurrence, where the proportions were derived from a master list of 17,112 currently active newsgroups downloaded from uunet (ftp.uu.net). We selected only "active" groups, which we defined as those groups for which there were at least 180 messages over 6 months, equivalent to 1 message per day. A final selection criterion was moderation: the groups selected were representative of the overall level of moderation in Usenet.

We collected header information about each message in each of those newsgroups over a 6–month period, from July to December 1996. For each message we extracted various types of information including: the email address of the message poster; the date that the message was posted, the subject line of the message; message length (number of lines in the body of the message); and thread depth. In cases where messages were cross-posted we also gathered information about the newsgroups that the message was posted to.

We first present descriptive data about newsgroup demographics, conversation strategies and interactivity. We then outline specific hypotheses about the relations between these factors, and present a causal model testing these hypotheses.

4.4 Descriptive Results

4.4.1 Demographics

Table 4.1 shows demographic statistics for the 500 newsgroups. For each newsgroup, we calculated the total number of messages that people posted over the 6–month interval, and the number of different people who posted to that newsgroup. Overall levels of message traffic were high, with each group on average receiving 4,299 messages (an average of 24 messages per newsgroup per day). In addition, each newsgroup attracted contributions from an average of 1,319 different posters. Together, these statistics provide evidence for mass interaction.

Table 4.1 Descriptive statistics for the 500 newsgroups over the 6 months of the study

	Data collected	Mean
Demographics	Number of participants	1319
	% messages from repeat posters	73
	Number messages	4299
Conversational strategies	Message length	44
	% messages that were cross-posted	34
	% messages that were FAQs	0.4
Interactivity	Thread depth	1.8

To calculate the familiarity of posters in a newsgroup, we used the criterion of repeat posting, i.e. whether a person posts more than once to a newsgroup. Our data show that in general a significant proportion of users are unfamiliar: 27% of messages are from "singleton posters" who contribute only once to a newsgroup. This raised the issue of whether newsgroups have participation inequality. Some participants must be contributing large numbers of messages, given the high proportion of singleton posters and that the mean level of contribution is 3.1 messages/poster. Figure 4.2 shows highly unequal levels of participation in each newsgroup. The right-hand side of the graph shows that the majority of people post only a few times, and the left-hand side reveals that there are a few people who post a large number of times. A final statistic bearing this out is that a tiny percentage (2.9%) of posters in each newsgroup account for an average 25% of the total posts (Figure 4.2).

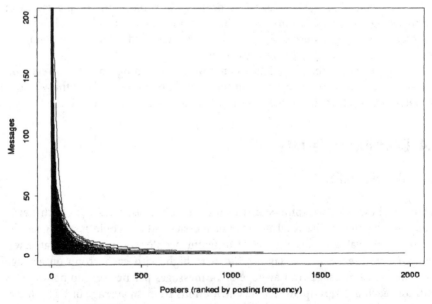

Figure 4.2 Levels of individual participation within newsgroups.

4.4.2 Conversational Strategies

We found cross-posting to be prevalent. On average 34% messages in each news-group were addressed to at least one other group, and the average cross-posted message targeted 3.1 other newsgroups. Cross-posting was not specific, either: news-groups were highly inconsistent in the set of external groups they cross-posted to. Each newsgroup overall cross-posted to a mean of 272 distinct groups. To further investigate the precision of cross-posts, we calculated the mean number of cross-posts per distinct cross-posted group. Strong links between groups would lead to a large number of cross-postings to a small number of groups and hence a high mean. However, the mean was 5.4. The absence of specific cross-posting argues against the view that there are strong communication ties between specific newsgroups.

FAQs were detected automatically by an algorithm which searched subject lines for the words "FAQ" or "Frequently Asked Questions". It excluded certain other special cases such as subject lines including the word "re". FAQs are a common feature of newsgroups, as shown by the fact that 54% of newsgroups had FAQs, although less than 0.5% of messages were FAQs. We also calculated average message length, which was 44 lines.

4.4.3 Interactivity

Finally we looked at interactivity. The average thread depth is 1.8 messages, sug-gesting a typical exchange in which the average message refers to approximately 2 other messages. A substantial proportion of messages (33%) had 2 or more responses, indicating frequent extended conversations. We also calculated a com-plementary measure of interactivity, the number of initiating posts (those with 0 references and thread depth of 1). A high proportion of initiating messages would indicate repeated failures to start conversations, or a prevalence of conversational dead-ends. We found that initiating messages are highly prevalent, accounting for over more than 40% of messages. This suggests a view of Usenet in which it is hard to start a conversation. Once a conversation starts, however, it then seems to attract multiple contributions.

4.5 Testing the Common Ground Model

We next use the common ground model to derive a specific set of predictions. Each of the conversational strategy variables:

- increased FAQ production
- decreased cross-posting
- longer messages

can be seen as an index of common ground. From our earlier arguments we would therefore expect demographics to affect common ground and hence conversa-tional strategies in the following ways:

- H1: Newsgroups that are larger in size will have more difficulty establishing common ground, we would therefore expect them to have (a) fewer FAQs; (b) more cross-posting; and (c) shorter messages.
- H2: Newsgroups containing many repeat posters (i.e. people who are familiar with the newsgroup) will establish common ground more easily, they will therefore have (a) more FAQs; (b) less cross-posting; and (c) longer messages.
- H3: Moderated newsgroups should more easily establish common ground, and hence have (a) more FAQs; (b) less cross-posting; and (c) longer messages.

We also expected conversational strategy variables to influence interactivity. If newsgroups can establish common ground through effective communication strategies, we should expect this to be manifested in terms of more interactive conversation as indicated by greater thread depth:

- H4: Newsgroups with more FAQs will have greater interactivity, as manifested by increased thread depth.
- H5: Newsgroups with less cross-posting will have greater interactivity, as manifested by increased thread depth.
- H6: Newsgroups with longer messages will have greater interactivity, as manifested by increased thread depth.

We should also expect demographic factors to have direct affects on interactivity:

- H7: Newsgroups that are larger in size will have less interactivity, as manifested by reduced thread depth.
- H8: Newsgroups containing repeat posters (i.e. people who are familiar with the newsgroup) will have greater interactivity, as manifested by increased thread depth.
- H9: Moderated newsgroups will have greater interactivity as manifested by increased thread depth.

We tested these predictions using the following causal model, which was tested using a series of regression analyses (Cohen, 1995):

Demographics → Conversational strategies → Interactivity

The overall analysis involved two steps. In the first we regressed each of the demographic variables onto the conversational strategy variables to test H1–H3, and second we regressed all variables onto interactivity to test H4–H9. Where relevant, variables were normalized to allow for the fact that there were different numbers of messages and participants contributing to each newsgroup. For several variables (e.g. cross-posting) we experimented with different operationalizations (e.g. mean number of cross-posts/message, mean overall number of groups cross-posted to), choosing the operationalization that best accounted for the variance in the regression equations.

4.5.1 Effects of Demographics on Conversational Strategy

Figure 4.3 shows the results of three regressions of demographics on conversational strategy. The numbers on the arcs represent the standardized β weights. For simplicity of presentation we show only significant relationships. Overall the

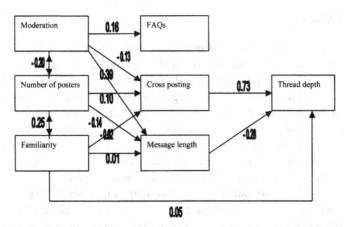

Figure 4.3 Causal model showing effects of variables in structural equation analysis, for demographic, conversational strategy, and interactivity variables.

models for each of the three factors was statistically significant. For message length ($F[3,496] = 41.3, p < 0.001, R^2 = 0.20$), for cross-posting ($F[3,496] = 11.3, p < 0.001$, $R^2 = 0.06$), and for FAQs ($F[3,496] = 5.89, p < 0.01, R^2 = 0.03$). We now discuss the specific predictions about the effects of each demographic factor. Although size had no effect on FAQs (H1a), predictions concerning hypothesis H1b and H1c were confirmed: newsgroups that are larger in size have more cross-posting ($t = 2.2, p < 0.05, \beta = 0.10$) and shorter messages ($t = 3.2, p < 0.01, \beta = 0.14$). The familiarity predictions H2b and H2c were also confirmed: newsgroups containing more familiar contributors had less cross-posting ($t = 4.5, p < 0.001, \beta = 0.02$) and longer messages ($t = 2.4, p < 0.05, \beta = 0.01$), although again there was no affect of familiarity on FAQs, so H2a was not confirmed. Finally predictions H3a,b, and c were all confirmed. Moderation led to more FAQs ($t = 3.5, p < 0.001, \beta = 0.16$) reduced cross-posting ($t = 2.8, p < 0.01, \beta = 0.13$) and longer messages ($t = 9.5, p < 0.001, \beta = 0.39$).

4.5.2 Effects of Demographics and Conversational Strategy on Interactivity

The full model was very successful at predicting interactivity ($F[6,493] = 133.9$, $p < 0.001, R^2 = 0.62$). However, two of the predictions about the effects of conversational strategy on interactivity were not confirmed. H5 predicted that newsgroups with less cross-posting will have greater interactivity, but in fact the less cross-posting there was in the group, the less the threading ($t = 23.3, p < 0.001$, $\beta = 0.73$). H6 predicted that newsgroups with longer messages will have greater interactivity, but in fact message length reduced interactivity ($t = 5.2, p < 0.001$, $\beta = 0.28$). There were no effects of FAQs on interactivity (H4).

Only one of the predictions about the effects of demographics on interactivity was confirmed, namely H8 – newsgroups containing familiar contributors will have greater thread depth ($t = 16.2, p < 0.001, \beta = 0.05$). Neither H7 nor H9, concerning the effect of FAQs and size, was validated.

4.6 Conclusions

We can draw a number of conclusions about mass interaction from this research. Although there are large numbers of people contributing to each newsgroup and large numbers of messages overall, the descriptive data show that the default mass interaction consists of a 43–line message referring to 2 previous messages. This indicates moderate but not large amounts of interactivity. This general view about interactivity should be tempered, however, by the fact that many attempts to initiate interaction were failures; over 40% of messages were initiating attempts. This suggests a problem of conversational inertia: it seems to be difficult to start a mass interaction but it is relatively easy to continue it once started.

We also found massive participation inequalities between different people in a given newsgroup. This is an important clarification of the view that the Internet is an egalitarian forum (King, 1997). It is true that anyone can post to a newsgroup, but the descriptive data clearly shows that conversations in newsgroups are dominated by a minority of highly verbose participants. Again this argues for a view that Usenet conversations do not strictly involve repeated levels of mass participation, as evidenced by the fact that 27% of messages are generated by people who contribute only once to the newsgroup. Overall, these results suggest that as far as active posting is concerned, mass interaction may be a misnomer. Typical conversations involve only small numbers of posters, and newsgroups are often dominated by cliques of verbose contributors. This participation inequality contrasts with research on face-to-face interaction and video-mediated communication which has shown much more equal levels of participation (O'Conaill, 1994). Participation inequality may not have wholly negative outcomes, however. The majority of Usenet participants may well be satisfied with making infrequent contributions, posting only about issues that are important to them. Such peripheral participation may enable people to remain in the background, monitoring general conversations until they spot a topic of direct relevance, or they need to pose a question of their own. This type of background involvement has been observed to be beneficial in the case of corporate email (Kraut, 1997) and interpersonal communication (Kraut, 1992). This form of participation has also been proposed as an important way for novices to learn about a novel topic (Kraut, 1992).

Although the conversational and participation data suggest a view in which conversation is carried out locally by a few participants, the cross-posting data suggest a slightly different perspective. It turns out that cross-posting is frequent, although it propagates potentially irrelevant messages and is thus contrary both to the common ground model and to Netiquette guidelines. Cross-posting can also inform us about the relations between newsgroups. When people do cross-post, they are unspecific about the groups they cross-post to, as indicated by the fact that the average newsgroup cross-posted to over 200 others. This in turn argues against the view that there are tight conversational links between different newsgroups (Smith, 1997).

We also tested a number of predictions derived from the common ground model. These were mainly verified for the effects of demographics on common ground. The demographic variables of moderation, familiarity, and smaller newsgroups all increased common ground as measured by increased message length and decreased cross-posting. The effects on FAQ production were less clear, however. Only moderation increased FAQ production, with neither familiarity nor size having an effect. This view argues against the view that FAQs are a "defence mechanism" arising from participants' desire to instil consensus in diverse or rapidly changing user populations. Rather, FAQs are most likely to arise under the orderly conditions induced by moderation.

What about the effects of demographics on interactivity? Here the common ground model fared much less well: Only familiarity directly increased threading, with neither moderation nor size having an effect. Furthermore, and contrary to our expectations, cross-posting increased interactivity. This is counter to both the common ground view and the Netiquette guidelines: both of these contend that cross-posting should dilute conversational focus and hence reduce interactivity. This result is consistent, however, with a different perspective on large scale interaction, namely weak ties (Constant et al, 1996; Granovetter, 1973). The positive effects of cross-posting on interactivity suggests that people exploit the mass distribution properties and diverse population of Usenet to go beyond a particular newsgroup to carry out their conversations. Combining the results about the effects of familiarity and cross-posting on interactivity indicates that there may be two complementary sets of circumstances that facilitate mass interaction. The first occurs when familiar participants share common ground and the second is where people seek out diverse perspectives by posting outside their newsgroup. Our final prediction about the effects of message length on interactivity was also disconfirmed: shorter messages actually promoted interactivity. How can we explain this? One possibility is consistent with communication overload (Whittaker and Sidner, 1996; Kraut and Attewell, 1997). Given the huge amounts of conversational traffic in Usenet, people are less likely to read, and hence reply to, long messages. Such an interpretation would be consistent with the Netiquette stricture ("avoid long postings").

Although moderation and FAQ production increased common ground, they had no effects on interactivity. Why was this the case? One reason why moderation does not increase threading may be that moderators increase conversational relevance by deciding that a new posting is tangential to the topic, and stopping the current thread. In doing so, however, they automatically reduce the amount of threading. A reason for the absence of expected conversational benefit of FAQs may be that FAQs have two contradictory effects. FAQs may promote conversation by providing access to information about group culture, conversational expectations and a précis of group conversational history. At the same time they may discourage newcomers from productively revisiting a previous conversation out of the mistaken belief that the topic has been exhausted. New research involving content analysis of FAQs and moderators' strategies is necessary to determine whether these suggestions are the case.

Our findings should also be qualified by a number of provisos. Our strictly quantitative analysis needs to be complemented by content analysis, as well as surveys of Usenet participants. The current analysis is silent about the effects of conversational content: which specific topics or conversational styles encourage large responses and which fail to elicit a response? What factors encourage or discourage flaming? What are people's reactions to flagrant examples of cross-posting? Surveys and interviews could also address people's attitudes to, and satisfaction with their Usenet interactions. Why do people contribute to certain discussions but not to others? How long do people lurk before they first post? And how is dominance viewed? Why do certain people post multiple messages and how are they perceived by others for doing so? Again some of these issues have been addressed in small scale studies, but more of this type of work is needed (Baym, 1993; Sutton, 1994). There are also issues about moderation and FAQ maintenance which are highly relevant for issues of group memory (Berlin et al, 1993): why do certain people take on the responsibility of moderating or maintaining FAQs, and what is their motive for doing so? Other issues that need to be addressed by content analysis include deliberate attempts to subvert Usenet conversation ("spamming, "trolling") or the generation of messages by artificial agents ("bots").

Finally there are issues concerning the use of thread depth to measure interactivity. One potential objection to using threading is it fails to include "backchannel" responses in email: Usenet users report that they sometimes reply to a public Usenet message privately in email. However, our interest here was in publicly observed mass interaction, and email conversations are not part of the public record. This argument also applies to the issue of "lurking", i.e. reading newsgroup messages without responding to them. Although lurking may be a prevalent behaviour, again it leaves no public conversational trace. Finally there is the question of "flaming". Deeply threaded Usenet interactions sometimes result from emotionally charged and occasionally personally abusive exchanges. However, this addresses the question of conversational content, an issue which we leave to future work.

What are the theoretical implications of these results? Our data shows that while the common ground model provides a good account of the effects of demographics on conversational strategy, it is much weaker at predicting interactivity. Two major modifications need to be made in applying the common ground model to mass interaction. The fact that shorter messages promoted interactivity suggests that a model of mass interaction also needs to incorporate the notion of conversational overload: participants have to filter large numbers of messages to find relevant information, with the consequence that long messages may be ignored. Our finding that cross-posting benefits interaction indicates that the model needs to take account of the benefits of both familiarity and diversity. On the one hand common ground can promote consensus, but conversations can grow stale through over-familiarity of topics and people. On the other hand, a diverse population may stimulate interaction but their widely disparate perspectives may mean that no conversational progress can be made.

Acknowledgements

We thank Marc Smith, Lyn Walker, and Julia Hirschberg for comments on early versions of this work.

References

Baym, N. (1993) Interpreting soap operas and creating community: Inside a computer-mediated fan culture, Journal of Folklore Research, 30, 143–176.

Berlin, L., Jeffries, R., O'Day, V., Paepcke, A., and Wharton, C. (1993) Where did you put it? Issues in the design and use of a group memory. In Proceedings of CHI'93, 33–30.

Clark, H. (1992) Arenas of language use. University of Chicago Press, Chicago.

Cohen, P. (1995) Empirical methods for artificial intelligence, Boston, MIT Press.

Constant, D., Sproull, L., and Kiesler, S. (1996) The kindness of strangers, Organizational Science, 7, 119–135.

Granovetter, M. (1973) The strength of weak ties. American Journal of Sociology, 78, 1360–1380.

Harrison, M. (1994) The Usenet handbook. O'Reilly, Boston.

Horton, M. (1993): Rules for posting to Usenet, news.misc,news.answers., FTP at rtfm.mit.edu.

King, J. Grinter, R and Pickering, J. (1997) The rise and fall of Netville. In S. Kiesler (Ed.), Culture of the internet. Erlbaum, NJ.

Kollock, P and Smith, M (1996) Managing the Virtual Commons In S. Herring (Ed.) Computer-Mediated Communication, John Benjamins, Philadelphia.

Kraut, R. and Attewell, P (1997) Media use in a global corporation. In S. Kiesler (Ed.), Culture of the Internet, Erlbaum, NJ.

Kraut, R., Fish, R., Root, B. and Chalfonte, B (1992) Informal communication in organizations. In R. Baecker (Ed.), Groupware and Computer Supported Co-operative Work, 287–314, Morgan Kaufman, CA.

Markus, M (1990) Towards a critical mass theory of interactive media. In J. Fulk and C. Steinfield (Eds.), Organizations and Communication Technology, Sage, CA.

O'Conaill, B., Whittaker, S., and Wilbur, S (1994) Conversations over video conferences, Human Computer Interaction, 8, 389–428.

Smith, M (1997) Measuring the social structure of the Usenet, Unpublished paper, University of California, Los Angeles.

Sproull, L., and Kiesler, S (1991) Connections, Boston, MIT Press.

Sutton, L (1994) Gender, power, and silencing in electronic discourse on Usenet, Proceedings of the 20th Berkeley Linguistics Society, University of California, Berkeley.

Whittaker, S. (1996) Talking to strangers: an evaluation of the factors affecting electronic collaboration, In Proceedings of CSCW96, ACM Press, NY.

Whittaker, S. and Sidner, C (1996) Email overload: exploring personal information management of email. In Proceedings of CHI96, ACM Press, NY.

Chapter 5
Conversation Map: A Content-based Usenet Newsgroup Browser
Warren Sack

5.1 Introduction

The Conversation Map system is a Usenet newsgroup browser that analyses the text of an archive of newsgroup messages and outputs a graphical interface that can be used to search and read the messages of the archive. The system incorporates a series of novel text analysis procedures that automatically computes (1) a set of social networks detailing who is responding to or citing whom in the newsgroup; (2) a set of "discussion themes" that are frequently used in the newsgroup archive; and (3) a set of semantic networks that represent the main terms under discussion and some of their relationships to one another. The text analysis procedures are written in the Perl programming language. Their results are recorded as Hypertext Markup Language (HTML, which is used to describe web pages), and the HTML is displayed with a Java applet. With the Java-based graphical interface one can browse a set of Usenet newsgroup articles according to who is "talking" to whom, what they are "talking" about, and the central terms and possible emergent metaphors of the conversation. In this paper it is argued that the Conversation Map system is just one example of a new kind of content-based browser that will combine the analysis powers of computational linguistics with a graphical interface to allow network documents and messages to be viewed in ways not possible with today's existing format-based browsers, which do not analyse the contents of the documents or messages.

Recent advances in computational linguistics and quantitative sociology make it possible to envision new designs for existing, network-based browsers and clients (e.g. web browsers, newsreaders, email clients, etc.). These new content-based browsers and clients will treat the contents of the messages and documents displayed and not just their formats. Roughly speaking, these new designs will incorporate the functionality of existing browsers together with text analysis and information retrieval capabilities more sophisticated than those now used in, for example, web-based search engines.

Originally published in *ACM Conference on Intelligent User Interfaces - 2000* (IUI'00), pp. 233–240. © 2000 ACM Inc. Reprinted by permission.

This paper describes the design of a prototype Usenet newsgroup browser, Conversation Map. The Conversation Map system employs a set of text analysis procedures to produce a graphical interface. With the graphical interface one can browse a set of Usenet newsgroup articles according to who is "talking" to whom, what they are "talking" about, and the central terms and possible emergent metaphors of the conversation. To allow this combination of social and semantic navigation (Dourish and Chalmers, 1994) the Conversation Map system computes a social network (cf. Wasserman and Galaskiewicz, 1994) corresponding to who is replying to (or citing) whose messages. The Conversation Map system also parses and analyses the contents of the newsgroup articles to calculate a semantic network (cf. Quillian, 1968) that highlights frequently used terms that are similar to one another in the Usenet newsgroup discussion. For example, if the discussion includes messages concerning "time" and other messages concerning "money" and these two terms ("time" and "money") are used in similar ways by the discussants (e.g. "You're wasting my time", "You're wasting my money", "You need to budget your time", "You need to budget your money") then the two terms will show up close to one another in the graphically displayed semantic network and so indicate the presence of a literal or metaphorical similarity between the terms (e.g. "Time is money"). In addition, the Conversation Map system analyses connections between messages to extract an approximation of the discussion themes shared between newsgroup participants.

The output of the text analysis procedures are automatically translated into interface devices that allow one to browse the Usenet newsgroup articles in ways that would be impossible with a conventional, "format-based" newsreader (e.g. RN, Eudora, or Netscape). One of the purposes of this research is to produce a better Usenet newsgroup browser for newsgroup participants and others who might like a quick way of discovering the terms and social structure of a newsgroup (e.g. sociologists and anthropologists of online text and social activity). The text analysis procedures are implemented in the Perl programming language and the graphical interface is programmed in Java. The example of the Conversation Map interface to be discussed in this paper can be found at http://www.media.mit.edu/~wsack/CM. Viewing the example Java interface requires a newer web browser (e.g. Netscape version 4.5 or better) and a operating system that supports Java 1.2 (e.g. Windows or Linux).

This paper is divided into three sections. The first section describes the graphical interface of the Conversation Map system, the second sketches out the text analysis procedures, and the third explains the Conversation Map system in the context of related work.

5.2 The Graphical Interface

Figure 5.1 was produced by the Conversation Map system after an analysis of over 1200 messages from the Usenet newsgroup soc.culture.albanian, a group devoted to the discussion of Albanian culture in general, but at this period in time (16 April 1999–4 May 1999) especially to the war in Kosovo. The following explanations of

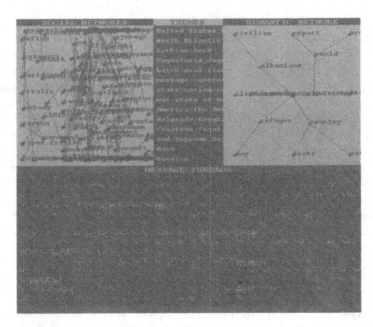

Figure 5.1 The Conversation Map main interface, with four panes: "social networks", "themes", "semantic networks", and "threads".

the interface will use images from the analysis of this newsgroup as an example. However, it should be clear that this is only one example. The Conversation Map system can be run on the message archive of any newsgroup concerning any topic and will produce a unique interface image for each and every newsgroup archive.

The interface is divided in two pieces:

- below the grey line labelled "message threads" is a graphical representation of the newsgroup messages that have been analysed by the Conversation Map system
- above the grey line is a display of the three-part analysis: (a) social networks; (b) discussion themes, and (c) a semantic network.

All parts of the interface are interconnected with the other parts of the interface, so clicking on one part will highlight parts of it, but will also highlight other parts of the interface too. To explain the parts and their interconnections, each part of the image shown in Figure 5.1 will be explained.

5.2.1 Social Networks

By automatically identifying who has either responded to or quoted from whom, the Conversation Map system calculates a social network given an archive of Usenet newsgroup messages. The nodes in the network represent people – i.e. participants in the online discussion – and the links represent reciprocating quotations or responses. Thus, if participant A responds to or quotes a message from participant B and then, later in the discussion, participant B quotes from or responds to a message from par-

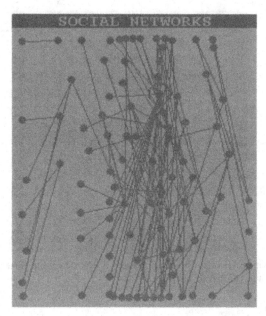

Figure 5.2 Conversation Map social networks, with names turned off.

ticipant A, a link is drawn between nodes labelled "A" and "B". In the calculated social networks, if A and B have reciprocated frequently, the link between them will be shorter than if they have only quoted from or responded to one another once or twice. By positioning the mouse over the social networks panel and then pressing the right mouse button, the names labelling the nodes of the social network can be turned off.

With the names off, it becomes easier to see that some participants are central to the newsgroup discussion and others are more marginal. The nodes with many connections represent participants who are both responding to and being responded to by many other participants. In other words, reciprocity is highlighted in the computed social networks. The layout algorithm used tends to push the central participants to the centre. By simultaneously holding down the shift key and the mouse button one can drag the nodes of the social networks around and get a better feel for the connectivity of various portions of the networks (Figure 5.2).

To turn the names labelling the nodes of the networks on again, press the right mouse button again (or, simultaneously the meta-key and mouse button if you have a one-button mouse) (Figure 5.3).

If one clicks the mouse button over one of the nodes in the networks, a small portion of a network is highlighted and the rest of the social networks disappear. The node selected (representing one participant in the newsgroup) and all the nodes linked to it are highlighted. At the same time, all of the threads in the archive are highlighted (with a light grey oval) in which the selected participant posted one or more messages.

By holding down the control key and simultaneously clicking the mouse button, a second participant in the social networks can be selected. The edge between the

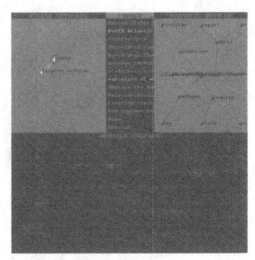

Figure 5.3 One participant selected. The social network is centred on one participant; all threads in which this participant has posted are circled.

two selected participants is highlighted, the threads where the two exchanged messages (or citations) are highlighted (in the case shown below, only one thread is highlighted), and, also, the discussion themes à propos of the messages exchanged by the pair are highlighted in the themes menu (in this case, two themes are visibly highlighted: the posters sent messages or quoted one another on the subject of the North Atlantic Treaty Organization (NATO) and the subject of war).

To make all of the social networks reappear, hold down the alt key and click the mouse button (Figure 5.4).

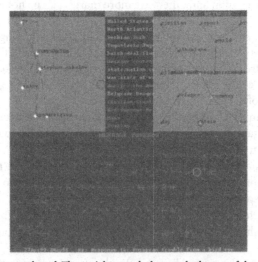

Figure 5.4 Two participants selected. The social network shows only the two of them; themes shared by both participants are highlighted.

5.2.2 Discussion Themes

If participant A mentioned the word "baseball" in a post that also quoted a part of a message from participant B wherein B wrote about the term "football", and then, later in the conversation participant B wrote about basketball in response to a message by A concerning soccer, then the link between A and B in the social network might be labelled with the term "sports" since baseball, football, soccer, and basketball are all sports. An analysis of discussion themes of this sort is done by the Conversation Map system.

A parenthetical note on "discussion themes": strictly speaking – i.e. according to the terminology of linguistics – the Conversation Map system does not identify discussion themes per se, but, rather, performs an analysis of lexical cohesion. Performing an analysis of lexical cohesion is only one step of many that would be required if – within linguistics – it was to be claimed that the Conversation Map system identified discussion themes. However, since an analysis of lexical cohesion is a necessary step in the determination of discussion themes, we will call the analysis an analysis of discussion themes for the sake of simplicity.

In the interface, the results of the discussion theme analysis are displayed as a menu of themes. When one clicks on the menu item "sports" the link between A and B is highlighted (along with the links between any other pairs of posters who are connected through a discussion of sports). We refer to this combination of the social network and a discussion themes analysis as an analysis of social cohesion (Sack, 1999). Following is a picture of the same social network shown in the previous figure along with the menu of discussion themes that link messages, and thus, people together in conversation about the larger topic of Kosovo and Albanian culture in general. The "NATO" item in the themes menu has been highlighted by

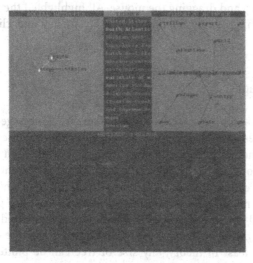

Figure 5.5 One theme, "North Atlantic Treaty Organization," selected. The theme only connects two pairs of posters, but it appears in many threads.

clicking on it with the mouse. Figure 5.5 shows which pairs of posters have exchanged messages concerning NATO. Again, the unhighlighted portions of the social networks disappear from view and the portions of the archive where NATO connects two or more messages together are highlighted in the lower portion of the interface.

Note that only two pairs of posters seem to have exchanged messages about NATO, but many threads in the archive use NATO as a lexical tie between messages. It is probably not the case that the four participants highlighted in the social networks are responsible for all of the threads concerning NATO. Rather, it must be kept in mind that a pair of posters is highlighted if and only if they have a two-way, back-and-forth exchange involving a given theme. In contrast, the criteria for highlighting a thread in the archive is less rigorous: a thread in the archive is highlighted for a given theme if the theme connects even one pair of messages in the thread.

Themes in the menu are listed according to the number of pairs of participants they connect in the social network. Thus "United States" is listed above "NATO" because "NATO" links only two pairs of posters whereas "United States" links three pairs. All of the themes down to "war; state of war; warfare" link two pairs; "America; the Americas" links one pair as do the rest of the following items in the menu.

Clicking on a theme is equivalent to searching the message threads, but the search performed differs from a conventional keyword search. A keyword search would find, for instance, every mention of the term "NATO". In contrast, the theme search criteria are more rigorous. The theme search criteria are only fulfilled if, for instance, "NATO" is mentioned in one message of the thread and then again in a response or quoting message later in the thread.

Multiple themes can be selected by holding down the control key while pushing the mouse button. The menu can be scrolled down by simultaneously holding down the shift key and dragging the mouse. All highlighted themes can be simultaneously unhighlighted by holding down the Alt key and clicking the mouse button.

5.2.3 The Messages

Threads in a newsgroup discussion consist of an initial message concerning some subject, a set of responses to the initial message, a set of responses to the responses, and so forth. Therefore, conceptually, a thread is a "tree" in which the initial message is the "root" and links between responses are the "branches" of the "tree". Graphically, a thread tree can be plotted as a "spider web" in which the initial post is placed in the middle, the responses to the initial post are plotted in a circle around the initial post, the responses to the responses are plotted in a circle around the responses, etc. One of the nice features of plotting the thread trees as "spider webs" is that, at least in theory, any size of tree can be plotted within a given amount of space.

In the bottom half of Figure 5.6, over 400 threads are plotted as spider webs constrained into rectangular (rather than circular) spaces. The threads are arranged chronologically from upper left to lower right. By passing the mouse over each thread, the start and end dates and the subject lines of each thread can be read in turn in light grey text written into the dark grey strip at the bottom of the interface.

Since each thread is allotted the same amount of screen space, a rough guide to newsgroup activity can be read off of the panel in which all of the threads are plotted. If a thread without many messages is plotted, the rectangle containing it in the panel appears as mostly black. Threads containing many messages, and thus a lot of activity, appear very green (dark in the figure).

In Figure 5.5 the threads in the archive where "NATO" is a theme of discussion are highlighted. It can be seen that the "NATO" theme is discussed in some of the busiest – i.e. largest – threads of the newsgroup archive.

In Figure 5.6, one thread from the archive has been selected with a mouse click. The thread selected has a white oval drawn around it. Note also that the dates when the messages of the thread were posted (27 April 1999–1 May 1999) and the subject line of the first message in the thread is printed in the dark grey strip at the bottom of the interface: "Re: Response to: European trouble from a bird eye". In addition, parts of the social network, the themes menu, and the semantic network have also been highlighted. In the social network, those participants who are part of the social networks and who also have posted to the selected thread are highlighted. In the themes menu, those themes which connect two or more messages in the selected thread are highlighted. In the semantic network, those terms which correspond to the highlighted themes are also highlighted. The connection between the themes and the terms in the semantic network will be more fully explained in the section below devoted to the semantic network.

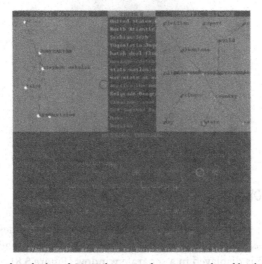

Figure 5.6 One thread selected. Many themes, and posters, are shared by these threads.

5.2.4 Message Threads

A thread can be opened and explored by double-clicking on it with the mouse. A double-click opens a separate window containing a larger version of the graphical display of the thread. Figure 5.7 illustrates an opened thread.

Normally, the nodes of a thread (representing messages in the thread) would be labelled with the names of the participants who posted them. In Figure 5.7, however, the names have been turned off (using the right mouse button or meta-click combination). In addition, some of the nodes of the thread have been moved around (by holding down the shift key and dragging the mouse).

The spider web shape of the thread tree can be seen. If the thread was perfectly balanced (i.e. if each message had exactly the same number of responses as every other message), then the graphical plot of thread would more closely resemble a symmetrical web. However, a symmetrical shape is more the exception than the rule. The initial message of the thread is plotted as the largest green node in the centre. In the thread shown above, the discussion theme "Croatia" has been highlighted. The menu of discussion themes can be scrolled by holding down the Shift key and dragging the mouse. Clicking on a discussion theme in the menu of themes highlights it in white; the portion of the thread in which it is used as a theme is also highlighted in white. In this case, it can be seen that three of the messages of the thread are connected together by the theme "Croatia".

Figure 5.7 Conversation Map thread view.

5.2.5 Message Display

In the thread shown above, a white circle around one of the nodes shows the position of the mouse. If the mouse is clicked, the text of the message (represented by the circled node) is displayed in a separate window (Figure 5.8).

The use of "Croatia" as a discussion theme that links two of the messages of the thread is visible in the display of the message shown above. "Montenegro" is mentioned in a quote from a previous message and "Croatia" is discussed in the present message. The discussion themes analysis procedure of the Conversation Map system connected these two terms together because, in the thesaurus used in the Conversation Map system (i.e. Wordnet version 1.6; Fellbaum, 1998), Montenegro is listed as a part of Croatia. The text of the message displayed above also illustrates two other features of the Conversation Map system as a Usenet newsgroup browser:

- Since quotations within messages are identified as a part of the analysis procedure for building the social networks, quotations within a given message are automatically highlighted as hypertext within the display of the text of the message. Clicking on the text of a quotation will open a new window containing the full text of the quoted message.
- Near the top of every message is a PREVIOUS and a NEXT label. If there is a • symbol listed next to the PREVIOUS label, clicking on the • will open a window containing the text of the message that precedes the current message. A message, A, is said to precede another message, B, if B is sent in reply to A. Since several messages might be sent in reply to a message, one or more •s might appear after a NEXT label. Click on each of the • symbols listed after the NEXT label to see all of the messages sent in response to the current message.

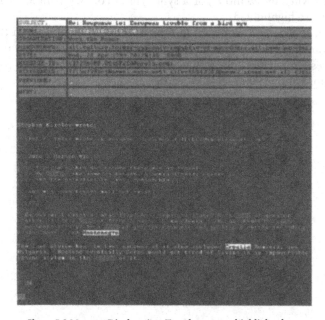

Figure 5.8 Message Display view. Two themes are highlighted.

5.2.6 Semantic Network

The upper right-hand corner of the main screen of the interface displays a semantic network (Figure 5.9). In the semantic network, if two terms are connected together, then they have been calculated to have been "talked about" in similar ways in the archive of newsgroup messages.

The central terms of a discussion are often connected to two or more other terms. Thus, in the soc.culture.albanian archive "people" is computed to be a central, perhaps neutral, term in the vicious argumentation that characterizes the content of many of the messages in the example archive. In this archive Albanians are "talked about" as people, Serbs are talked about as people, refugees are talked about as people, as are governments and countries. In other words, it appears to be the case that all sides of the argument (which is predominantly an argument pitting the Albanian view of the Kosovo situation against the Serbian view) can agree that the more general term "people" is applicable to both Serbs and Albanians.

The graphical interface uses the same spider web algorithm to lay out the semantic network as it uses to display the thread trees. Note that the algorithm sometimes overlaps nodes of the graph. In Figure 5.9, the nodes of the semantic network have been rearranged for legibility by holding down the shift key and dragging the mouse.

Nodes of the semantic network can be selected by clicking the mouse. For example, if the term "country" is selected, all of the themes synonymous with country are highlighted in the themes. Simultaneously, all of the participants in the social network connected by the highlighted themes are also highlighted, and all of the threads wherein "country", or a synonym of country, is used as a discussion theme are also highlighted.

To better understand why a given term appears where it does in the semantic network, double click on the term to see all of the associations it has in the archive of messages. Double-clicking on the term "country" produces a web page containing the information (Figure 5.10).

Figure 5.9 Conversation Map semantic networks.

The associations displayed in Figure 5.10 were calculated by the Conversation Map system. The Conversation Map system parses and analyses the contents of the newsgroup messages to calculate the semantic network. In the semantic network, terms that are similar to one another in the newsgroup messages are connected together by a line. To calculate which terms are similar to one another, the Conversation Map system compares the list of associations for each term against the list of associations of every other term. For example, if the discussion includes

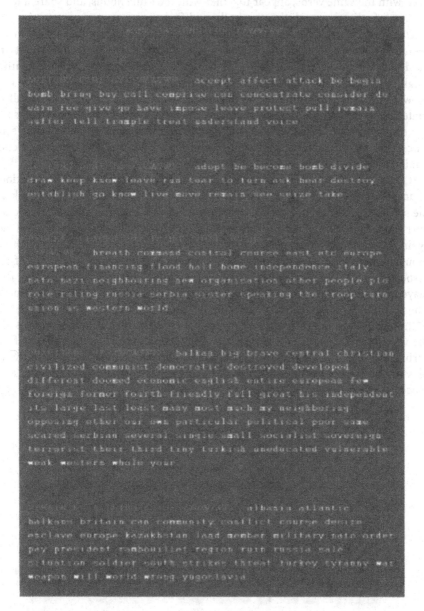

Figure 5.10 Word association map for the word "country," separated by category.

messages concerning "time" and other messages concerning "money" and these two terms ("time" and "money") are used in similar ways by the discussants (e.g. "You're wasting my time", "You're wasting my money", "You need to budget your time", "You need to budget your money") then the two terms will show up close to one another in the graphically displayed semantic network and so indicate the presence of a literal or metaphorical similarity between the terms (e.g. "Time is money"). Specifically, two terms are "talked about" in similar ways if they are often used with the same verbs, appear together with the same nouns, and share a large number of adjectives with they are both modified.

The word associations, which can be viewed by double-clicking on a term in the semantic network, is a complete list of the verbs, adjectives, and nouns that are used with the given term. Each of the word associations can be "opened" with a single click. If the verb "consider" is clicked on from the display shown above, a web browser window containing the following table appears. This table shows all of sentences in the archive of messages where the term "country" has appeared as the subject of the verb "consider". To see the message that contains an example sentence, click on the sentence and a new web browser window will be opened containing the text of the message (Figure 5.11).

It is also possible to compare the associations of one term with the associations of another term. Return to the main window displaying the semantic network. In the semantic network, hold down the control key and click the mouse twice, once over the term "country" and then over "nation". Now, hold down the control key again and move the mouse over one of the two selected terms, and double click the mouse. A new window is created, which displays the difference and union of the associations for "country" and "nation". Associations unique to "country" are displayed in green. Associations unique to "nation" are shown in silver. And, associations common to both "country" and "nation" are written in white. Clicking on any of the terms listed in green or silver will create a window of example sentences like the window shown above for the examples of "country" used as the subject of the verb "consider". If any of the white terms is clicked on, a similar window of examples will be created containing sentences using the term "country" and other sentences using the term "nation".

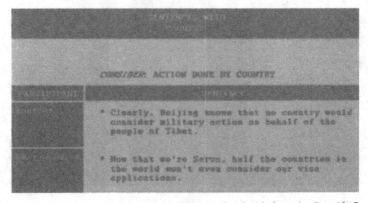

Figure 5.11 Selected sentences with the word "country," and with the action "consider".

By comparing terms' intersecting associations it is possible to begin to explore questions like these: In this conversation, how are countries like nations, people like countries, or Serbs like Albanians?

5.3 The Text Analysis Procedure

The analysis procedure of the Conversation Map system performs the following steps on an archive of Usenet newsgroup messages in order to compute the social and semantic networks described above:

1 Messages are "threaded".
2 Quotations in the messages are identified and their sources (in other messages) are found.
3 The "signatures" of posters are identified and distinguished from the rest of the contents of each message.
4 An index of posters (i.e. newsgroup participants) to messages is built.
5 For every poster, the set of all other posters who replied to the poster – or quoted from messages authored by the poster – is recorded. Posters who reply to or quote from one another are linked together in the social network. Reciprocity is therefore highlighted in the computed social network.
6 The words in the messages are divided into sentences, tagged with part-of-speech information, and their roots are identified. To divide the words into sentences, a tool built at the University of Pennsylvania is used (Reynar and Ratnaparkhi, 1997). To accomplish the part-of-speech tagging, a simple trigram based tagger has been constructed. The morphological analyser built for the Conversation Map system uses a freely available morphology and syntax database (Karp, Schabes, Zaidel, and Egedi, 1992).
7 Discourse markers (e.g. connecting words such as "if", "therefore", "consequently", etc.) are tagged in the messages. The Conversation Map system employs a list of discourse markers compiled by Daniel Marcu (1997).
8 The sentences of the messages are parsed. The parser is a re-implementation of the parser described in (Grefenstette, 1994).
9 An analysis of lexical cohesion is performed on every pair of messages where a pair consists of one message of a "thread" and another message that either immediately follows the first message in the thread (i.e. is a reply to the first message) or follows the first message in the thread and contains a quotation from the first message. This analysis produces a series of lexical ties between messages that can be understood as a crude approximation to the theme of the conversation in a sequence of messages. The lexical database WordNet (Fellbaum, 1998) is used in the lexical cohesion procedure. See Halliday and Hasan (1976) for a definition of lexical cohesion. See Hirst and St-Onge (1998) for an example implementation of a somewhat analogous lexical cohesion routine.
10 By using the index created in step 4 with the results of step 9 a set of lexical ties are computed for every pair of posters who have replied to and/or quoted from one another over the course of time represented by the Usenet newsgroup

archive under analysis. These aggregated lexical ties are layered on top of the social network computed in step 5. The result is that most of the links between pairs of posters are labelled with one or more lexical ties (i.e. one or more "discussion themes"). The combination of social networks and lexical cohesion results is called social cohesion. The social cohesion analysis procedure developed for the Conversation Map system is partially described in (Sack, 1999).

11 The lexicosyntactic context of every noun in the archive is compared to the lexicosyntactic context of every other noun in the archive. Nouns that are used or discussed in the same manner are calculated to be similar and are placed close to one another in the semantic network. An algorithm similar to the one described in Grefenstette (1994) is used. Once all of the noun-noun pairs have been compared and a nearest neighbour for each noun computed, a subset of the semantic networks computed are selected for display by ranking the semantic networks. The top-ranked semantic network contains a set of terms (used as "discussion themes") that connect the greatest number of poster pairs linked in step 10. In this manner, information about the social networks of the newsgroup is used as a kind of "lens" to select an important subset of the semantic information. Effectively, this type of interlacing of the social and semantic information supports social and semantic navigation (Dourish and Chalmers, 1994) in the interface generated for the newsgroup.

5.4 Related Work

Several other content-based Usenet newsgroup readers have been built with text analysis procedures simpler than those incorporated into the Conversation Map system discussed in this paper. For example, Isahara and Ozaku (1997) describe an intelligent network newsreader that performs a sort of example-based, relevance feedback procedure to select small collections of messages from an archive given an example message. The intelligent network newsreader also contains a method for identifying sub-threads within larger threads by analysing the content of the messages in a thread (Uhcimoto et al, 1997). However, systems of this sort (cf. Sheth, 1993) are mostly concerned with filtering messages rather than with one of the problems addressed by the Conversation Map system: How can all of the messages in an archive be graphically displayed and organized according to content of the messages and the social structure representative of the participants' interactions?

Many of the computational techniques developed for the analysis of Usenet newsgroups do not take the linguistic content of the messages into account at all using, instead, exclusively information that can be garnered from the headers of the messages; see, for example, Smith (1997). Other work does employ some keyword spotting techniques to identify and sort the messages into categories but does not involve the analysis of grammatical or discourse structures; see, for instance, Donath et al (1999).

Work that does use the contents of the messages for analysis often does not take the threading of the messages into account, or, if it does, does not pay attention to the social network produced by newsgroup participants (e.g. Best, 1998). Or, if the work does take the threading and citation information into account it does not necessarily use any of the linguistic contents of the messages to compute the graphical display (cf. Cannon and Szeto, 1998).

Research that has combined content analysis with an analysis of co-referencing of messages and discussion participants has often employed non-computational means to categorize the contents of messages (e.g. Berthold et al, 1998). Some of the most interesting work that analyses message threading, participant interaction, and the form and content of messages is often ethnographically oriented, sociolinguistic analyses of newsgroup interactions that is done without the assistance of computers and is so, necessarily, on the basis of a reading of only a small handful of messages (e.g. Herring et al, 1995). Ideally one could program the computer to emulate the latter sort of analysis, but that will require many advances in the field of computational linguistics. What is unique to the text analysis procedures of the Conversation Map system is the automatic construction and combination of social and semantic networks that, together, provide a means for exploring both the social and semantic structure of a Usenet newsgroup.

The novel text analysis procedures in combination with a graphical interface make the Conversation Map system an example of a new sort of content-based browser. Earlier examples of content-based browsers (e.g. Rennison, 1994) used simpler text analysis procedures akin those employed in information retrieval systems. New content-based browsers, clients, and readers (like the Conversation Map system) will incorporate more sophisticated text analysis (and probably, eventually, image analysis) techniques.

5.5 Conclusions

The Conversation Map system is an attempt to construct a prototype, content-based Usenet newsgroup browser that shows not only the terms being discussed but also how the discussion conducted in the newsgroup constitutes a set of social relations between participants. The text analysis procedures of the Conversation Map system produce (1) a set of social networks, (2) a list of high-frequency "discussion themes", and (3) a set of semantic networks. These three results are displayed in a Java-based graphical interface. Using this interface one can get a quick overview of some of the social and semantic structures of the newsgroup discussion.

The prototype system is being developed with two different groups of users in mind:

- The Conversation Map system could be used as a newsgroup reader by newsgroup participants. This use would require that a newsgroup be archived (as is done at sites like, for instance, www.dejanews.com) and the Conversation Map system run periodically on the archive. The graphical interface of the Conversation Map system would then provide newsgroup participants an alternative way of reading the archive of past messages.
- The Conversation Map system is being developed in coordination with a small set of professional users, i.e. anthropologists, sociologists, and others, who are professional discourse analysts interested in having a tool that provides them

with a first cut at their data. Specifically, the Conversation Map system allows them a means to quickly overview thousands of newsgroup messages and so provides a place to start doing closer readings of parts of the archive. One example collaboration of this sort involves Joseph Dumit at MIT, an anthropologist of science and technology. Together we are attempting to use the Conversation Map system to explore a set of newsgroups concerned with health and medicine (Sack and Dunit, 1999). While the Conversation Map system is currently being used as an archive interface by a small number of newsgroup participants, the development, refinement, and evaluation of the Conversation Map system is currently being accomplished more through a process of participatory design with professional discourse analysts.

References

Berthold, M., Sudweeks, F., Newton, S., Coyne, R. (1998) "It makes sense: Using an autoassociative neural network to explore typicality in computer mediated discussions" In F. Sudweeks, M. McLaughlin, and S. Rafaeli (editors) Network and Netplay: Virtual Groups on the Internet (Cambridge, MA: AAAI/MIT Press, 1998).

Best, M. (1998) "Corporal ecologies and population fitness on the net." Journal of Artificial Life, 3(4), 1998.

Cannon, S. and Szeto, G. (1998), Parasite, http://parasite.io360.com/index.html and http://www.cyber-geography.org/atlas/topology.html, 1998.

Donath, D., Karahalios, K., and Viegas, F. (1999) "Visualizing Conversations" Proceedings of HICSS-32, Maui, HI, January 5–8, 1999.

Dourish, P. and Chalmers, M. (1994). "Running Out of Space: Models of Information Navigation." Short paper presented at HCI'94 (Glasgow, UK, 1994).

Fellbaum, C., ed. (1998) WordNet: An Electronic Lexical Database (Cambridge, MA: MIT Press).

Grefenstette, G. (1994), Explorations in Automatic Thesaurus Discovery (Boston: Kluwer Academic Publishers).

Michael A.K. Halliday and Ruqaiya Hasan. (1976) Cohesion in English (New York: Longman).

Herring, S., Johnson, D., DiBenedetto, T. (1995) "'This discussion is going too far!': Male resistance to female participation on the Internet" In K. Hall and M. Bucholtz (editors) Gender Articulated: Language and the Socially Constructed Self (New York: Routledge, 1995).

Hirst, G. and St-Onge, G. (1998) "Lexical Chains as Representations of Context for the Detection and Correction of Malapropisms" in Christiane Fellbaum (editor) WordNet: An Electronic Lexical Database (Cambridge, MA: MIT Press, 1998).

Isahara, H. and Ozaku, H. (1997) "Intelligent Network News Reader" In Proceedings of IUI'97, Orlando, FL.

Karp, D., Schabes, Y., Zaidel, Z., and Egedi, D. (1992) "A Freely Available Wide Coverage Morphological Analyzer for English" In Proceedings of COLING-92, 1992.

Marcu, D. (1997). The Rhetorical Parsing, Summarization, and Generation of Natural Language Texts, Ph.D. Thesis (Toronto: Department of Computer Science, University of Toronto, December 1997).

Miller, G. (1995) "WordNet: A Lexical database for English". Communications of the ACM. November 1995, 39–41.

Quillian, M. (1968) "Semantic Memory" In M. Minsky (editor) Semantic Information Processing (Cambridge, MA: MIT Press, 1968).

Rafaeli, R. and Sudweeks, F (1998). "Interactivity on the Nets" In F. Sudweeks, M. McLaughlin, and S. Rafaeli (editors) Network and Netplay: Virtual Groups on the Internet (Cambridge, MA: MIT Press/AAAI Press, 1998).

Rennison, E. (1994). "Galaxies of News: An Approach to Visualizing and Understanding Expansive News Landscapes" In Proceedings of UIST'94, 1994.

Reynar, J. and Ratnaparkhi, A. (1997) "A Maximum Entropy Approach to Identifying Sentence Boundaries" In Proceedings of the Fifth Conference on Applied Natural Language Processing, March 31–April 3, 1997. Washington, D.C.

Sack, W. (1999) "Diagrams of Social Cohesion" In Descriptions of Demonstrated Systems, Association for Computational Linguistics, ACL'99, University of Maryland, College Park, June 1999.

Sack, W. and Dumit, J. (1999) "Very Large Scale On-Line Conversations and Illness-based Social Movements," presented at the conference Media in Transition, MIT, Cambridge, MA, October 1999.

Sheth, B. (1993). NEWT: A Learning Approach to Personalized Information Filtering, MIT Master's Thesis, 1993.

Smith, M. (1997). Netscan: Measuring and Mapping the Social Structure of Usenet. Presented at the 17th Annual International Sunbelt Social Network Conference, Bahia Resort Hotel, Mission Bay, San Diego, California, February 13–16, 1997.

Uchimoto, K., Ozaku, K. and Isahara ,H. (1997) "A Method for Identifying Topic-Changing Articles in Discussion-type Newsgroups within the Intelligent Network News Reader HISHO" In Proceedings of Natural Language Processing Pacific Rim Symposium, Phuket, Thailand, December 2–4, 1997.

Wasserman, S. and Galaskiewicz, J., editors. (1994) Advances in Social Network Analysis: Research in the Social and Behavioral Sciences (Thousand Oaks, CA: Sage Publications).

Chapter 6
Silent Participants: Getting to Know Lurkers Better

Blair Nonnecke and Jenny Preece

6.1 Introduction

Why do lurkers lurk and what do they do? A number of studies have examined people's posting behaviour on mailing lists (Sproull and Kiesler, 1991), bulletin board systems (Preece, 1998) and Usenet newsgroups (Smith, 2000) but studying lurkers is much harder because you don't know when they are there or why. Although lurkers reportedly make up the majority of members in online groups, little is known about them. Without insight into lurkers and lurking, our understanding of online groups is incomplete. Ignoring, dismissing, or misunderstanding lurking distorts knowledge of life online and may lead to inappropriate design of online environments. E-commerce entrepreneurs are particularly eager to find out why people lurk, in order to understand better how to entice them to participate in commercial interactions.

To understand lurkers better we carried out in-depth interviews with 10 online group members. From these interviews, 117 possible reasons for lurking were discovered. In addition we identified 5 primary lurking activities and a number of key lurking strategies. From this analysis we conclude that lurking is a strategic activity that involves more than just reading posts. On the basis of these findings we propose a new definition for lurking.

6.2 Rethinking Lurking

A generally accepted definition of an online lurker is anyone who reads but seldom if ever publicly contributes to an online group. In many types of online groups, lurking is possible because the technology provides access to group dialogue without being visible or forced into public participation. There are exceptions, such as multi-user dimensions (MUDs) and object oriented MUDs (MOOs), in which members are visible and participation is assumed. However, in email-based discussion lists (DLs, aka LISTSERVs and lists) and newsgroups, one can participate through lurking. This is particularly true of public newsgroups, where formal membership is not required and access is through a newsreader. DLs are somewhat different as they typically require that individuals join and provide a valid email address. The focus of our work has been on DLs, but many of our findings will be important in understanding lurking in other online contexts.

DLs, newsgroups, and Web-based bulletin board systems (BBSs) have experienced rapid growth as the number of Internet users climbs. As of May 2001, there are more than 177,000 DLs using LISTSERV's server software. The 124,000,000 members of these DLs send in excess of 28,000,000 messages per day (L-Soft International, 2001). Whittaker, Terveen, Hill, and Cherny (1998) cite similarly large numbers for Usenet newsgroups. The growth and prevalence of online groups, coupled with the relative ease of gathering persistent and traceable messages, has made online groups a fertile ground for research. The following are a few of the areas so far studied: the development of friendship (Parks and Floyd, 1996), the perception and quality of community (Roberts, 1998), factors affecting interaction within newsgroups (Whittaker et al, 1998), and the development of empathy in health support groups (Preece, 1998; Preece and Ghozati, 1998). Each of these studies was on the basis of examining individuals participating in public spaces, i.e. those who post. None examined their chosen area from a lurking perspective, even though lurkers are reported to make up over 90% of online communities (Katz, 1998; Mason, 1999).

Given that lurkers are both unstudied and apparently in the majority, knowing more about them will have benefits in many areas. For example, their sheer number suggests they are an important area to study from an e-commerce perspective. As group development becomes an important component of commerce on the Internet, understanding lurkers will become an essential part of doing business. Many e-commerce enterprises present group facilities and a community-oriented face, e.g. the Ask Dr. Weil Web site (Weil, 2001). Every lurker is a potential customer. For example, Amazon.com has been very successful in creating an online retail environment in which lurkers can make purchasing decisions on the basis of how others have purchased in the past and on reviews supplied by other customers. Amazon.com has leveraged the information gained from those willing to post reviews into purchasing-support tools for the lurker and poster alike. From a usability perspective, improvements in tools and group design will fall out of a better understanding of lurkers and their activities. For lurkers and their communities, knowledge of lurking will have the benefit of demystify lurkers' roles, value, and activities.

Researchers also have opinions about lurkers that need to be verified. For example, Kollock and Smith (1996) describe lurkers as "free-riders", i.e. non-contributing, resource-taking members. Knowing more about lurkers and their lurking will show whether this is an accurate description.

Definitions for lurker and lurk provide insight into how lurking is viewed. The online *Jargon Dictionary* (2001) defines the term, lurker, as:

> One of the "silent majority" in an electronic forum; one who posts occasionally or not at all but is known to read the group's postings regularly. This term is not pejorative and indeed is casually used reflexively: "Oh, I'm just lurking". Often used in "the lurkers", the hypothetical audience for the group's flamage-emitting regulars. When a lurker speaks up for the first time, this is called "delurking".

This definition suggests that lurking is the normal behaviour of the majority of the population and that lurking can be defined in terms of the level of participation, either as no posting at all or as some minimal level of posting. In contrast to the *Jargon Dictionary*, *Merriam-Webster Online* (2001) provides a pejorative definition for the term, lurk:

> a: to lie in wait in a place of concealment especially for an evil purpose b: to move furtively or inconspicuously c: to persist in staying

These contrasting perspectives reflect an inadequate understanding of the lurker in online discussion forums. The former definition evokes the image of a benevolent yet responsible Net citizen, but the traditional definition implies something much more sinister. Evidence for the former is anecdotal and, without appreciating the nature of online lurking, the latter definition may be inappropriate.

In studying public participation levels in health and software support DLs, it was found that lurking is "normal" in the sense that everyone is likely to lurk at least some of the time and frequently most of the time (Nonnecke and Preece, 2000). We have also come to understand that describing lurkers from a single point of view, e.g. as free-riders, misses much of the diversity of lurking as will be described in this chapter Nonetheless, an operational definition for the term "lurker" is helpful in discussing the phenomena of lurking. To that end, we base our definition on whether a person publicly participates in a group or community, i.e. a lurker is anyone who rarely or never participates publicly in online groups and communities. At the end of this chapter, we will revisit the definition and offer improvements.

6.3 Lurkers in Discussion Lists

While lurkers exist in many online environments, our primary focus will be on DLs. DLs were chosen because of their popularity, and just as importantly, for a technical reason which aids the study of lurking. Membership levels can be determined in DLs, something which is difficult to do in other asynchronous group environments such as newsgroups and BBSs. Knowing membership levels is crucial to determining lurking levels as the number of lurkers in a DL is the total membership minus the number who post. In the case of DLs, those who post can be counted by tracking the authors of the posted messages. In order to understand lurking in DLs, the remainder of this section provides a brief overview of how DLs function.

DLs are automatic devices for sending and receiving messages among members of a group. They are also asynchronous communication tools in which members can choose when to view their messages, if at all. DLs facilitate delivery of email to a set of subscribed members using a broadcast model. Anyone who sends email to the central server effectively broadcasts the email to all members of the DL. Individuals can respond to received email via the server, which in turn broadcasts the reply to all members. There may be an intermediate step in which messages are moderated. This can introduce delays in propagation or the elimination of some email, depending on how the moderation is handled. At the member's option, the email may be received individually or in the form of a digest (a group of messages).

An important aspect of DL messages is their persistence. In this case, "persistence" means the continued availability of messages, often for an indefinite period of time, and not only in each member's email storage but also in private, public, and corporate locations. For example, many DLs keep all messages in a central public archive that can be easily searched. Email may also be intercepted or backed up and held in corporate databases. Being both persistent and dispersed means DL messages are searchable and manipulable, and may be available to non-group members.

DL messages contain header information that includes sender, date, and subject. The header information allows messages to be sorted and managed using a variety of software. For example, users of the email client Eudora can follow a thread by sorting messages by author, subject, and date. In addition, each message contains content and, frequently, a signature. Both the header and message content make great fodder for searching. Searching can range from members searching their own locally maintained email to a researcher searching for quoted text through the use of crawler-based search engines, e.g. Google Search (Google.com, 2001) Because copies of messages may reside in many locations outside the subscriber's control, access is effectively wide open. The messages can be searched for content, originator, or in many other ways.

DL email may be read in isolation and the flow and intent of the messages can be distorted through the redistribution of individual messages or parts of copied messages. For all intents and purposes, email from DLs may be mutated from dialogue to data and back to content, without the originator having control over the process or use. An example of unintended use is the trolling of DLs for the purpose of creating address lists, which are then sold to spammers and legitimate businesses. The copies may also be used in the way they were intended, e.g. as an accessible resource for the group, for finding specific information, and for following conversations.

At the individual level, people manage their incoming email, including their DL email, in many different ways (Whittaker and Sidner, 1996). Some people have high volumes of email, others have low volumes. Some people read all messages and others do not. Some people file messages while others keep all their messages in a central inbox. How people manage their email has an effect on how they manage their DL messages. As a result, it is unlikely that members of a DL see or treat their messages in a uniform manner. This is different from Usenet newsgroups, where messages are viewed in browsers specifically designed for Usenet messages. Usenet differs in another important way; unlike DLs, Usenet groups typically do not require membership. Both of these differences are likely to have an effect on how people interact with a group, e.g. membership in a DL may carry with it certain perceived responsibilities, and using a browser to view messages rather than an email client may be less intrusive on everyday use of email. A fuller understanding of these important differences is beyond the DL focus of this chapter and open to future research.

In addition to a group's DL, group members are frequently supported through related Web sites, electronic forums such as chat-rooms and BBSs, and frequently asked questions (FAQs) which are created out of a need to support the group and are seen as a crystallization of the group's wisdom. Web sites are becoming central gateways to a number of different group information and communication tools, e.g. FAQs and BBSs.

6.4 Interviews and Initial Discoveries

To study lurkers, we used in-depth, semi-structured interviews. The primary goals of the study were to understand why lurkers lurk and what they do. We sought to elicit information about lurkers from online community members with the assumption that many of the interviewees would be lurkers as well as participants. The study was intended to provide a better understanding of lurkers and lurking, and was not intended to be exhaustive or by any means the last word on the subject. Rather it was an initial probing, which could become the basis for further work.

The interviews were designed to gain as broad a picture as possible. While generally following a script, questions in the open-ended interviews focused on issues brought up by the interviewee. These new areas of interest would form a background of investigation for subsequent interviews.

Participants were selected at random from two physical communities in which members were known to be Internet users. Given the relatively high incidence of lurkers reported by Mason (1999), it was assumed that the majority of participants would more than likely be lurkers. Ten participants were drawn from 2 locales, 5 men and 5 women, ranging in age from early 20s to early 50s; all had at least one university degree. The intention with the small sample size was to balance for age and gender, rather than examine age or gender issues. All participants were members of at least one online group, and were not pre-selected for lurking or for their level of experience with online communities. All the people asked participated in the study; 3 were well known to the researchers, and 7 were not. Face-to-face or phone-based, open-ended interviews lasted between 45 minutes and 2 hours, and focused on the participant's participation in online groups. Prompting was minimal, and the interviewer did not validate whether a group or topic was worth discussing.

Several things became very obvious after the first couple of interviews. For one, the semi-structured interviews worked very well. By emphasizing the online groups and then having the participant describe their participation in the group, it was possible to understand lurking, not just in terms of lurking behaviour, but also in terms of participation in general. Understanding the types of groups they joined, the reasons they joined, their activities and the duration of their membership painted a very rich picture of their lurking and participation. For most participants, talking about a particular group experience proved to be a good anchor for their discussion.

A number of participants had a very good understanding of why and how they participated. For these participants, it was often easier for them to describe their strategies and then give examples using a specific group. Their approach to explaining their knowledge and experience while different from the anticipated interview structure, in no way lessened the value of their input.

One conclusion drawn from the study is that lurking is a strategic and idiosyncratic activity driven by an individual's needs and background. The participants were well educated and comfortable in talking about their use of the technology and how it affects them, and were in all likelihood more comfortable with the technology than the average online group member. If a different set of participants had been used, then the results would likely be biased in some other way. For example, studying lurking habits of teenagers could lead to very different results. It is likely that teenagers may be much more adventurous in their use of technology and would probably seek different kinds of interaction.

The collection of specific quantifiable information was less important than the exploration of the issues during the interview. Given that this first study was not intended to carry the burden of quantifying lurkers and their behaviours, this was a reasonable approach. A simple count did show that everyone was a lurker. Some participants lurked all the time, some lurked in specific DLs, and others lurked at specific times. Discovering that lurking was so prevalent was an important finding.

The participants' stories of their group participation hold potential for describing lurking in a way that could make the lurking experience more accessible to community developers and tool designers. Given the dearth of lurker information for grounding group and community design, these stories could provide a means of establishing and fostering environments suited for lurking.

Of the groups described by participants, 30 of the 41 were ones in which the 10 participants lurked. These findings support suggestions that lurking is a common activity in online groups. Twenty-five of the 41 groups listed were DLs (Table 6.1). Of this group, 21 were described as DLs in which the participants lurked. (Finding that DLs are widely participated in and that participation is largely in the form of lurking was one of the deciding points in favour of using DLs in a follow-up demographic study;Nonnecke, 2000; Nonnecke and Preece, 2000.)

Reasons for lurking were varied, with participants providing 117 reasons, and what lurkers did while lurking was equally varied. The most obvious conclusion to be drawn from the interviews is that lurking cannot be characterized by the single

Table 6.1 Group types and whether lurking occurred

Participant	DL	BBS	Newsgroup	Chat	MOO	Lurked/total
			Group type			
P1	LLL		LLL			6/6
P2	LLLL					4/4
P3	L					1/1
P4	LLLLLL		L		P	7/8
P5	LLLL-PP					4/6
P6	L	L-P				2/3
P7	L-PP	L				2/4
P8		LL		PP		2/4
P9	L	P	P	P		1/4
P10		L				1/1
Lurked/total	21/25	5/7	4/5	0/3	0/1	30/41

L, lurked in a group; P, posted in a group.

behaviour of not posting. Neither can lurking be described as reading without posting, as lurking frequently occurs without the reading of individual messages. For example, lurking can take the form of culling and organizing messages for later use. Rather, lurking is a complex set of actions, rationales and contexts, i.e. situated action. It would be convenient for designers and community builders if specific reasons for lurking could be cited as more important than others; however, the participants in this study painted a very broad picture of why they lurked. Individuals appeared to be guided by their own reasons, needs, and stage of membership. By examining their stated reasons for lurking, it is possible to get a sense of the issues involved.

6.5 Why Lurkers Lurk

There is no single answer to why lurkers lurk. For example, one participant belonged to a broad range of DLs, having joined them for both personal and business reasons. The motivations for joining each DL was different (e.g. as part of a hobby or required by work), participation in the DLs was for the most part limited to lurking. Lurking was comfortable and enabled him to attain his goals given the nature of the DLs, each DL having high volumes of quality postings representing both depth and breadth of knowledge. In neither group was the participant motivated to post for information. Instead, he took a more general wait-and-see approach. Participants described their needs/wants met by lurking. The following were mentioned by at least 50% of the 10 participants (the number in brackets indicates the number of participants citing a particular need):

- conversations/stories (8)
- entertainment (7)
- access to expertise/experience (6)
- information without interaction (5)
- community (5).

The following reasons for lurking were mentioned by at least 50% of the participants:

- they wished to preserve their anonymity in order to ensure privacy and safety (8)
- there were work-related constraints preventing them from posting (8)
- the volume of messages was too low or too high (5)
- the quality of messages was poor (5)
- they were shy about posting (5)
- they had limitations on their time (5)

And, they lurked while:

- leaving the group (6)
- getting to know the group (5).

To understand better why lurkers lurk, the 117 given during the interviews collected and then aggregated. This resulted in a set of 8 categories that will now be used to discuss why lurkers lurk:

- satisfy personal needs
- satisfy information needs
- learn about the group
- leave a group quietly
- maintain privacy and safety
- reduce noise and exposure
- act within constraints
- act in response to group dynamics

6.5.1 Satisfy Personal Needs

When DLs were joined for personal reasons there was a correspondingly strong motivation to get as much out of the DL as possible. Entertainment was a common theme and took a variety of forms. Just as some people enjoy receiving snail mail, several participants enjoyed receiving email, indicating they liked having new email in their inbox. This gave them a sense of connection and also something to do in their free time. Others mentioned being attracted to controversy and debate, including watching flaming from the sidelines. Curiosity and learning were high on many peoples' list of reasons for joining and lurking in a DL. Humour was also appreciated and for several participants was the primary reason for belonging to specific DLs. Anecdotal evidence suggests that membership of this kind leads to much out-of-group communication, although this was not specifically mentioned by these participants.

Others joined DLs with many of the same members as their non-electronic-based organizations. In their opinion, this complemented and strengthened relationships. DLs also provided a convenient way to track events and announcements. One participant who belonged to such a DL read all messages and deleted all but the announcements for physical meetings. This brings up an important distinction between DLs and distribution lists. DLs foster group communication, whereas distribution lists are used to disperse information from a single source and typically do not include the functionality for list members to interact publicly.

Some participants are attracted to health-support DLs as a source of empathy (Preece, 1998). At least one participant in our study felt empathy strongly while lurking. DLs can also act as a mechanism for putting people in contact with one another through more private channels. For example, peers, expertise, and finding people beyond a local geographic community were described as reasons for joining a DL. Topics of specific interest to participants also drew them into joining DLs. Participants often described members of DLs as interested and focused. Relationships developed out of belonging to the DL, although no long-lasting friendships were reported, as found elsewhere (Parks and Floyd, 1996). Several participants indicated they developed a sense of community through lurking.

6.5.2 Satisfy Information Needs

Satisfying information needs was important to the participants. In some cases, information was more important than interaction. In addition to email-based messages, archives were used by several participants, especially if they were readily searchable. In a more passive way, the turnover of information through members' dialogue was also informative. In this way, participants were able to identify experts and if need be, seek expertise directly from these individuals.

Participants sought three types of information: factual information (e.g. job postings or solutions to technical problems); different viewpoints arising from different levels of expertise; and access to personal experiences of others. Participants also mentioned breadth and depth of expertise as being important, as was finding "authentic" information on the basis of an individual or group experience. Timely information was also considered quite important both in the sense of it being current, and that it meet the participants' immediate needs. Getting information from people living in the Middle East during the Gulf War was given as an example of timely information.

Professional needs, such as keeping abreast of conferences and work being done by peers and colleagues, were cited. Understanding who is doing what and where appears to be an important part of keeping abreast of a professional community.

6.5.3 Learn About the Group

Half of the participants lurk on joining a group and use this time to evaluate the group for its fit or value to them, and to come up to speed on the individuals in the group, dialogue styles, the language of the group, and its rules (implicit and explicit). The following is a list of group attributes which lurkers use to understand a group:

- terminology or special language
- posters (players and archetypes)
- rules (implicit and explicit)
- responsibilities related to being a member of the DL (implicit and explicit)
- style(s) of interaction, e.g. confrontational, humorous, etc.
- response of members to delurkers
- style and intrusiveness of moderation
- response time to messages
- volume and quality of postings.

For these participants, lurking was a preferred method of doing this. For many, it reduces the risk of making a faux pas or being rejected.

Group characteristics and behaviour can effectively act as filters to the public posting and thus have an effect on lurking. For example, a new group member may join a DL with the intention of observing before deciding on their form of participation and whether to remain a member. If there was a mismatch between their expertise and that of the group, then this initial period of lurking was used to determine this before unsubscribing or remaining subscribed. Participants wanted to know whether they would be able to add value to the DL, or whether postings by others would make their contribution redundant.

Several participants mentioned watching how others were treated on posting for the first time, i.e. on delurking. Several aspects of the delurking process stood out for them. One is how the delurker carried out the delurking action, i.e. how they presented themselves to the group for the first time. The other is how the group received them. It is interesting to note that lurkers evaluated the welcoming quality of the group on the basis of the public response. They knew little if anything of the private responses engendered by the delurking. This points out how important these public spaces are to both lurker and poster alike, especially in the initial phase of joining when the group is being evaluated for its fit to the participant.

Most participants described the process of understanding the DL as a period of intense reading of most, if not all, posts. This occurred whether the posts were available as separate emails, digests, or archives. In several cases, reading of current posts was supplemented by searching and reading archives. During this period, which ranged from days to months, participants worked at identifying the topic or topics of the DL and determining whether this was a good fit for their needs.

In the process of doing the interviews, it became obvious that knowing a group and the individuals in it was very important to several of the participants. These participants were able to describe their tactics in detail. These included looking at previous posts by an author (using archives or other means), examining email addresses for personal or corporate information, following threads to understand the nature of the discussion and participants, and using signatures and related Web sites to find out more about posters.

6.5.4 Leave a Group Quietly

In contrast to lurking after joining there is lurking when leaving a group. Participants were asked to describe both current and past groups. As a result, a glimpse into why they left groups emerged. Six of the 10 participants indicated that they lurked in the process of leaving a group. None of the participants mentioned publicly saying goodbye to the group; rather, the leaving took the form of reduced public participation and reading of messages. Many indicated that a lack of time was an important element in leaving a group. However, groups cited as largely information interchange houses (e.g. software application help groups) were frequently left because they no longer supplied information in sufficient quantity or quality. This was largely a result of groups repeating topics, and the participants becoming more expert in their knowledge. Others left because they were less in need of what the group could offer. For one participant, belonging to a health-support group was less important once his health was no longer an issue. At that point he started to pay less attention to the group, to the point of not reading posts. This points out how lurking can change depending on the stage of membership, i.e. intense reading of posts in the beginning and virtually no reading at the end. Because the participation is in the form of lurking, this change in participation may go unnoticed in the group. For some participants, the practice of lurking makes leaving a DL easier. For these participants, public posting is an implicit pledge to ongoing participation, and if no such pledge exists, leaving is simpler as no explanation is required.

6.5.5 Maintain Privacy and Safety

Participants were generally aware that messages in many DLs can persist indefinitely through publicly accessible archives. In addition, maintaining privacy is generally up to the list member, e.g. through the use of secondary anonymous email accounts. Unlike the participants in this study, less technically knowledgeable DL members may be unconcerned with these issues. The persistence of messages and a lack of built-in privacy in DLs inhibited posting of personal information by most participants, and in one case, a participant's employer prohibited posting for these very reasons. For some individuals, their notoriety makes posting problematic, e.g. few government officials post to public DLs.

Members and potential members of a DL should have a clear understanding of the implications of posting, i.e. loss of privacy. Part of that understanding lies in knowing whether the DL is publicly archived, whether there are membership criteria that have to be met in order to join the DL, and whether a list of members is publicly available. At present the majority of DLs do not provide membership lists.

Safety is also a concern for some lurkers. Participants who had concerns about safety expressed it at two different levels. The first relates to a fear of violence, i.e. that someone or some agency can use posted information (or mere membership in a DL) to find someone or something about someone. The second relates to the fact that if you don't post you can't offend, and therefore will not become a target of flaming. The safety and privacy issues are different, but they both result in lurking.

One option for ensuring privacy and safety is the use of anonymous email hosting services such as hotmail.com. These services provide mechanisms for anonymously posting and receiving messages. There is a conundrum; participants were interested in maintaining their own privacy yet wanted to know more about other members. For example, a poster's address and signature were mentioned as a means of understanding the poster, and one participant wanted to find DL members of a similar age and gender.

6.5.6 Reduce Noise and Exposure

As one participant expressed it, when you lurk, you can have curiosity without exposure. In contrast, several participants indicated that it is much more difficult to lurk in chat-rooms than DLs as chat-rooms are synchronous environments where participants are normally visible and thus approachable.

Some DLs discourage lurking, at least at the outset, suggesting in their introductory message that newcomers should provide a description of themselves and post it to the DL. Other DLs specifically state that posting is not required. In either case being aware of the rules of the DL is often an important part of participation. However, where to find the rules is not always self evident. In some DLs, a related web site will be linked at the bottom of each message. However, few of the participants in this study indicated they read the rules or guidelines. This does not appear to be a case of rule intolerance, as lurking was cited as a way of understanding the groups discourse norms and standards of etiquette.

Most participants realized that DLs and other online forums are regularly pilfered for email addresses, which are then sold or used directly to spam. Not one participant said they look forward to receiving spams. Spammers can obtain messages directly from the messages themselves or by querying the DL server for a list of members.

As a first level of defence, members' addresses should be made difficult to access. Owners of DLs can easily restrict access to the DL membership list. Similarly, DL server software can be set up to prevent the distribution of email from non-members. Some DL members take their protection one step further and provide incorrect return addresses in their email. This may foil spamming, but it also makes legitimate communication, such as side-posting, more difficult.

6.5.7 Act Within Constraints

Apart from the areas already discussed, such as the stage of the membership and the fit between member and group, constraints on lurkers' activities were primarily related to time or work. These constraints are largely external in nature. For example, one person was prohibited by his employer from posting and another participant belonged to a group because it was part of his job. In this latter case, the employer did not require or even expect the participant to post.

Like anything else in life, when someone is busy in one area, the time available for another area is reduced. Being involved with a community through posting can take more time. In recognition of this, several participants mentioned that they did not post because they knew that it would likely lead to a dialogue, which in turn would require them to continue. There is an awareness that posting has responsibilities. One participant indicated he was uncomfortable when someone would post to a group and a response was not forthcoming. They mentioned this was a situation in which they considered delurking or sending a private response. Several participants made the interesting observation that it is much easier to ask a question than to respond to one. This was particularly true in a group that was technical in nature. This would suggest that a member of a group may lurk as a respondent and post as a questioner.

One constraint that is typically under the control of both the DL owner and the member is the format in which the messages arrive. The participants who mentioned receiving DL messages in digest format indicated the digests were more difficult to follow and less exhaustively read. A digest could therefore be considered a barrier to participation in all its forms, not just to posting.

6.5.8 Act in Response to Group Dynamics

There are two other points related to the behaviour of the group that have an impact on lurking. The first is related to groups in which there are periods of posting followed by mass lurking with only a small proportion of the group posting. It is as if the group collectively lurks during lulls in posting and collectively rallies into a posting frenzy on a periodic basis. From at least one participants' perspective, these lulls are useful as the high levels of posts take a fair amount of work and are generally quite valuable. The other point is that large groups appear to be easy to lurk in. This is certainly true in groups that are synchronous such as MUDs and MOOs. In a follow-up demographic study (Nonnecke, 2000), lurking levels in DLs were shown to increase as membership levels increased.

For many, lurking is a methodical process and substantial effort can be invested in managing, selecting, and reading messages. How this takes place is dependent on the individual and the group. For example, individuals with little or no time are less likely to read all messages from groups with high message rates. In describing acceptable message rates, several participants suggested that more than half a dozen messages a day is too many. It is not clear that this is the case for all users or for all types of lists.

Of the 10 participants in this study, at least 4 were predisposed to lurk in all of their online environments. This suggests that no matter how groups present themselves, there will be a portion of the members who will lurk. On the other hand, there appears to be a class of members who are predisposed to post publicly. It is certainly the case in many DLs that there is a constant discourse by many of the same people. Anyone who has spent time in a DL will be able to tell you approximately how many participants post daily. They may even be able to name these individuals. How concentrated this group of primary posters is in terms of overall membership levels is not known, and is likely to vary between online communities.

6.6 What Lurkers Do

Lurking involves many different activities. It is not just reading of posts and perhaps sending an occasional post, as suggested by the *Jargon Dictionary*. If this group of participants is representative of the general online population, management of messages is a very important lurking activity. The activities described by the participants are not passive in the sense that the reader waits for email and then responds, but involve strategies for determining what to read, delete or save. In general, activities were goal driven and somewhat idiosyncratic. Some of the idiosyncrasy may be a result of variation in tools (email-clients). For example users of non-GUI email clients such as Pine (on UNIX operating systems) tended to not use folders or secondary mail boxes, but instead deleted messages on a regular basis. Variation in lurking also appears to be related to the skills of the lurkers and their goals.

It is clear that lurkers' activities are carried out methodically and that individuals are capable of explaining not only their methods, but also the strategies they employ. For example, none of the participants read all messages all the time, and depending on the experience within the community they might not read any of the messages. Some participants were able to describe an overall set of strategies that they employed, e.g. delete all messages except for those related to announcements. Others appeared to be much more dependent on the context of their lurking. For example, if they were short of time, they would delete whole threads, confident that the information would come up again at a later date.

Participants had other priorities in their lives; DL reading/following was frequently not the most important task of the day and certainly not the one in which they wished to spend most of their time, or even a good portion of it. In the context of their lives, lurking in a DL is one of many activities filling their day. Participants employed the following strategies to deal with messages:

- maximize return on effort
- keep information manageable
- identify DL email amongst other email
- follow threads
- decide to read or not to read

The next five sections will discuss each of these activities as they relate to lurking.

6.6.1 Maximize Return on Effort

In general the participants were interested in getting the most out of the time they had for lurking. Even if they lurked to entertain themselves, they still wished to do this as efficiently as possible. This typically meant spending less rather than more time with DLs. They used a number of methods to do this. If they belonged to more than one DL, they limited themselves to the number of DLs they could handle. It was clear that too many DLs meant that the value of one or more of the DLs would be reduced.

The asynchronous and persistent nature of DLs means that lurkers can go back through archived messages at any time and either search for particular information or browse the messages. For some lurkers this is an efficient way of finding pertinent information.

Although many of the DLs described by participants had 20–30 messages/day, participants were generally happier with fewer messages. Factors affecting the amount of time required to lurk on a DL include the quality and size of the messages, the motivation in belonging to the DL, the volume and type of email received from other sources, and the time available. In the examination of a number of introductory messages provided by DLs and related web sites, none mentioned how many messages a subscriber might expect.

6.6.2 Keep Information Manageable

Manageable meant different things to different participants, but was often related to comfort. For several participants, comfort came from keeping their inbox small, i.e. they were able to see all retained messages at once. The process of picking through the messages was an important part of their management process. Not surprisingly, understanding how inboxes are used is critical to developing design solutions.

Filters to sort messages into secondary mail boxes was not commonly used by participants. A number of reasons were stated: not trusting the effectiveness of the filters, potential burying of important email, and no knowledge of filtering tools or the process of creating effective filters. Filtering mechanisms should be examined with an aim to making them verifiable, trustworthy, and simpler to learn and use.

6.6.3 Identify DL Email Amongst Other Email

Identification of DL messages is an important mechanism for scanning and process-ing email in the inbox and elsewhere. Differentiating one DL's messages from another, and those in turn from non-DL email was an effort for participants. Recognizing this as a problem, some DLs use an identifying prefix in the subject header to indicate that a message is from a particular DL, e.g. the MORE cycle DL prefixes all subject headers with "more:". The current ad hoc approach of using pre-fixes may be good enough, but could be improved upon. A related issue, although not raised by the participants, is the use of prefixes to identify different types of mes-sages, e.g. "Q:" for question. The use of prefixes helps identify a message's origin and intent, but it may also make the subject heading more difficult to read.

Existing header information is sufficiently descriptive to be used in separating messages from different DLs and non-DL email. However, filtering tools remained largely unused by the participants. Whittaker and Sidner (1996) found the inbox to be an important repository for messages. Their findings suggest that the low use of filters may not reside solely in the act of filtering, but on other factors, such as the fear of losing track of important information.

6.6.4 Follow Threads

A thread is a conversation of multiple messages linked by a repeatedly used subject header. Participants were able to follow threads in newsgroups and BBSs because these systems were designed with threaded conversation in mind. Participants used threading either to follow a particular discussion or to determine whether a line of discussion was worth reading. This particular facility is poorly implemented or non-existent in most email clients. In addition, threading in email clients is different from that in newsgroups or BBSs. Even when messages can be sorted by subject header in an email client, the results are presented as a list of messages related by subject header. In both BBS and newsgroups, messages are related in a tree like manner, with the relationships between individual messages being apparent to the user. For this reason, email-based threading might better be called clumping.

For threading to be of value in email clients, threading must be effectively rep-resented in the UI, e.g. threading on the basis of subject header and date, and keeping the most active threads in the most visible position in order for the thread activity to remain observable to the user. GUI-based email clients can show thread-ing on the basis of the subject headers, but the results are frequently cumbersome and confusing. Alternative solutions need to be examined.

Additional problems occurred when receiving DLs as digests. Digests reduce message clutter in the inbox, but they eliminate thread visibility. Current email clients are unable to show threading in digests although specialized digest readers such as Digester (TECHWR-L, 2001) show promise in this area.

6.6.5 Decide to Read or Not to Read

Determining what to read is an important activity for any lurker. Deciding whether a message was worth reading differed between participants, and for a given participant often differed between DLs. The following criteria were described:

- read all if participant is new to the DL
- read if the subject heading shows potential value
- read if the author is known
- read all messages in a thread if the middle message of a thread is interesting
- read messages if thread is long (i.e. quality of messages and thread is somehow related to the length of the thread)
- read messages with confusing subjects
- read or not read an obvious flame

Several participants deleted all or most messages (read or not read) as a matter of course, whereas others kept messages, either by leaving them in the inbox and relying on the read flags to indicate their status, or by manually placing them in secondary folders. The delete process was most common among users of text-based email clients.

A rich set of cues was used in deciding whether to read a message. The fact that messages are persistent and asynchronous means that a message does not have to be read at the time of receipt. It also means that the decision as to whether a particular message is read will often be on the basis of other messages, e.g. other messages in the thread or the quantity of messages in the inbox.

6.7 Lurkers as Participants

We find that the subject of lurking has strong universal appeal to researchers and non-researchers alike. That appeal no doubt comes from the fact that each and every one of us has either lurked, is lurking, or will lurk in the future. As one researcher said, "you've got it wrong, lurking is normal, it is the people who post who are abnormal" (B. Wellman, personal communication, May, 1999). Taking that perspective, it is difficult to equate lurkers with free-riders. Earlier in this chapter, it was mentioned that Kollock and Smith (1996) described lurkers as free-riders, which classifies them for their lack of public participation and their use of resources without giving back to the group. Even when lurking is narrowly defined, e.g. one post per month or fewer, the vast majority (81%) of DL members are lurkers (Nonnecke and Preece, 2000). This being the case, one might ask how do online groups survive in the face of almost universal free-riding?

One explanation is that lurking is not free-riding, but a form of participation that is both acceptable and beneficial to online groups. Public posting is only one way in which an online group can benefit from its members. Members of a group are part of a large social milieu, and value derived from belonging to a group may have far-reaching consequences. For example, information supplied in health-support groups may end up enlightening a member. When the group member then uses that information to seek better medical care, physicians and other health-care professionals also benefit from this knowledge. The online group is just one way in which the member communicates with others. Online groups are one of many places for interaction, and although it may not seem like it from a research perspective, life for most members is more than life in the online group.

A second explanation is that a resource-constrained perspective may not apply to online groups where the centralized cost of servicing 100 members is not much different from that of serving 1000, or even 10,000. In large DLs the danger could be in not having enough lurkers. If everyone posted in large DLs, there would be a flood of messages that could make interaction very difficult. Thus, an important topic for future research is to examine how critical mass of membership is associated with lurking. An important question will be "what is the optimum number of posts to number of lurkers in any particular online community?" The following are but some of the reasons for valuing lurkers:

- **Lurkers work at knowing the group:** Participants described putting substantial effort into understanding a group. This work benefits both the group and the lurker by providing the lurker with the knowledge of whether the group is a good fit for them and provides the lurker with an understanding of the social dynamics of the group. These are important consideration taken by the lurker.
- **Lurkers try not to add to the chaos:** Many of the participants found that groups can be chaotic environments. Examples of this chaos include high levels of posts, duplicate posts by different authors, and irrelevant or inflammatory comments. Lurking is a form of participation that does not add to the chaos.
- **Lurkers extend the group:** Participants generally described groups in which the topics were of interest to them. Often these groups were related to other aspects of their life in which they were well connected. For example, several participants described DLs in which they lurked as part of their job and that found information was then used to inform themselves or others. In another example, one of the participants had a passion for history and as a result joined a number of military history groups. This participant lurked in some groups but not in others, and as a result, information from one group would sometimes become the fodder for discussion in another online group or in an offline setting. Other participants joined groups on the basis of friends recommending they join. Belonging to an online group is just one expression of a web of related activities. Contributions can and do take place outside a group's public space in the form of disseminating information, contacting individuals within a group, and introducing others to a group.
- **Some lurkers side-post:** Several participants said they made connections to individuals outside the online groups. These connections are a valid form of communication and have value for the individuals and thus the group as a whole. Reasons for side-posting varied and included a desire to contact individuals rather than the

whole group, not wanting to get involved in a public dialogue when time was of the essence, and feeling more comfortable in one-on-one emails.

● **Lurkers make a commitment:** Joining a DL appears to be somehow different from browsing a BBS or a newsgroup. For several participants, the process of joining and either explicitly or implicitly agreeing to the rules of the group is a form of commitment. For these participants, making a commitment to join a DL and then lurking did not feel in any way like free-riding. Rather, it was a way of assessing a group and determining the group's value to the member and the member's value to the group.

6.8 Lurkers with a Sense of Community

Several participants said they felt a sense of community while lurking. This goes against the preconceived notion that you must be an active poster to be part of a community. For one participant, a sense of community was extremely strong. This came about through a number of avenues – the participant's need to find community within a self-help group, the stories found within the community's web space, private postings and responses by members of the community – and the character and nature of the dialogue engendered a sense of trust and care. The fit between this participant and the community was good, and the outcome was a very strong sense of community, a sense that was developed without posting. Even though this participant has not actively lurked in the community for over a year, there was still a sense of belonging to this community.

This is curious as it flies in the face of what many consider to be the defining elements of community. Definitions of community (Erickson, 1997; Whittaker et al, 1997; Roberts, 1998; Preece, 2000; Wellman and Gulia, 1999) commonly incorporate the following:

● notion of membership
● relationships between members
● commitment and reciprocity
● shared values
● collective goods
● duration.

Not all definitions assume that it is necessary to contribute publicly (e.g. Preece, 2000), however, most tend to make this assumption. To understand how lurkers can have a sense of community, each of the above attributes is examined from the perspective of the lurker. The underlying assumption in this discussion is that online groups may be communities.

6.8.1 Notion of Membership

Participants were members of the groups they discussed. This was demonstrated by their knowledge of the community and the effort they put toward learning about the community. Belonging to a community is often a process of coming to know the members, traditions, rules and language. Participants mentioned this process and also mentioned that lurking was a way in which they learned about the group and eventually considered themselves to be members. It may be that for some people and at certain stages of membership (e.g. being a new member) lurking is an indirect way of saying they are not yet members, but are trying to be.

6.8.2 Relationship Between Members

Forming personal relationships with community members was important to some of the participants in some of their communities. For other participants, becoming a member of the group and forming a personal relationship was not necessarily part of the participants' desires or needs. For example, finding out a piece of information did not have to incorporate the development of a personal relationship. It could, but this was not required. In groups in which the partici-pant's goal was strictly informational, then a sense of community was not felt. However, where personal relationships were pursued, often outside the public space (e.g. through email), then a sense of community was possible. It is also pos-sible that a lurker can feel they know someone very well from their public postings and in that way feel kinship with that person. The non-reciprocal relationship of the poster and the lurker provides a sense of community for the lurker, even if it bends the concept of communities being reciprocal in nature.

6.8.3 Commitment and Reciprocity

It was obvious that the participants with the sense of community were very committed to their communities. This was shown in their effort to understand the community, often through the careful reading of messages and side-posting to members. Many lurkers are willing to support individuals in their dialogue outside the public spaces. For example, Katz (1998) experienced a deluge of private and sup-portive responses from lurkers when he was verbally lambasted in a BBS. Similarly, several participants in this study sent private messages of support to group members.

6.8.4 Shared Values

Most of the communities mentioned by participants are topic-based. These topics draw interested parties into them, either by sharing or becoming familiar with a common set of values, knowledge, or practices. This effort expended in becoming knowledgeable about a group is in a sense a measure of the respect for the com-munity. In health-support groups, members' dialogue and stories allow other members to share in their experience and identify with the authors (Preece, 1998).

6.8.5 Collective Goods

It is unclear how lurkers contribute to the collective goods of the community. It may be that their contribution lies outside the public dialogues, e.g. in other ways such as sharing their experience with others outside the online community. They may spread the word and act to enlarge the community by drawing in new members. This broad interpretation of goods includes the community itself and the persistent dialogue, i.e. resources and information.

In noisy or chaotic groups, lurking allows the collective goods, i.e. the already existing messages and dialogue, to be more easily perceived by the whole group. Participants were aware that public participation was not always good for the group. Several participants said they knew others would voice similar views and adding a message to the dialogue would not add value to the discussion.

6.8.6 Duration

As already mentioned, the participants were committed to understanding the community and spent a considerable period becoming familiar with the community and following the conversations.

Although it is a bit of a stretch to say that the lurkers met all the criteria for being members of the community, some nonetheless had a sense of community. For them, having a sense of community was likely different from them being members of the community. Even they would probably make that differentiation.

6.9 Summary

While work on this area was taking place, a question was put forward at a number of conferences and workshops on online groups and communities: does anyone know of any research on lurkers? Nobody came forward with a name of a paper or an author. However, many came forward with opinions, ideas, and personal experiences. Non-researchers have shown a similar interest in lurkers and lurking. The participants in the first study were very interested in having their opinions heard, and friends and family of the authors have been similarly enthusiastic about sharing their lurking experiences. It is obvious that the topic has strong universal appeal, which no doubt comes from the fact that each and every one of us has either lurked, is lurking or will lurk in the future. As we mentioned earlier, this was highlighted by one researcher who claimed that posting is abnormal, not lurking (B. Wellman, personal communication, May, 1999).

On the basis of the results from the interview study it is safe to say that lurking is widespread. All participants said they lurked and some lurked all the time. This was corroborated in a demographic study (Nonnecke and Preece, 2000) where more than 55% of the DL members lurked with no posts (81% if lurking is defined as one post per month or fewer). This is lower than the often-quoted figure of 90% (e.g. Mason, 1999), but nevertheless it represents a large number of participants.

A driving question of our work is, why do lurkers lurk? The unexpected out-pouring of 117 reasons gives a sense of the complexity of lurking. This complexity is increased when one considers the many activities of lurking. The participants' activities and rationales offer insight into all group members. Message selection, deleting, archiving, and reading are activities common to all members, not just lurkers. Lurking is not the single simple action of not posting. Even public partic-ipants do not post all the time. In their moments of non-posting, they can be con-sidered lurkers.

Contrary to what has been said elsewhere (Kollock and Smith, 1996), lurkers do not appear to be free-riders. Their non-public participation as lurkers is both ben-eficial and an acceptable part of online participation. Traditional definitions on participation emphasize public participation with very little understanding of non-public participation. Viewing online groups and communities through public participation alone casts lurkers in an unfavourable light.

Lurkers are capable of having a sense of community. If judged by traditional def-initions of community membership, they do not meet all the requirements. However, much of their community mindedness and membership does not appear in the online public forum. This may be true for all members of online communi-ties. That is, the online public interaction of the community may represent only a small portion of a community's total interaction. In any case, whether lurkers meet the definition of community members is a moot point, as they can and do feel a sense of community.

The term "lurker" is frequently used pejoratively and usually refers to anyone who never posts or posts infrequently. As we have come to understand, lurking is non-public participation. Lurking is a situated action with many personal and group-, work-, and tool-related factors affecting the activities and level of public and non-public participation. Lurking is "normal" in the sense that everyone is likely to be a lurker at some point in time. Lurkers are heterogeneous in most respects except in their lack of public posting. Therefore, in the absence of an understanding of the context in which lurking takes place, lurker is a somewhat meaningless term. Instead of using the term, lurker, the term non-public partici-pant (NPP) should be used. It is not pejorative and suggests there are other forms of valid participation other than public posting.

Part of this study focused on understanding how participants viewed lurking in general and their own lurking behaviour in particular. An initial abstract on lurkers was distributed to some of the participants. One participant responded with the following comment:

> Maybe it's a sign of my own mild discomfort around being a lurker, but I found it reassuring to recognize myself and my behaviour within the continuum you describe, and to see lurking treated seriously, with both acceptance and respect. As a lurker, I'm used to observing from the sidelines and participating vicariously, and it's strangely gratifying to read an article that speaks directly to that experience. It's almost like suddenly feeling part of an (until-now) invisible community of lurkers.

This participant was not alone in feeling there is a stigma associated with lurking, although the degree of stigmatization varied from individual to individ-ual. Giving lurkers recognition as valid and beneficial participants will benefit both lurkers and the community as a whole. Several participants expressed a fear that if all lurkers were to contribute publicly, the groups would become chaotic and unpleasant from the increased volume of messages.

Understanding lurking will be incomplete without further studies of individuals and their groups. Longitudinal studies of an ethnographic type will provide a wealth of information on lurking and participation in general. Work has till now focused on public participation in online groups (e.g. Mason, 1999). Broadening the ethnography to cover non-public interaction, and non-online interaction will reveal even more about lurkers' community involvement. Broadening the research beyond DLs, to other online forums will provide us with an understanding of how different technologies affect participation.

Demographic studies employing message logging will further improve our perspective. Logging has the advantage of being able to monitor thousands of groups, groups selected not only for their topic type, but on size, interactivity, and other features. Web-based surveys show promise in understanding group dynamics by similarly polling large numbers of lurkers across many groups. Our current interest in surveys is in understanding the life-cycle of participants, in particular the transitions between lurking and posting, and the role of lurking when joining and leaving a group. Other areas where logging and surveys will be of value include:

- high traffic and its impact on participation
- group topic and how this relates to lurking
- frequent posters and their relationship to group health
- membership turnover and the role of lurking in that process
- gender differences and lurking, especially in high-traffic groups.

Learning about how these silent participants behave and why they don't post is fundamental for understanding social interaction online. It is all too easy to forget that almost everyone lurks at some time and that there are usually more lurkers than people posting. The dearth of studies about lurking is testament to how overlooked this activity is. Fortunately for us, lurkers willingly respond to the inquisitive researcher.

References

Google.com (2001) All About Google (http://www.google.com/about.html).

Jargon-Dictionary (2001) Lurker (http://info.astrian.net/jargon/terms/l/lurker.html).

Katz, J. (1998) Luring the Lurkers , In: Slashdot (http://slashdot.org/features/98/12/28/1745252.shtml).

Kollock, P. and Smith, M. (1996) Managing the virtual commons: cooperation and conflict in computer communities. In: Herring, S. (ed) Computer-Mediated Communication: Linguistic, Social, and Cross-Cultural Perspectives. John Benjamins, Amsterdam.

L-Soft-International (2001) Record sites (http://www.lsoft.com/news/default.asp?item=statistics).

Mason, B. (1999) Issues in virtual ethnography In Ethnographic Studies in Real and Virtual Environments. In: Buckner K (ed) Inhabited Information Spaces and Connected Communities. Edinburgh.

Merriam-Webster Online (2001) Lurk (http://www.m-w.com/cgi-bin/dictionary?book=Dictionary &va=lurk).

Nonnecke, B. (2000) Lurking in email-based discussion lists. South Bank University, London.

Nonnecke, B. and Preece, J. (2000) Lurker Demographics: Counting the Silent. In: ACM CHI 2000, The Hague.

Parks, R.M. and Floyd, K. (1996) Making friends in cyberspace. Journal of In: Computer-Mediated Communication (http://jcmc.huji.ac.il/vol1/issue4/parks.floyd.html).

Preece, J. (1998) Empathic Communities: Balancing emotional and factual communication. In: Interacting with Computers: The interdisciplinary Journal of Human-Computer Interaction 5:32–43.

Preece, J. and Ghozati, K. (1998) Empathy online: A review of 100 online communities. In: Association for Information Systems, 1998 Americas Conference, Baltimore, MD.

Roberts, T.L. (1998) Are newsgroups virtual communities? In: ACM CHI 98, Los Angeles, CA.

Smith, M. (1999) Invisible Crowds in Cyberspace; Measure and Mapping the Social Structure of USENET. In: Communities in Cyberspace: Perspectives on New Forms of Social Organization, Routledge Press, London.

Sproull, L. and Kiesler, S. (1991) Connections: New Ways of Working in the Networked Organization. MIT Press, Cambridge, MA.

TECHWR-L (2001) Information about David Castro's Digest Reader software (http://www.raycomm.com/techwhirl/digestreader.html).

Whittaker, S., Isaacs, E. and O'Day, V. (1997) Widening the net. In: SIGCHI Bulletin 29:27–30.

Whittaker, S. and Sidner, C. (1996) Email overload: Exploring personal information management of email. In: ACM CHI'96, Vancouver, BC.

Whittaker, S., Terveen, L., Hill, W. and Cherny, L. (1998) The dynamics of mass interaction. In: ACM CSCW 98, Seattle, WA.

Part III
Enhancing Spaces

Chapter 7
Computer Mediated Communication Among Teams: What are "Teams" and How are They "Virtual"?

Erin Bradner

7.1 Introduction

This chapter is concerned with computer-mediated communication among virtual teams. A focus on social factors in small-group interaction is required to adequately answer the question: what is a "virtual team" and how can it be said to be "virtual?" Understanding the role of social factors in small-group interaction is important since governments and corporations around the world are increasing their reliance on information technology as a surrogate for face-to-face interaction among distributed teams. Work in this area is particularly timely since, as "virtual teaming" has been on the rise, research in small groups has declined (Gladstein, 1984; Ilgen, 1999). A survey of social science research on small groups will conceivably help software designers design "group friendly" electronic environments for virtual teams. It is the first step towards knowing, for example, when a 3D rendered virtual collaboration environment would better support collaboration than email, a conference call, or a face-to-face meeting. It is anticipated that work in this area will also inform management on the social-psychological impacts of distance on small group collaboration.

7.1.1 Approach

It has not been determined empirically that any set of critical constructs describes small groups better than large groups, or workgroups better than social groups. In fact, the field of group dynamics is based on the assumptions that general laws concerning human interaction within groups are identifiable and can be used to analyse all types of groups. Group dynamicists assert: "the various criteria that have been used to identify 'types' of groups should be conceived as variables that may enter into a single general theory of groups" (Cartwright and Zander, 1968). Thus the approach of this chapter is to draw upon literature from various disciplines – sociology, social psychology, management science, organizational behaviour, industrial relations – to inform an understanding of cohesion among groups.

Because it is good scientific practice to study the intellectual lineage of a concept before applying it, section 7.2 begins with a brief history of small-group research and the origins of the concept of "social group". It then defines virtual teaming with respect to social science definitions of "groups", "small groups" and teams in the organizational context. Section 7.3 presents a discussion of group cohesion as it is defined in the social science literature. Implications of physical collocation on cohesion is also discussed. Section 7.4 applies these concepts to empirical data of the use of computer-mediated communication technologies (CMC).

7.2 Small-group Research: History and Definitions

> The set of research on teams embedded in organizations represents more of a portfolio model than a neatly bound paradigm. (Ilgen, 1999)

7.2.1 Interdisciplinary Interest in Groups

As implied by the quote above, research on teams has not been associated exclusively with any one academic discipline. In the social sciences, intellectual veins of small-group research can be followed in sociology, social psychology and more recently, cognitive science. Early research on small groups in the work place arose out of the scientific management movement. This research agenda took a mechanistic perspective on the relationship between worker and task. Economic implications surrounding the influence of physical environment on human performance spurred the National Academy of Sciences to fund, in 1924, the well-known Western Electric Company experiments at the Hawthorne Works in Chicago. The objective of the Hawthorne studies was to identify the "relation of quality and quantity of illumination on efficiency in industry" (Sundstrom and Sundstrom, 1986). Ironically, the Hawthorne studies are seen as the seminal work in the field of human relations. This is ironic because the implicit assumption of the Western Electric researchers was deterministic – that environment, in this case illumination, determined production. While searching for a dependency relationship between environment and production, the Hawthorne researchers found that social factors strongly influenced production. They attributed production variability to employee attitudes and to socially negotiated standards of production (i.e. norms) that arose among informal social groups.

It has been said that the failure of the Hawthorne studies to find a direct correlation between lighting and production widened the focus of industrial psychologists to include employees' attitudes, interpersonal relations and groups (Sundstrom and Sundstrom, 1986). The heyday of small-group research was the 40–year period after the Hawthorn studies. In the latter part of this period, the seminal ideas of Kurt Lewin (Lewin, 1948, 1951) were applied to theories of social comparison process (Festinger, 1954), cooperation and competition (Deutsch, 1949) social power (French, 1959), and the social psychology of groups (Thibaut

Table 7.1 Definitions of groups and teams

Reference	Field	Definition
Lewin (1948)	Social psychology	"Groups are sociological wholes; the unity of these sociological wholes can be defined operationally in the same way as a unity of any other dynamic whole, namely by the interdependence of its parts."
Rabbie (1991)	Social psychology	"A group becomes a compact 'we-group' or 'social group' to the extent that individuals are subjected to the experiences of a common fate, perceive themselves to be interdependent with respect to their common goals and means to attain those goals, view themselves (and are considered by others) as a distinctive social unit, can directly communicate with one another and engage in cooperative fact-to-face interactions in an effort to achieve a group product or a common outcome."
Hare (1962)	Sociology	"For a collection of individuals to be considered a group, there must be some interaction. In addition... four features of group life typically emerge: shared motive or goals..., norms, stabilized roles, and a network of interpersonal attraction."
Goodman et al. (1978)	Organizational behaviour	"Groups [are] collections of individuals who interact with each other in pursuit of some common goal."
(Homans, 1950)	Sociology	"A group is a number of persons who communicate with one another often over a span of time, and who are few enough so that each person is able to communicate with all the others, not at second hand, through other people, but face-to-face."
Mink, Mink, & Owen (1987)	Human resource management	"Groups are three or more persons in a combination of mental energy... groups form to engage in a task – to work."
Sundstrom & Sundstrom (1986)	Environmental psychology	"A group is social entity that represents more than the collection of individuals who make it up."
Bales (1950)	Social psychology	"A small group is defined as any number of persons engaged in interaction with each other in a single face-to-face meeting or a series of such meetings, in which each member receives some

Table 7.1 *Continued*

Reference	Field	Definition
		impression or perception of each other member…"
Sayles (1958)	Industrial relations	"The work group is the primary focus of registering discontent as well as the organizational mechanism for releasing productivity. Being able to identify in advance the work groups that will support or attack management or union programs, the administrator gains a major tactical advantage."
Mohrman, Cohen, Mohrman, & University of Southern California. Center for Effective Organizations (1995)	Management	"Teams have responsibility for a "whole" part of the work. These teams have been described a "empowered," because in theory they do not have to seek hierarchical approval for many of their decisions about how to do their work… sometimes referred to as "self-managing," because they perform for themselves many of the tasks that management used to perform, such as scheduling and monitoring performance."
Haywood (1998)	Management	"… the primary factor that distinguishes a virtual team from other types of teams is that one or more of the team members is geographically separated from the other members."
(see p. 141)	–	A virtual team is a small group using technology to communicate with one or more geographically remote member… members operate in an organizational context, assume differentiated roles, are interdependent, and produce some intellectual or physical product for which members have collective responsibility.

and Kelley, 1959). A hotbed for small-group research, the University of Michigan was the birthplace of the field of group dynamics (Cartwright and Zander, 1968). In his 1966 600-page survey of small-group research, McGrath summarized the history of small-group research in this way:

> The 1930s emphasized national problems such as leadership…and contained the broad theorizing of Kurt Lewin. The postwar 1940s were times of application and amplification. We entered the, 1950s with vigour and increased resources, scurrying to conduct research on matters learned about during the war… . That decade saw a research boom which has continued into the 1960s. (McGrath, 1990)

In a more recent survey of small-group research, McGrath (1997) identified the following seven fields producing research on small groups: organizational behaviour, speech communications, political decision-making, group therapy, family studies, human relations, and management. Recent work on self-managed work teams reported by Sundstrom, DeMuse, and Futrell (1990) comes from the field of organizational behaviour. Table 7.1 lists several definitions of "group" and "team" from the relevant literature.

7.2.2 What Is a Group?

There is little agreement in the literature about how to define a group. Size, function, extent of in-group communication, persistence over time – these are only a few of the dimensions of groups. Interaction is one criterion commonly used to distinguish a collection of individuals, such as a crowd waiting for a New York subway, from a "social group". Proponents of the interaction theory believe human interaction defines a group. Simply stated: "for a collection of individuals to be considered a group, there must be some interaction"(Hare, 1962). Interactionists believe that once interaction is enabled, four properties of groups emerge:

- **Shared goal:** Members of a group share one or more motives or goals that determine the direction in which the group will move.
- **Norms:** Members develop a code of behaviours, or norms, which set boundaries within which interpersonal relations may be established and activity carried out.
- **Roles:** Relative position and responsibilities of group members stabilize over time.
- **Cohesion:** Explicit "likes" and "dislikes" of members for one another refines group membership and creates a network of interpersonal attraction (adapted from Hare, 1962).

Alternatively, social identity theorists maintain that affiliation, not interaction, defines a group. Individuals identifying with a group, defines the group (Tajfel, 1978). Another school of thought maintains that interdependence is the essential property of a social group (Lewin, 1948; Rabbie, 1991). According to this line of thinking, a group exists if members perceive themselves to be interdependent with respect to a common goal and means to attain the goal (Rabbie, 1991).

Although an interesting topic, the ontology of groups is not the focus of this chapter. However, an examination of group theory is germane to a study of virtual teams to the extent that it uncovers implicit assumptions about distance and collaboration within groups. For example, it is important to note that the definition of "groupness" provided by the interdependence school presumes face-to-face interaction:

> A group becomes a compact we-group to the extent that individuals ... can directly communicate with one another and engage in cooperative face-to-face interactions in an effort to achieve a group product or a common outcome (Rabbie, 1991).

According to Hare (1962), the most commonly used definition of a small group is that given by Bales:

> A small group is defined as any number of persons engaged in interaction with each other in a single face-to-face meeting or a series of such meetings, in which each member receives some impression or perception of each other member ...
> (Bales, 1950)

Face-to-face interaction is explicit in this definition as well. Although it is not possible to know precisely why physical collocation is explicit in these definitions, one can guess that face-to-face interaction was prescribed by the research questions and protocols used by these researchers to study small groups. It suffices to say that classical theories of small-group interaction should be cautiously applied to the study of geographically distributed teams. With that in mind, in this chapter discussions of theory are separated from discussions of implications raised by theory and regarding collocation.

7.2.3 Workgroups in Organizations

A collection of frequently cited definitions of the terms "group", "workgroup" and "team" is listed in Table 7.1. The definition of "workgroup" proposed here is drawn from Hackman (1990). He defines three essential attributes:

- Workgroups are real groups. They are intact social systems, with boundaries, interdependence among members and differentiated member roles.
- They have one or more tasks to perform. The group produces some outcome for which members have collective responsibility and whose acceptability is potentially assessable.
- They operate in an organizational context. The group, as a collective, manages relations with other individuals or groups in the larger social system in which the group operates. (Hackman, 1990)

The fact that workgroups are embedded in organizations produces interesting questions about all manner of issues concerning human interaction. Since the organizational context does not distinguish virtual teams from other workgroups, adopting an "organizational" perspective does not provide the intellectual currency to warrant extensive discussion here. However, it is important to note that implicit in Hackman's definition and all preceding definitions of "groups" discussed here, is the assumption that people first orient towards their common goal then determine the means, i.e. process, to achieve that goal. Arguably appropriate for analyses of social groups (e.g. a street gang or Mothers Against Drunk Drivers), this assumption is troublesome when applied to groups in the organizational context. It is troublesome because people at work are often not granted the latitude to orient towards a goal; goal orientation is explicitly or implicitly mandated in their job description. So too is group participation.

7.2.4 What Is a Team?

One approach to defining work teams is to consider the dichotomies often used to classify groups (work/social; informal/formal, etc.). Teams are small groups in which participation is either implicitly or explicitly mandated by management. In teams, formal roles are prescribed by the organizational structure (managers don't stop being managers when they work in a team). Informal roles, such as team peacemaker, are emergent. Like the workgroups defined above, teams are real groups, have a task to perform and operate in the context of an organization. Lastly, time matters in teams (McGrath, 1990). Work teams have a task; that task is planned and carried out over a period of time.

7.2.5 What's Virtual About Virtual Teams?

A debatable, but commonly held, assumption about teams is that they outperform individuals, especially when performance requires multiple skills, judgements, and experience (Katzenbach and Smith, 1993). The trend towards re-engineering organizations around teams (Ilgen, 1999) has occurred in parallel with the proliferation of computer-mediated communication, the rise in telecommuting, and increased reliance on information technology in organizations. The teaming trend and "wiring of the workplace" have lain the organizational and technological ground-work for virtual teams. Findings from a survey of teams in U.S. companies indicate that 66% had at least one member who was permanently assigned to a location geographically distant from the rest of the team (Kinney and Panko, 1996). Among these distributed teams, 31% of the members were not collocated with the others on their team. Although recent academic studies of virtual teaming at Boeing Corporation (Poltrock and Engelbeck, 1997) and management texts (e.g. Haywood, 1998) have identified some features of virtual teams that may distinguish them from collocated work teams, the only distinguishing factor considered here is geographic distance mediated by communication technology.

Thus, a virtual team is a small group using technology to communicate with one or more geographically remote members. A "significant" time period connotes at least half the life-span of the team. In practice, it often constitutes the entire life-span. In addition, members of virtual teams operate in an organizational context, assume differentiated roles, are interdependent, and produce some intellectual or physical product for which members have collective responsibility. Thus, "virtual" is shorthand for "virtual collocation". It connotes technology-mediated communication which may or may not involve an artificial environment provided by a computer, i.e. "virtual reality". Technology-mediated communication in virtual teaming may be as elaborated as a 3D rendered electronic environment or as mundane as a conference call.

7.3 Cohesion in Groups

> There is virtually no end to the list of symptoms one could use to characterize a group. (Weick, 1979)

The focus of this chapter is on virtual teams in the workplace. Related issues not addressed are the implications of the organizational context of groups (Gladstein and Caldwell, 1988), the division of cognitive labour across workers and tools (Hutchins, 1990), the influence of leadership on group decision quality (Maier and Solem, 1952) development (Gersick, 1988) performance (Steiner, 1972), and norm formation (Phillip and Dunphy, 1959). For discussions of these topics and the interesting questions therein the reader is directed to the references provided. The issue addressed here is cohesion. According to the definition of virtual team constructed in Section 7.1, the absence of collocation is a defining property of virtual teams. Since "virtual" is synonymous with "virtual collocation", implications of collocation are discussed with regard to the formation of norms and cohesion. In this section, collocation is discussed in terms of issues directly implied by the social science theories cited above.

7.3.1 Cohesion Defined

Cohesion has been defined as "the tendency of group members to stick together" (Sproull and Kiesler, 1991), as "in-group favoritism" (Tajfel, 1978) and as the sum of all forces that act on individuals to stay in a group (Festinger, 1968). Since the focus of this study is workgroups and not social groups, the notion of cohesion as in-group favouritism is not examined here. Considered here are conceptualizations of cohesion which impact aspects of group decision making, specifically consensus. The effects of cohesion on productivity are examined in the next section.

How cohesion influences interpersonal attraction among group members is an interesting question. Leon Festinger examined this question in his laboratory experiments in the 1950s (Festinger, 1954). In his seminal study, Festinger assembled small groups of subjects and introduced a controversial topic to them. He required each subject to write their opinion on the issue on a piece of paper. He convinced the subjects that he had accurately computed the distribution of opinions and gave each subject a copy of the results. Some subjects received results indicating their opinion was held by a majority of the group members. Others received results indicating their opinion was quite contrary to the majority. After the experiment, each subject was asked how well they liked others in their group. In each of eight different experimental conditions, subjects who felt others held contrary opinions were less attracted to members of their group.

The notion of attraction is just one component of cohesion. Another component is uniformity of opinion, or consensus. As an extension of the experiment reported above, Festinger asked subjects to rate their confidence in their opinion after discovering the opinions of others in their group. Findings show that those who learn they hold a minority opinion become less confident in their opinion and are prone to change their opinion. Festinger generalizes these findings in this way: "The availability of comparison with others whose opinions or abilities are somewhat different from one's own will produce tendencies to change one's evaluation of the opinion or ability in question (Festinger, 1954). This hypothesis, taken with the finding that a person will be less attracted to groups of others who hold opinions contrary to their own, suggests that uniformity of opinion, if not cohesion, is self-perpetuating.

Another way to articulate Festinger's findings is to say that a group creates a socially persuasive force that acts to reinforce the majority opinion. This is the essence of "groupthink", a term coined by Irving Janis in 1972. Groupthink is: "a mode of thinking that people engage in when they are deeply involved in a cohesive group, when the members' strivings for unanimity override their motivation to realistically appraise alternative courses of action" (Janis, 1972). The canonical example of groupthink is the Bay of Pigs invasion of Cuba. This decision made by U.S. President John F. Kennedy and his cabinet, best described as a grave political fiasco, is viewed by Janis as a "defective decision" caused by groupthink. Janis reports that Kennedy and his cabinet reached consensus at the time the decision was made, although it was later revealed that certain members did not support the decision.

It is not precisely known what was said, implied, or otherwise communicated outside the Oval Office such that consensus was reached on the decision to launch the Bay of Pigs invasion. However, Janis uses this event to abstract several sources of groupthink: illusions of invulnerability, stereotyping outsiders, bounded rationality, belief in inherent morality, self-censorship, and direct pressure on dissenters (Janis, 1972). Festinger supplies empirical evidence to support two of these so-called sources of groupthink. He reports that his studies "have shown clearly that the presence of disagreement in a group leads to attempts to influence others who disagree and also to tendencies to change one's own opinions to agree more with the others" (Festinger, 1954).

7.3.2 Collocation and Cohesion

If Festinger's findings are correct, self-censorship and direct pressure on dissenters are inherent properties of collocated groups. In an interesting study of automobile factory line workers (Walker and Guest, 1952), workers were asked to list the names of others in their workgroup. This study showed that workers almost invariably listed 10 people in their group. It is not the size, but the consistency in the composition of the group that is interesting. Workers reported that their groups consisted of the two pairs of workers occupying the position immediately before theirs, the person directly across from them, and the two pairs of workers occupying the position immediately after theirs. This continued systematically down the line. Although it is clear that these groups were the product of individual perceptions (Sundstrom and Sundstrom, 1986), what is not clear from this study is if proximity or task interdependence, both of which are dictated by the structure of the assembly line, alone contributed to the common conceptualization of the workgroup.

Walker's factory line workers are examples of what human relations experts call "occupational groups" (Sayles, 1958). Sayles summarized findings from his groundbreaking fieldwork in this quote:

> Frictions and discontent at the work place are reduced when the work team incorporates [i.e. collocates] all individuals whose work is highly interdependent. [When separated] the intimate communications and self-control mechanisms of the workgroup do not function efficiently: one individual tends to blame another

(whom he does not know) for failure to complete the work quota and for other shortcomings of coordination. Recriminations build onto on another and grievances follow … . Where the work unit is artificially divided by some physical communications barrier, work-derived discontents are constantly boiling over and giving these areas a reputation for erratic behaviour. (Sayles, 1958)

Exemplified by Sayles' work, studies of informal groups that arise from on-the-job interaction with co-workers have been the focus of much research in the field of industrial relations since the Hawthorn studies (mentioned above). The reader may recall from our earlier discussion that the Hawthorne studies established that workgroups can exert social pressure to produce at or below management expectations. Furthermore, in the Hawthorne studies, group members who produced above quota were called "rate busters". They were pressured by others to reduce their output so as not to raise management expectations. This finding spawned numerous scholarly studies of occupational status and organizational design (Sayles, 1958). This body of work examined the relationships between collocation and cohesion by measuring job satisfaction, incidence of grievance, and incidence of worker insurgence. Keen interest in these issues arose because the serial nature of assembly operation makes it particularly vulnerable to strikes and slowdowns. Most studies produced in this time period concluded that physical collocation fostered increased cohesion among both informal and formal groups.

7.4 Computer-mediated Communication and Virtual Teams

Organizations will tacitly create agreements about the relative level of informality that is acceptable in electronic messages. These unspoken agreements can have an impact on both the anxiety level of the users and the communication strategies they use. (Ehrlich, 1987)

If collocation fosters cohesion, do virtual teams, by definition, have low cohesion? To review, a virtual team is a small group using technology to communicate with one or more geographically remote member. A type of "workgroup", virtual teams operate in an organizational context. A type of "group", virtual teams assume differentiated roles, are interdependent, and produce some intellectual or physical product for which members have collective responsibility. Cohesion is the tendency of group members to stick together. An interesting question to ask is if cohesion of virtual teams suffers as a direct consequence of being distributed and using CMC to mediate communication. In the paragraphs below, two types of CMC technologies and their implications on group cohesion are discussed.

7.4.1 Chat in the Workplace

This section discusses a qualitative study of the use of a proprietary chat system called BABBLE by six groups in a large U.S. corporation (Bradner, Kellogg, and Erickson, 1999). Six groups at the IBM T.J. Watson Research Centre (USA) were studied, including a Software Engineering, Staff, and Human Resources group, a professional and a social cohort, and "the BABBLE Lab" group (which developed the system). Group size ranged from 5 to 175 people. The Software Engineering, Staff, and Human Resources groups were collocated (i.e. had adjacent offices) and organizationally bound (i.e. members belonged to the same department). Cohorts were geographically distributed but shared professional or social interests. The BABBLE lab's members were co-located and organizationally bound.

7.4.2 The BABBLE Interface

BABBLE is a chat-like communication tool in which typed messages are transmitted across a TCP/IP network, stored on a server and displayed to each client. BABBLE allows its users to engage in synchronous or asynchronous textual conversations, and provides visual feedback regarding who has recently participated in a conversation (see Erickson et al, 1999).

The panes of the BABBLE window (Figure 7.1) display the following information: a list of all connected users; the social proxy (a minimalist graphical representation of user activity); a list of topics (user-defined conversation areas); the current topic (i.e. text of the conversation). Messages appear in the order posted.

Three features of BABBLE distinguish it from other chat systems. First, BABBLE conversations are persistent: the conversations stay on the server permanently, thus permitting asynchronous conversations and activities. A user who is not online when a comment is made can see it later, and can scroll back through the entire history of a conversation. Second, a minimalist graphical representation called a social proxy is used to provide information about who is currently present in the conversation. The proxy uses a large circle to represent the conversation, and coloured dots (aka "marbles") to represent individuals. A marble inside the circle represents a user who is "in" the displayed conversation; a marble outside the circle is in some other conversation. When a user interacts with BABBLE – either by

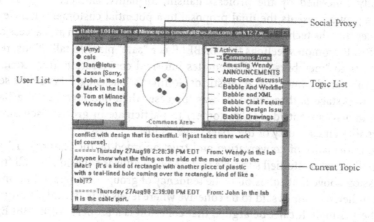

Figure 7.1 The BABBLE interface.

posting a message, or simply by scrolling or clicking on the interface – her marble rapidly moves towards the centre of the circle; with inactivity the marble will slowly drift out to the inner edge of the circle. In Figure 7.1, five participants have recently "spoken" or "listened", two have been idle, and one is in a different conversation. The third distinguishing feature of BABBLE is that it lacks technical mechanisms for enforcing behaviour. Originally intended for small workgroups, it provides no technical means for "kicking" people off, creating private topics, etc. With the exception of private, one-to-one chats, all BABBLE conversations were visible to everyone in a deployment group. Although various usage conventions have arisen, all negotiation and enforcement of such conventions is social.

7.4.3 Cohesion and Workplace Chat

In much the same way that levels of accountability vary between groups, so do levels of formality and informality in communication. Interviews of BABBLE users revealed that BABBLE promotes "informality" in conversation. This informality results, in part, from the access control mechanisms built in to the system. It also results from the sociability and trust that exists among group members who use BABBLE. With respect to access control, a firewall exists to restrict access to IBM users, and separate BABBLE servers are configured for each group to ensure that users can access only the BABBLE topics created by their group. It can be argued that these technical features of BABBLE, i.e. the firewall and access control, enable a cyber analogy of what Goffman calls the "backstage" (Goffman, 1961). Goffman proposes that

> if a [group's] performance is to be effective it will be likely that the extent and character of the cooperation that makes this possible will be concealed and kept secret (ibid, p. 104).

The informality of communication, indecision, uncertainty, and imperfection that characterizes a collaborative work of drafting a business proposal, for example, is carefully concealed by the professionalism, formality, and certainty portrayed when a group presents the final proposal to a potential customer. Interview data indicates that the technical properties of secure communication and access control of BABBLE promotes feelings that BABBLE is a "safe" place to talk. Thus, restricting access to "members only" promotes informal conversation, free exchange of ideas, and social banter characteristic of Goffman's "backstage". When the security of the backstage is threatened, as was the case when one member of a BABBLE group invited an outsider (a customer) to participate in group discussions, the informality and security of the "backstage" is lost.

The informality of conversation and trust afforded by the features of BABBLE among the groups studied suggests that BABBLE affords cohesion. Recall from the discussion above that cohesion is the tendency of group members to like and trust one another. A group is said to be cohesive where levels of trust and affinity among members is high. It can't be argued that cohesion is a property of BABBLE, much as it can't be argued that accountability is a property of BABBLE. Yet, trust and mutual attraction are implicit in the comments that some BABBLE users make when they describe their experience using BABBLE with members of their workgroup. These users report that conversation in BABBLE is "more relaxed" and "less obtrusive" than conversation via email or the phone. These groups use BABBLE to keep others abreast of their decisions and activities – to keep one another "in the loop", so to speak. The fact that these groups prefer a communication medium such as BABBLE – that is informal, enables free exchange of ideas and provides synchronous access to one another – suggests they are cohesive. Cohesion, thus, is a property of these groups that use BABBLE. It is technologically enabled by the features of BABBLE and socially enabled by the trust and mutual attraction that exists among members of these groups.

Interview data show that the technical properties of secure communication and access control promoted the feeling that BABBLE was a "safe" place to talk. Informants stressed that restricting access to "members only" promoted informal conversation, a free-flowing exchange of ideas, and social banter.

> I think [BABBLE is] less formal. I treat it less formal. I wouldn't write mail about someone else's bug unless I check very very carefully that it is indeed in their code. It's funny but it's OK to write things [in BABBLE] that are not 100% finished … not that thought through … half-baked ideas are OK. Somehow it's much more like conversation. (software engineer)

Users also said that they were less careful about the mechanical aspects of writing using BABBLE (e.g. as compared to email) because they knew that BABBLE discussion was confined to the group. For example:

> When you are in BABBLE it seems like a more relaxed atmosphere and you don't have to watch your spelling, you don't have to have your sentence structure perfect and all that. [In email] you feel like everything has to be correct. (recruiter)

That BABBLE provides a safe sanctuary becomes quite evident when members perceive that quality being threatened. This occurred in the Software Engineering group when a client joined BABBLE. Several core members voiced strong concerns that the client's presence threatened the integrity of their BABBLE, for example:

> Peter asked the person in Lyon to be on all the time. So I think to myself, "is she listening to every word?" Once you start being very careful [about what you say] then you start to lose something essential to the discussion. (software engineer)

These concerns are serious because BABBLE's access control is all or none: once "outsiders" are allowed in, they can see everything. Conversely, because BABBLE makes user actions visible via the social proxy, and provides ways of finding out who has been in a topic, "outsider" behaviour can be monitored.

To summarize, this discussion examined communicative practices of small groups using a proprietary chat tool. The cohesion fostered by the tool is evidenced by a candid and informal tone of conversation and by the frequent and explicit acts of keeping others "in the loop". These practices emerge from the technical features of the BABBLE environment and the social dynamics of each workgroup.

7.4.4 Instant Messaging in the Workplace

We turn now to another kind of computer-mediated communication technology used the workplace: instant messaging (IM). This section discusses qualitative study of 20 workplace users of IM across three technology organizations (Nardi, Whittaker, and Bradner, 2000). A defining characteristic of all instant messaging applications, including those studied which were AOL's Instant Messenger and Excite's PAL, is the use of "buddy lists" to initiate messages and show status. Status indicators vary among systems; most show "log in" and "log out" at a minimum. When a user sends a message to a buddy, the message appears either expanded in a small pop-up window on the recipient's screen or minimized in the buddy's task bar (Figure 7.2). The following paragraphs explore ways in which the design of IM affords different aspects of cohesion such as social bonding and impression management, discussed below.

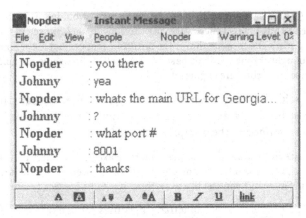

Figure 7.2 An example of information exchange via IM.

7.4.5 Cohesion in IM: Social Bonding

One use of IM that was observed in the workplace is social bonding. IM users reported monitoring their buddy list for activity, not to exchange messages, but simply to "know who is around". In this case, IM was used to produce a feeling of closeness with others, rather than to exchange information. Users described the connectedness they experience from using IM with comments such as: "You feel like you're not the only one working on a weekend... You feel like you're in this world together so this creates a little universe" and "You can see when people log in and out... you get a visual image in your mind of that person and I feel closer to the people I work with as a result of that".

Collocated workers maintain a sense of the presence of others through opportunistic encounters in shared spaces such as coffee rooms or hallways (Fish, Kraut, Root, and Rice, 1992; Bly, Harrison, and Irwin, 1993; Tang, Isaacs, and Rua, 1994;

Dourish and Bly, 1993; Olson and Olson, 2000). But for people collaborating at distance, such encounters are rare. One IM user, with colleagues on the opposite coast of the U.S., explained that IM can partially address this lack of connectedness: "I tell people about [IM] because it helps overcome some social problems you experience when you're a thousand miles away from your co-workers. Things like forgetting that they're there".

7.4.6 Impression Management

Another use of IM is impression management. The concept of impression management refers to the way in which we actively guide and control the impressions others form of us (Goffman, 1961). An interesting instance of impression management that IM mediates is responsiveness. Many of the workers studied felt they could ignore instant messages without offending the sender. They were able to do this because the features of IM don't allow the sender to know for certain whether the intended recipient is there or not. As a result, failing to respond is not necessarily interpreted as rude or unresponsive. IM therefore provides plausible deniability about one's presence. A software developer commented, "One thing I like about [IM] is that I'll see a message but I won't have to acknowledge my presence. So I'll respond to them later when I have time."

Informants reported that there were fewer costs associated with delaying a response to an IM, compared with other media. If the message is temporarily ignored, it stays up on the user's computer screen as a reminder. It can be responded to later by simply typing into the window. A web page designer said: "You can choose if you want to respond. It's like voicemail but more accessible. I can choose not to respond for a while. It [the message] is still sitting there. I don't have to go in, get my messages. It's a nice, clean, easy way to communicate."

In contrast, people often feel compelled to answer the phone because they do not know the identity of the caller or their reason for calling (although this is mitigated somewhat by caller-ID). Alan observed, "So the phone can be a very intrusive thing, whereas IM is a lot friendlier because it's just a quick thing of, 'Are you there and available' or very short questions. I don't mind that interruption. With a phone call, you don't know if it's really urgent because there's no way to know who's calling, whether it's urgent and what the topic is." An IM is also typically from someone on the user's buddy list. It is therefore already partially screened and less likely to be an irrelevant distraction.

Together, ease of screening, delayed responding, and plausible deniability of presence allow recipients much more control over responding than with face-to-face interaction or the phone. This greater control redresses the fundamental communication asymmetry in informal communication. Instead of conversations taking place at the convenience of the initiator, IM allows genuine impression management about whether and when to talk. The conversational contract can be negotiated on a more equal footing between initiator and recipient than with face-to-face or phone interaction. This may explain why IM is often used to negotiate availability for phone calls and face-to-face conversations.

Thus, I can maintain the impression that I am conscientious and responsive to another's needs without immediately responding to a colleague's instant message because I know that my colleague doesn't know if I have seen the message and am deliberately ignoring it, or if I have not seen it at all. Some level of plausible deniability is acceptable in a white-collar office but little to no deniability is tolerable in the control room of a nuclear submarine, for example. A similar logic holds that using IM to selectively block others from communicating with you is probably not acceptable in a white-collar office, but is perfectly acceptable in the social context of teenage banter. Blocking is a feature of most IM tools. It allows users to selectively block others from receiving updates to their log-in status. Users who have been blocked will perpetually see the blocking user as "not logged in" on their buddy lists. One IM user at Insite corporation reported blocking her mother from seeing her in IM because, as she put it:

> It was hideous... she was so excited she could call me up that easily, she went overboard. I was on a deadline and it was going BING!, BING!, BING! in the background. I shut it off and made myself hidden [from her]. I didn't want to hurt her feelings, but I didn't want to have to worry about that again. (web site designer)

By using the blocking feature in IM, this user cut communication with her mother, plausibly denied that she was accessible via IM, and maintained the impression that she was still quite happy to communicate with her mother when communication was mediated by other technologies. Some researchers have examined IM use in social contexts, specifically among teenage users in the home (Grinter, 2000). They found that the plausible deniability afforded by the blocking feature of IM was instrumental in the construction and maintenance of conversational cliques. Grinter compares adult use with teenage use and found that teenagers rely heavily on the blocking features of IM to create deniability:

> Specifically, they [teenagers] needed to create the illusion that they were not available to their friends at times, and they used access control [i.e. blocking] to achieve this. The difference between adult and teenage use of IM suggests that adults can hide behind the ambiguity of the wide range of uses of the computer, and their importance of accomplishing "work"... the teenagers used access control to attain their required unavailability. (Grinter, 2000)

7.4.7 "Open" Conversation

Lastly, the near-synchronous, perpetually "open" channel of communication that exists in IM once an IM connection is made between two buddies affords what social linguists call an "open" conversational system (Kendon, 1977). Open conversations are created when one enters the workplace in the morning, greets co-workers, and begins to work. The conversation is said to be "open" until the end of the day when a "terminal exchange" takes place such as "goodbye: goodbye". In effect, when we greet others on arriving in the morning, they tacitly consent to a social contract that permits us to approach them, at any point later in the day, and begin discussing business matters without formally greeting them a second time.

Once a conversation is "opened", it is mutually agreed that discussion can be resumed, paused, and re-purposed without requiring additional formal greetings or other explicit addresses.

Likewise, in instant messaging, during any given day, once an initial message is sent and received a conversation is "open" until one or the other buddy explicitly closes the communication by saying something like "goodbye". Alternatively, if the recipient fails to respond for an extended period of time the message initiator concludes that the recipient has left the vicinity of the computer. Subjects discussed these "open" IM conversations with statements like: "I never feel on IM that I've got to find something to say back. It's okay if it sits there and we don't talk for a while" and "You [IM] for five minutes and then you do something and communicate again. It doesn't have to be a continuous, make sure you've got everything thought through [conversation]".

IM participants seemed to create a virtual environment similar to a shared physical office, where people engaged in work-related tasks, interspersing sporadic interchanges throughout their individual work (Heath and Luff, 1991, 1992; Dourish, Adler, Bellotti, and Henderson, 1996; Bradner et al, 1999; Churchill and Bly, 1999; Olson and Olson, 2000). In IM, messages are persistent and visible, which helps preserve ongoing conversational context. These observations are similar to the "virtual shared office" that is characteristic of open video links (Dourish et al, 1996; Kraut and Attewell, 1997). However, the key differences between IM and video are that IM supplies a record of conversation which provides thematic context for ongoing "open" conversations and affords plausible deniability of presence.

7.5 Summary

In her early study of computer-mediated communication in the workplace, Ehrlich reported: "Organizations will tacitly create agreements about the relative level of informality that is acceptable in electronic messages. These unspoken agreements can have an impact on both the anxiety level of the users and the communication strategies they use" (Ehrlich, 1987). The data reported in this chapter help to answer questions such as: "Why do organizations create norms of informality?" and "How do communicative norms such as informality give rise to cohesion in groups?" More generally, the qualitative data reported here demonstrated how specific technical properties of different CMC systems (chat and IM) interact with the social characteristics of groups to enable a variety of communicative practices.

This chapter has also demonstrated that social science knowledge of collocation among groups has several implications for virtual teams. Empirical studies suggest collocation fosters cohesion and separation fosters discontent (Sayles, 1958) and groupthink (Janis, 1972). Other empirical studies show that permitting communication between opponents as they play a game significantly increases the likelihood that a cooperative strategy will be adopted. When communication is not possible, a competitive strategy is more commonly adopted (Rabbie, 1991). Thus, there is some evidence that direct communication fosters a norm of cooperation.

But is technology-mediated communication "direct" communication? This is another unanswered question. Over the past 20 years, significant inroads have been made towards understanding the technical dimensions of computer-mediated distance collaboration (e.g. Poltrock and Engelbeck, 1997; Mark, Grudin, and Poltrock, 1999). Along the way, efforts to unite sociological and technical perspectives on small-group interaction have been made (e.g. Galegher, Kraut, and Egido, 1990). The long-term goal of this research should not be to outline how to digitally reconstruct the physical experience of collocation but to go beyond "being there". That is to say, the goal should be to capitalize on social and technical affordances to better support distance collaboration. This chapter offers a principled understanding of social-psychological dimensions of interpersonal interaction (e.g. cohesion) in groups. This understanding can help software designers generate socially informed software requirements. In other words, the question that motivated this chapter, i.e. "What is a team and how can it be said to be virtual?" is the first question software designers should ask when collecting functional requirements for software to support virtual teaming. It is wise to start with this question because it engages the social issues surrounding distance collaboration among small groups which are likely to impact adoption (cf. Grudin, 1994). Finally, this chapter reveals a gap in small-group research – there seems to be a lack of empirical studies which examine the extent to which fundamental theories of small-group interaction (e.g. social comparison, groupthink) describe communication among geographically distributed groups.

References

Bales, R.F. (1950). Interaction process analysis : a method for the study of small groups. Cambridge, Mass.: Addison-Wesley Press.

Bly, S.A., Harrison, S.R., and Irwin, S. (1993). Media Spaces: Video, Audio, and Computing. Communications of the ACM, 36(1), 28–47.

Bradner, E., Kellogg, W., and Erickson, T. (1999). Adoption and Use of Babble: A field study of chat in the workplace. Paper presented at the Conference on Computer Supported Cooperative Work (CSCW 2000), Copenhagen, Denmark.

Cartwright, D., and Zander, A.F. (1968). Group dynamics; research and theory. (3d ed.). New York,: Harper and Row.

Churchill, E., and Bly, S. (1999). "It's all in the words": Supporting activities with lightweight tools. Paper presented at the Conference on Supporting Group Work (GROUP '99).

Deutsch, M. (1949). An Experimental Study of the Effects of Co-operation and Competition Upon Group Process. Human Relations, 2, 129–152.

Dourish, P., Adler, A., Bellotti, V., and Henderson, A. (1996). Your Place or Mine?: Learning from long-term use of audio-video communication. Computer Supported Cooperative Work, 5(1), 33–62.

Dourish, P., and Bly, S. (1993). Portholes: Supporting awareness in a distributed work group. Paper presented at the Conference on Human Factors in Computing (CHI '93).

Ehrlich, S. (1987). Strategies for encouraging successful adoption of office communication systems. ACM Transactions on Office Information Systems, 5, 340–357.

Erickson, T., Smith, D., Kellogg, W., Laff, M., Richards, J., and Bradner, E. (1999). Socially translucent systems: Social Proxies, persistent conversations and the design of 'Babble'. Paper presented at the Conference on Human Factors in Computing (CHI '99), Pittsburgh, PA.

Festinger, L. (1954). A Theory of Social Comparison Process. Human Relations, 7, 117–140.

Festinger, L. (1968). Informal Social Communication. In D. Cartwright and A. Zander (Eds.), Group Dynamics (3 ed.,). New York, NY: Harper and Row.

Fish, R., Kraut, R., Root, R., and Rice, R. (1992). Evaluating video as technology for information communication. Paper presented at the Conference on Human Factors in Computing (CHI '92).

French, J. (1959). The Basis of Social Power. In D. Cartwright (Ed.), Studies in Social Power (pp. 150–167). Ann Arbor, MI: Research Center for Group Dynamics, University of Michigan.

Galegher, J.R., Kraut, R.E., and Egido, C. (1990). Intellectual teamwork: social and technological foundations of cooperative work. Hillsdale, N.J.: L. Erlbaum Associates.

Gersick, C. (1988). Time and Transition in Work Teams: Toward a New Model of Group Development. Academy of Management Journal, 31, 9–41.

Gladstein, D. (1984). Groups in Context: A Model of Task Group Effectiveness. Administrative Science Quarterly, 29, 499–517.

Gladstein, D., and Caldwell, D.F. (1988). Beyond Task and Maintenance. Group and Organizational Studies, 13, 468–494.

Goffman, E. (1961). The Presentation of Self in Everyday Life. New York: Anchor-Doubleday.

Grinter, R. (2000). "Working" from Home: Why Teenagers Use Instant Messaging : unpublished.

Hackman, R. (Ed.). (1990). Groups that Work (and Some that Don't): Creating Conditions for Effective Teamwork. San Francisco, California, USA: Jossey-Bass Publications.

Hare, A.P. (1962). Handbook of small group research. New York: Free Press of Glencoe.

Haywood, M. (1998). Managing virtual teams : practical techniques for high-technology project managers. Boston: Artech House.

Heath, C., and Luff, P. (1991). Disembodied Conduct: Communication Through Video in a Multi-Media Office Environment. Paper presented at the CHI'91.

Heath, C., and Luff, P. (1992). Collaboration and control. Computer Supported Cooperative Work, 1, 65–80.

Homans, G.C. (1950). The human group. New York,: Harcourt Brace.

Hutchins, E. (1990). The Technology of Team Navigation. In J. Galegher and R. Kraut (Eds.), Intellectual Teamwork: Social and Technological Foundations of Cooperative Work. . Hillsdale, NJ: Lawrence Erlbaum.

Ilgen, D.R. (1999). Teams Embedded In Organizations. American Psychologist, 54, 129–139.

Janis, I.L. (1972). Victims of groupthink; a psychological study of foreign-policy decisions and fiascoes. Boston,: Houghton Mifflin.

Katzenbach, J.R., and Smith, D.K. (1993). The wisdom of teams : creating the high-performance organization. Boston, Mass.: Harvard Business School Press.

Kendon, A. (1977). Studies in the behavior of social interaction. Bloomington: Indiana University.

Kinney, S., and Panko, R. (1996). Project Teams: Profiles and member perceptions. Paper presented at the 29th Hawaii International Conference on Systems Sciences, Maui, HI.

Kraut, R.E., and Attewell, P. (1997). Media use and organizational knowledge: Electronic mail in a global corporation. In S. Kiesler (Ed.), Research Milestones on the Information Highway (pp. xvi, 463). Mahwah, NJ: Lawrence Erlbaum Associates Publishers.

Lewin, K. (1948). Resolving social conflicts: Selected papers on group dynamics 1935–1946. New York: Harper.

Lewin, K. (1951). Field theory in social science; selected theoretical papers. ([1st] ed.). New York,: Harper.

Maier, N., and Solem, N. (1952). The Contribution of a Discussion Leader to the Quality of Group Thinking: The Effective Use of Minority Opinions. Human Relations, 5, 277–288.

Mark, G., Grudin, J., and Poltrock, S. (1999). Meeting at the Desktop: An Empirical Study of Virtually Collocated Teams. Paper presented at the Computer Supported Cooperative Work (CSCW '99), Copenhagen, Denmark.

McGrath, J. (1990). Time Matters in Groups. In J. Galegher and R. Kraut (Eds.), Intellectual Teamwork: Social and Technological Foundations of Cooperative Work. Hillsdale, NJ: Lawrence Erlbaum.

McGrath, J. (1997). Small Group research, that once and future field: An interpretation of the past with an eye for the future. Group Dynamics, 1(7–27).

Mink, O.G., Mink, B.P., and Owen, K.Q. (1987). Groups at work. Englewood Cliffs, N.J.: Educational Technology Publications.

Mohrman, S.A., Cohen, S.G., Mohrman, A.M., and University of Southern California. Center for Effective Organizations. (1995). Designing team-based organizations : new forms for knowledge work. (1st ed.). San Francisco: Jossey-Bass.

Nardi, B., Whittaker, S., and Bradner, E. (2000). Interaction and Outeraction: Instant Messaging in Action. Paper presented at the Computer Supported Cooperative Work, Seattle, Washington.

Olson, G.M., and Olson, J.S. (2000). Distance Matters. Transactions on Computer Human Interaction (TOCHI), 15, 139–179.

Phillip, J., and Dunphy, D. (1959). Developmental trends in small groups. Sociometry, 22, 162–174.

Poltrock, S., and Engelbeck, G. (1997). Requirements for a Virtual Collocation Environment. Paper presented at the Conference on Supporting Group Work (GROUP '97), Phoenix, Arizona.

Rabbie, J., M. (1991). Determinants of Instrrumental Intra-group Cooperation. In R.A. Hinde and J. Groebel (Eds.), Cooperation and Prosocial Behaviour (pp. 238–262). Cambridge, UK: Cambridge University Press.

Sayles, L.R. (1958). Behavior of industrial work groups: prediction and control. New York,: Wiley.

Sproull, L., and Kiesler, S. (1991). Connections: New Ways of Working in the Networked Organization. Cambridge, MA: MIT Press.

Steiner, I.D. (1972). Group process and productivity. New York,: Academic Press.

Sundstrom, E., DeMuse, K., and Futrell, D. (1990). Workteams: Applications and Effectiveness. American Psychologist, 45(2), 120–133.

Sundstrom, E.D., and Sundstrom, M.G. (1986). Work places : the psychology of the physical environment in offices and factories. Cambridge, MA: Cambridge University Press.

Tajfel, H. (1978). Differentiation between social groups : studies in the social psychology of intergroup relations. London ; New York: Published in cooperation with European Association of Experimental Social Psychology by Academic Press.

Tang, J., Isaacs, E., and Rua, M. (1994). Supporting distributed groups with a Montage of Lightweight interactions. Paper presented at the Computer Supported Cooperative Work (CSCW'94).

Thibaut, J.W., and Kelley, H.H. (1959). The social psychology of groups. New York,: Wiley.

Walker, C.R., and Guest, R.H. (1952). The man on the assembly line. Cambridge, MA: Harvard University Press.

Weick, K.E. (1979). The social psychology of organizing. (2d ed.). New York: Random House.

Chapter 8
CoWeb – Experiences with Collaborative Web Spaces

Andreas Dieberger and Mark Guzdial

8.1 Introduction

CoWebs, short for collaborative webs, are web-based collaborative tools that have been in continuous use at Georgia Tech and many other places for several years. Originally CoWebs were relatively simple but flexible web servers that allowed everybody to easily modify content. Their openness, and the fact that every user has essentially the same rights and abilities in the space, distinguishes CoWebs from many other collaborative systems.

Over the years a number of variants of CoWebs have been developed and used in educational and other settings, be it to support anchored discussions, collaborative writing, to maintain case libraries, to share information, or to serve as simple brainstorming devices.

A peculiarity of CoWebs is their openness. In many CoWebs the ownership of space is not strictly pre-determined, but it evolves out of peoples' interactions with the space and with other users. Similarly, most CoWebs do not enforce a strict author/reader distinction. Instead, these and other roles often emerge over time, out of the use of the tool.

8.2 History of the Swiki and the CoWeb

Conceptually, CoWebs are on the basis of the WikiWiki Web (or simply "Wiki") by Ward Cunningham (see http://c2.com/cgibin/wiki or Leuf and Cunningham, 2001). A Wiki invites users to edit any page within the site and to add new pages. In order to do so only a regular web browser is required, and the user does not have to download any special plug-ins or software, as the text is edited in a regular HTML text area.

The Wiki is an unusual collaborative space because of its total freedom, ease of access and use, and because of its total lack of predetermined structure. As every user has exactly the same rights on the Wiki, it is an inherently democratic space, not requiring accounts or passwords or the like.

The original CoWeb was created by Mark Guzdial on the basis of these ideas. While the Wiki is implemented in Perl, Mark based his system on Squeak, a cross-platform open source freeware version of Smalltalk. Squeak (see http://www.squeak.org/ or Guzdial, 2001) runs on virtually any server platform available, which makes the CoWeb widely available. The focus of the CoWeb has been on use in higher education. In reference to the Wiki, Mark called his system Swiki (for Squeak Wiki). The name CoWeb emerged later, as an easier term for teachers and students to understand. We will use the terms Swiki and CoWeb interchangeably in this chapter.

There are a number of differences between the Swiki and the original Wiki. Like the Wiki, most CoWebs look like fairly traditional web sites, except for a set of buttons, which allow users to do things not possible on most web sites. For example, people can edit pages, look at the history of a page, check what other pages link to a page, and so forth. In recent version of the CoWeb it is also possible to lock pages, to upload files (images or other documents to work on), etc. An example of a typical CoWeb page is shown in Figure 8.1.

A CoWeb doesn't have to look like this, though, as the system is very open to adaptations and modifications. Internally, the original Swiki was based on Squeak's pluggable web server (PWS). Recent versions of the CoWeb designed by Jochen Rick from Georgia Tech are on the basis of a new server, called Comanche, implemented by Bolot Kerimbaev (also from Georgia Tech). The PWS and Comanche support lightweight creation of artefacts. This permits, for instance, creation of items using embedded Squeak and then serving these items directly through the Swiki.

For example, it is relatively easy to create sounds (Squeak has tremendous sound capabilities) or images and to pass these objects directly to Comanche to be

Figure 8.1 A typical CoWeb page.

served. Comanche handles all type conversions and the associated MIME-typing, which makes it quite easy to develop new kinds of dynamic web resources or to enhance the Swiki with new collaborative functionality.

8.3 Content Creation on the CoWeb

Another difference between the Wiki and the CoWeb lies in how pages are edited. The Wiki provides a simple text notation (mark-up) to format pages. The Swiki also provides such a simple notation, but in addition it also supports HTML. Knowledge of HTML is not necessary to contribute on a CoWeb, though. For example, ordinary line breaks get converted into paragraphs. This allows users to copy and paste text into a Swiki page and never to worry about formatting.

For more elaborate formatting of content, users can employ either HTML or the text mark-up mentioned above. Starting a line with an exclamation mark turns it into a header (the more exclamation marks, the larger), starting a line with dashes turns these lines into list items, and separating items with vertical bars turns them into a simple table.

Creation of new pages and links to other pages is very easy and non-threatening as well, which might be one of the keys to the success of the Swiki. Putting an asterisk before and after any text (for example: *my reference list*) will mark the text with a page creation button. Once that button is clicked, the text turns into a link to a new page with the title "my reference list", and the page opens directly in the editor, ready to accept new content. Figure 8.2 shows what editing content in a CoWeb looks like. It shows the content of the CoWeb page from Figure 8.1.

Figure 8.2 Editing in a CoWeb (editing the CoWeb page shown in Figure 8.1).

Note the line consisting of only a plus sign "+" in Figure 8.2. This text mark-up item represents the "insert here" form shown in Figure 8.1, essentially a text box with an "Add to this page" button. It allows users to provide additional content on the page without having to "edit the page". These insert here forms have at least four advantages over editing the entire page:

- In large pages it is not necessary to find the place where to add text.
- It is possible to define exactly where text should be added (at the bottom for a comments list, for example) and it is possible to have more than just one of these insertion forms on a page. Of course it is still possible to edit the page if a user wants to modify existing content or add to a different location.
- The "insert here" forms are less threatening to new users than actually editing an entire page, especially as Web users are not used to the concept of being able to modify pages on the Web.
- It is possible to lock a page to ensure no text gets accidentally deleted and still allow people to add to the page.

The last point brings up the issue of security on the CoWeb. Surprisingly, security hasn't been a major problem in either the Wiki or the CoWeb. Both systems have a backup mechanism, which can be easily used for damage recovery. For example, using the page history function users can access every version of a page since it was created and to see exactly what parts have changed. From this view it is a simple step to retrieve material that was maliciously or – more frequently – accidentally modified and restore an earlier version of the page.

8.4 Typical Uses of CoWebs

The CoWeb's flexibility allows it to be used for a variety of activities. It could be used primarily by one person, for example to build a collection of quick notes and ideas from wherever the person has access to the Internet. More interesting, though, are uses that stress the collaborative aspects of the CoWeb.

The Swiki is a simple and lightweight collaboration tool, in strong contrast to most other CSCW systems, which tend to employ more or less static predetermined roles, permissions, and authorization. We will discuss some of these aspects in a later section. Because of its openness and the use of simple web pages and web forms, most of a CoWeb's features can be mastered in a matter of minutes. This makes the CoWeb a non-threatening and forgiving tool for collaboration.

In Guzdial, Rick et al (2000), Mark Guzdial identifies four general categories of CoWeb use:

- collaborative artefact creation
- review activities
- case library creation
- distributing information.

8.4.1 Collaborative Artefact Creation

Artefact creation is a goal in many classes where students use CoWebs. In some cases, the resulting web site itself is the artefact created. In other cases, the artefact is an analysis, or report, which is collaboratively marked up and commented on. The CoWeb can also be used to collect pieces of text, which are then put together in an external document to form the beginning of a final, collaborative artefact.

Alternatively, CoWeb users might be working on non-textual external artefacts (for example a multimedia presentation) and use the CoWeb mostly for coordination, planning, and distributing versions of the presentation.

A prime example of artefact creation was the construction of a collaborative adventure game a number of years back. The game was of the simple "choose-your-own-path" type, essentially a hypertext where each link described what to do next. According to the Catalogue of CoWeb uses (Guzdial, 2000), the game originated the night before a big assignment was due, and has been extended over time and re-created by other students. Artefacts of this kind are not planned. The fact that they can be created at all is proof for the openness and flexibility of the tool.

Other examples of CoWeb uses in this category are the collaborative creation of glossaries or FAQ lists or any type of collaborative writing. Note that glossaries and FAQs are not only artefacts, but also distributed information, as discussed below.

8.4.2 Review Activities

CoWebs are frequently used for review activities. For example, colleagues at the Swedish Institute for Computer Science (SICS) used a Swiki to help organize a conference workshop. Activities in the CoWeb included not only collecting ideas and suggestions for the workshop (a collaborative artefact creation type of activity) and distributing information to the programme committee, but the actual reviews of the submitted papers. To achieve this, the submitted papers were uploaded to the Swiki, a list of reviewers was assigned to each paper and reviewers linked their reviews directly to the submitted paper. This set-up allowed reviewers to see other reviewers' comments on a paper and respond to them, which, in a couple of cases led to interesting discussions already before the workshop. It also permitted reviewers to get an overview of the materials they did not have to review. Certainly, activities of this kind require limiting access to the program committee of the workshop.

In the academic setting, review activities might be performed both by internal (peers, other students, teachers) as well as external users. One of the most successful CoWebs at Georgia Tech was used in an architecture class, where expert architects reviewed students' "pin-ups" online (Zimring, Khan et al, 1999). The key to activities of this kind is again the simple set-up of access to a CoWeb and the fact that no special hardware or software is needed to work with a CoWeb.

Yet another example of these types of activities was used in a multimedia project at Georgia Tech, called "Griffith in Context", by Ellen Strain and Greg VanHoosier-Carey. In this project, an interactive CD on the basis of Griffith's film *Birth of a Nation* is being created. Several experts were interviewed to create voice-overs for video segments of the movie. A modified CoWeb permitted the experts to review the video segments along with their voice-overs. Although this set-up required significant modifications to the standard CoWeb, it is again proof for the flexibility of the CoWeb architecture mentioned before.

8.4.3 Case Library Creation

In an educational setting, CoWebs are frequently used as persistent spaces across offerings of a given course. As such, contributions to the CoWeb of students in one semester become information sources, and even advice, to later students. Students post assignments, resources, and even "letters to future students" in the CoWeb, to serve as cases for others. For example, a class on object-oriented design at Georgia Tech gives extra credit for students who write up their class projects in a form that is useful to future students. The class projects have to have received a A grade or better in order to be able to post them, as future students are most interested in studying successful past projects. Useful cases include corrections to what was graded down on the project, descriptions of the design process, analyses of strengths and weaknesses of the project, lessons learnt, etc.

Cases posted have included tutorials, new projects, descriptions of group processes, and so forth. If case libraries grow large enough, multiple solutions to similar problems eventually occur, which are especially useful.

Case libraries can be useful also in any non-educational setting, where similar or identical problems have to be solved over and over again. In such a setting the CoWeb would function as a simple organizational memory. However, like with most organizational memory tools, the trick is to re-find a previous solution, because frequently users do not know what exactly to look for.

8.4.4 Distributing Information

As the CoWeb is essentially a web site, it is easy to create links to external resources. Creation of URL lists is therefore a simple and easy to achieve form of distributing information on a CoWeb. Other types of information that can be easily distributed using a CoWeb include organizational information, as in the workshop example above, or images, such as scanned in design sketches.

If the information flow is mostly one-way, such that one person posts information and everybody else just accesses it, a CoWeb would might not appear to offer a tremendous advantage. However, employing a CoWeb in such a situation permits users to comment directly on information, offer suggestions, create links to additional materials, or correct mistakes.

In an early CoWeb one of us posted information and didn't notice that a link was broken, owing to a typo. Somebody else simply hit "edit this page" and fixed the problem. In an ordinary web site fixing this mistake would involve sending email to the owner of the page who then would eventually fix the problem. A lot of time might pass until a problem is fixed, with incorrect information being online all that time. On the CoWeb, the time from finding the problem to fixing it was at most a few minutes. Enabling users to fix problems right away as in this example, gives them a sense of ownership of the information space. We will say more about this in the section on emerging roles below.

In an educational context, connecting students with instructors and managing class context are important activities. Again, the CoWeb permits to easily create links to additional information or artefacts to the point that – in some classes – students agreed that they learned as much from each other as from the teacher (Guzdial, Realff et al, 1999).

8.4.5 Other Uses for CoWebs

A fifth use of CoWebs could be seen in its use as a tool for experimenting with collaboration per se. An example of this use was the social navigation Swiki one of the authors created by modifying a standard CoWeb. Social navigation is a systems design approach, which tries to make people aware of each other's activities. In that sense social navigation is about awareness support. However, social navigation also encompasses activities involving social filtering and touches on collaborative work in general. Examples would be to see which texts in a digital library are popular, or being guided to relevant information in an FAQ on the basis of what my colleagues (who supposedly have similar interests and needs) found interesting. For more information on social navigation, see Dieberger (1997) and Munro, Höök et al (1999).

The social navigation Swiki was designed to enhance awareness of other CoWeb users (Dieberger and Höök, 1999). We observed (confirmed in a later user study of the system) that a CoWeb, even when bustling with life, appears pretty "dead" at first sight. The reason is that a CoWeb is essentially just another web site with a couple of extra buttons – at least until a user starts experimenting with the special CoWeb features, and looks at what has been modified, for example.

To increase awareness of what is going on in the CoWeb the social navigation CoWeb annotates all links inside the CoWeb with activity markers. These markers indicate when the page behind the link was last modified and also whether it was recently accessed. The last point is a major change in the user experience because users leave traces of their activities in a CoWeb even if they are not modifying content. Simply looking at a page causes activity markers to appear!

In one situation we observed how the activity markers could change the users' experience and therefore their actions on the CoWeb: the social navigation CoWeb provided access to the log file. This allowed users check for recent activity in the CoWeb as a whole without causing activity markers to appear. Originally the log was meant as an administration tool only. We found, though, that the log was deliberately used to avoid leaving markers. This behaviour occurred, for example, when somebody wanted to check whether other people had read a recent contribution to a page already, but without hyping that page by accessing it over and over again.

We used a three-level approach to all markers, indicating the amount of activity and the how recently modifications had been made by using different coloured

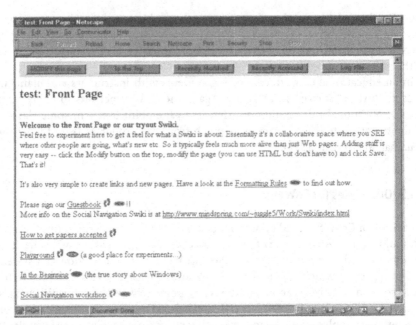

Figure 8.3 A social navigation Swiki page. Note that this CoWeb deliberately hides some of the standard CoWeb features.

markers. Additionally, we marked pages that had not been accessed for a very long time with a special marker. A "recently accessed" page, akin to the recently modified page, complemented the design and allowed people to find active pages without having to hunt them down by following links (Figure 8.3).

Our set-up had a number of problems. One of them was the choice of using link markers to indicated activity (the presence of markers changes the design of the page). Other issues we encountered were typical awareness support issues, such as how do you define a page that is "active", considering the fact that different areas in a site might have very different "rhythms" and rates of change.

A similar approach to incorporating social navigation information was again used in a more recent CoWeb, in Colleen Kehoe's 2cool CoWeb at Georgia Tech. This system used link colours to indicate how recently pages have been modified. This approach managed to avoid some of the issues in the social navigation CoWeb, though it's still not clear how visitors used the information on how recently pages have been modified. An interesting direction for future research is to explore how large-scale (e.g. the 2cool CoWeb was used by an architecture class with over 150 students) social navigation CoWebs would actually be used.

Another example for using a CoWeb to experiment with new collaborative applications was the collaborative radio system by Aibek Musaev at Georgia Tech. Aibek created a collaborative jukebox. Users of the Collaborative Radio would create a radio program assembled from uploaded sound files. On the basis of a regular schedule, the CoWeb would play the program, one sound file at a time. Connecting a low-power FM transmitter to the server turned the CoWeb into a true collaborative radio station. Users could tune into the program from any ordinary FM radio in the vicinity of the server. Although it was not considered a tremendous success, the collaborative radio demonstrates that collaboration on CoWebs does not have to be text-based.

Yet another example which does not exactly fit the four categories above, is the use of CoWebs in the Classroom 2000 project (now called E-Class). In this set-up classroom lectures are captured in multiple media, including slides and associated audio. The material posted on the web, by itself, would be static. By linking these slides to pages in a CoWeb, E-class allows students and teachers to engage in discussions of parts of a lecture even after the end of the lecture and it further allows them to post follow-up and background information that possibly was not available at the time of the lecture (Abowd, daPimentel et al, 1999).

8.5 Emerging Roles in CoWebs

The development of the CoWeb has been rapid, with a half dozen releases per year. The majority of that development has been driven by user requests, but in meeting those requests, the developers made a conscious effort to identify who the user was and what role they were performing (Guzdial, Rick, and Kerimbaev, 2000). From that effort, we have been able to identify a set of roles that we hypothesize may not be unique to CoWebs-rather, they might appear whenever a large scale, open collaborative system is in place. An obvious example role is the author, but others include:

- **Purpose agents** who are pursuing a particular agenda through use of the collaboration space. In the case of the CoWebs, the purpose agent is the teacher who designs particular educational activities in the CoWeb. The purpose agent rarely actually implements the designs – that's the role of the central user (the graduate student teaching assistant, in our CoWeb context). But the purpose agent wants an overview of what's happening. That's where facilities like the Recent Changes list comes into use. In a business context, for example, the purpose agent might the manager of a group who wants to use the collaboration space for solving some problem.
- **Central users** are the main web site designers in the CoWeb. They set up the look and feel of the site, as well as implementing the collaborative activities. For them, the CoWeb developers provided features like being able to rename pages (which is almost unique to the CoWeb among most Wiki clones) because that makes it easier to restructure and reuse a CoWeb.
- **Peripheral users** are people who just come to visit the CoWeb or who want to leave comments or critiques. In the CoWeb context, these are sometimes expert practitioners who contribute their time to review architecture or engineering projects. The peripheral users want to know as little as possible about the CoWeb, but they want easy navigation and ease of adding text. The CoWeb developers created features that make it easier to navigate the site (like automatic reverse links from each page) and to add to a page (e.g. an optional "add to page" box that appears when viewing a page). Peripheral users in a business context might be upper management who want to review activity in the collaborative space.

It's an open question, left for future research, whether these roles really do appear in other collaborative settings.

8.6 The Future of the CoWeb

The CoWeb is growing away from a strictly textual medium. Many academic departments rely on media formats that do not work well in plain HTML, e.g. mathematicians and engineers use equations extensively, and architects need annotatable graphic (even better, 3D) representations. Increased bandwidth and connectivity makes it more reasonable to provide support for other kinds of media in the CoWeb.

We have been exploring the creation of CoWeb plug-ins using a cross-platform language, Squeak, which the CoWeb itself is written in. Through these plug-ins, we have created a maths equation editor (Figure 8.4) where users can create equations using a drag-and-drop interface. They then drag the finished equation into the "Save" area, name it, and then insert the equation (by name) into their pages. Similarly, we have developed an image editor plug-in which allows users to paint on an image and retrieve previous versions of the image. The CoWeb plug-ins are our first foray into true collaborative multimedia.

One could easily imagine extensions that enhance a CoWeb as a social navigation tool. Many web sites seem to take the route towards more social information spaces, prime examples being Amazon, eBay and other eCommerce sites (Dieberger, Dourish et al, 2000). Similar to these sites, a future social navigation CoWeb could incorporate feedback schemes for content provided on the CoWeb.

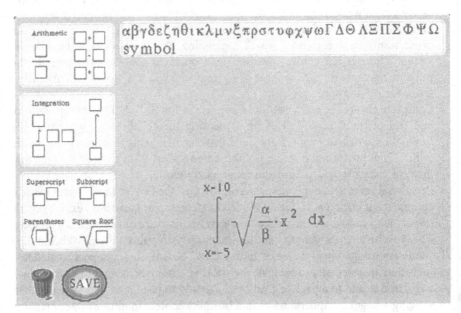

Figure 8.4 An Equation Editor in a CoWeb.

Examples might be a simple rating scheme or maybe even voting support for reaching decisions on the CoWeb. Such functionality would not be very difficult to implement, because of the CoWeb's open architecture.

As the CoWeb is a kind of social space already it might be useful to associate people with their contributions. Typically such functionality might introduce some form of identification or authentication, which could significantly change the character of the CoWeb. Currently, CoWeb users often put their "signature" under a contribution by typing their name between asterisks, thus creating a link to a personal page. From the personal page it is then possible to find all contributions of that person by listing the pages "linking to this page". Such signatures are based on conventions and there is no guarantee that nobody has modified a text above a signature.

Once rating information is available it would be possible to incorporate this information in the typical CoWeb functionality. For example when listing pages that link to the current page these pages could be sorted by their rating. Like the activity markers in the original social navigation Swiki, link colours or rating markers could annotate links directly to show the rating of a target page.

Aside from such changes, possible future extension might introduce some form of awareness support. Currently, CoWeb users are left unaware if another user is reading the same page at the same time or whether several people are modifying pages about a shared topic. It would be conceivable to build awareness support into the CoWeb in order to give a better indication of other people in the space at the same time. Ideally we would also want to interact with these people once we are aware of them. The question is how much such additions would change the CoWeb experience and if a CoWeb with a chat box on every page or topic would still be a CoWeb.

8.7 Summary

In this chapter we have given an overview of the CoWeb or Swiki. The CoWeb is implemented in the highly portable open-source freeware language Squeak and supports lightweight collaboration. It essentially looks like a web site, but it allows users to easily add content or modify existing content. CoWebs are unusual collaborative spaces because of their total freedom, ease of access and use and because of their lack of predetermined structure. All users have the same rights on the server, they don't require accounts or passwords, and everybody can modify any part of the information in the CoWeb and create new links and pages. Contributing to a CoWeb requires only a standard Web browser and knowledge of HTML is not necessary. We think that these minimal requirements are one of the reasons for the CoWeb's success.

Unlike most other CSCW tools, the CoWeb does not define strict roles in collaboration. Instead roles such as purpose agents, central users, and peripheral users tend to evolve out of the interactions with the CoWeb. We have described a number of typical uses for CoWebs, like collaborative artefact creation, case libraries, distributed information, review activities to show the variety of usage scenarios we observed. Some of these scenarios required (sometimes substantial) modifications of the CoWeb server. That applications like the "Griffith in Context" project were even possible demonstrates the flexibility and openness of the CoWeb architecture.

References

Abowd, G., M. daPimentel, et al. (1999). Anchoring Discussions in Lecture: An Approach to Collaboratively Extending Classroom Digital Media. Proc. of CSCL'99.

Dieberger, A. (1997). "Supporting Social Navigation on the World Wide Web." International Journal of Human-Computer Studies 46: 805–825.

Dieberger, A. and K. Höök (1999). Applying Social Navigation Principles to the Design of Shared Virtual Spaces. Proc. of WebNet'99. Honolulu, HI.

Dieberger, A., Dourish, P., et al. (2000). "Social Navigation: Techniques for Building More Usable Systems." interactions 7(6): 36–45.

Guzdial, M., M. Realff, et al. (1999). Using a CSCL-driven shift in agency to undertake educational reform, Proc. of CSCL'99, Palo Alto, CA, pp. 211–217.

Guzdial, M. (2000). Catalog of CoWeb uses. GVU Technical Report GIT-GVU-00–19, accessible from: http://www.cc.gatech.edu/gvu/reports/2000/abstracts/00–19.html.

Guzdial, M. (2001). Squeak – Object-Oriented Design with Multimedia Applications. Upper Saddle River, NJ, Prentice Hall.

Guzdial, M., J. Rick, B. Kerimbaev (2000). Recognizing and Supporting Roles in CSCW. Proc. of CSCW'2000, Philadelphia, PA, ACM Press, pp. 261–268.

Leuf, B. and W. Cunningham (2001). The Wiki Way – Quick Collaboration on the Web. Boston, MA, Addison-Wesley.

Munro, A.J., K. Höök, et al., Eds. (1999). Social Navigation of Information Space. Computer Supported Cooperative ork. London, Springer.

Zimring. C., S. Khan, D. Craig, S. ul-Haq and M. Guzdial (1999). CoOL Studio: Using simple tools to expand the discursive space of the design studio. Design Thinking Research Symposium, MIT, Cambridge, MA.

Chapter 9

From PHOAKS to TopicShop: Experiments in Social Data Mining

Brian Amento, Loren Terveen and Will Hill

9.1 Introduction

We live in an age of information abundance. The Internet in particular confronts us with endless possibilities: web sites to experience, music to listen to, conversations to participate in, and every conceivable consumer item to buy. Not only are there vast numbers of possibilities, but they also vary widely in quality. People thus face a difficult information management problem: they cannot hope to evaluate all available choices by themselves unless the topic of interest is severely constrained.

One information management task many web users perform is topic management – gathering, evaluating, and organizing relevant information resources for a given topic. Sometimes users investigate topics of professional interest, at other times topics of personal interest. Users may create collections of web information resources for their own use or for sharing with co-workers or friends. For example, someone might gather a collection of web sites on wireless internet services as part of a report she's preparing for her boss and a collection on *The X-Files* as a service to her fellow fans. Librarians might prepare topical collections for their clients, and teachers for their students (Abrams, 1998).

Current web tools do not support this task well; specifically, they do not make it easy to evaluate collections of web sites to select the best ones or to organize sites for future reuse and sharing. Users have to browse and view sites one after another until they are satisfied they have a good set, or, more likely, they get tired and give up. Browsing a web site is an expensive operation, both in time and in cognitive effort. And bookmarks, the most common form of keeping track of web sites, are a fairly primitive organizational technique.

Our approach to this problem combines social data mining (Terveen, 2001) with information workspaces (Card, 1991). As a type of recommender system (Goldberg, 1992; Resnick, 1997; Shardanand, 1995), social data mining systems mediate the process of sharing recommendations. In everyday life, when people have to make a choice without any personal knowledge of the alternatives, they often rely on the experience and opinions of others. They seek recommendations from people who are familiar with the choices they face, who have been helpful in the past, whose perspectives they value, or who are recognized experts. Social data mining systems extract information from computational activity records that can be used to recommend items. For our application, we need information to help people evaluate web sites. To help with the topic management problem, social data mining could be applied to web usage logs (Pitkow, 1997; Wexelblat, 1999) (answering the question "Which sites are visited most by other people?"), online conversations (Hill, 1996; Vieagas, 1999) (answering the question "Which sites are talked about most by other people?"), or the structure of the web itself (Aggarwal, 1999; Bharat, 1998; Chakrabarti, 1998; Goldberg, 1992; Pirolli, 1996) (answering the question "Which sites are linked to most by other people?"). TopicShop uses the final strategy.

Once the information has been extracted, it must be made available to users. TopicShop provides an information workspace in which collections of sites can be explored, ordered by any of the extracted features, added to a personal collection, grouped into subsets, and annotated.

We report here on two interrelated experiments. The first answers the question: "Is the information that TopicShop extracts about web sites valuable?" The answer is yes – we found that features on the basis of the number of incoming hyperlinks to a site, as well as simple counts of various type of content on a site, correlate well with expert quality judgements. The second study answers the question: "Is user task performance enhanced by the TopicShop interface?" The answer again is yes. TopicShop users were able to select significantly more high-quality sites, in less time and with less effort. Further, they were able to organize the sites they selected into more elaborate personal collections, again taking less time. Finally, they easily integrated the two tasks of selecting sites and organizing the selected sites.

This chapter is organized as follows. We first discuss related work and use it to situate our approach. Second, we describe the details of the TopicShop system. Third, we describe the two studies we just mentioned. Fourth, we discuss areas for future work. Finally, we conclude with a brief summary.

9.2 Previous and Related Work

9.2.1 Social Data Mining

The motivation for the social data mining approach goes back at least to Vannevar Bush's "As We May Think" essay (Bush, 1945). Bush envisioned scholars blazing trails through electronic repositories of information and realized that these trails could subsequently be followed by others. Everyone could walk in the footsteps of the masters. In our work, we have formulated a similar intuition using the metaphor of a path through the woods. However, this metaphor highlights the role of collective effort, rather than the individual. A path results from the decisions of many individuals, united only by where they choose to walk, yet still reflects a rough notion of what the walkers find to be a good path. The path both reflects history of use and serves as a resource for future users.

Social data mining approaches seek analogous situations in the computational world. Researchers look for situations where groups of people are producing computational records (such as documents, Usenet messages, or web sites and links) as part of their normal activity. Potentially useful information implicit in these records is identified, computational techniques to harvest and aggregate the information are invented, and visualization techniques to present the results are designed. Thus, computation discovers and makes explicit the "paths through the woods" created by particular user communities. And, unlike ratings-based collaborative filtering systems (see Chapter 10), social data mining systems do not require users to engage in any new activity; rather, they seek to exploit user preference information implicit in records of existing activity.

The "history-enriched digital objects" line of work (Hill, 1992, 1994) was a seminal effort in this approach. It began from the observation that objects in the real world accumulate wear over the history of their use, and that this wear – such as the path through the woods, or the dog-eared pages in a paperback book, or the smudges on certain recipes in a cookbook – informs future usage. "Edit wear" and "read wear" were terms used to describe computational analogues of these phenomena. Statistics such as time spent reading various parts of a document, counts of spreadsheet cell recalculations, and menu selections were captured. These statistics were then used to modify the appearance of documents and other interface objects in accordance with prior use. For example, scrollbars were annotated with horizontal lines of differing length and colour to represent amount of editing (or reading) by various users.

Other work has focused on extracting information from online conversations such as Usenet. PHOAKS (Hill, 1996) mines messages in Usenet newsgroups looking for mentions of web pages. It categorizes and aggregates mentions to create lists of popular web pages for each group. Donath and colleagues (Viegas, 1999) have harvested information from Usenet newsgroups and chats and have used them to create visualizations of the conversation. These visualizations can be used to find conversations with desirable properties, such as equality of participation or many regular participants.

Still other work has focused on extracting information from web usage logs. Footprints (Wexelblat, 1999) records user browsing history, analyses it to find commonly traversed links between web pages, and constructs several different visualizations of this data to aid user navigation through a web site. Chalmers and colleagues (Chalmers, 1998) tale the activity path – e.g. a sequence of URLs visited during a browsing session – as the basic unit. They have developed techniques to compute similarities between paths and to make recommendations on this basis – for example, to recommend pages to you that others browsed in close proximity to pages you browsed.

9.2.2 Mining the Web

Most relevant to the concerns of this chapter is work that mines the structure of the World Wide Web itself. The web, with its rich content, link structure, and usage logs, has been a major domain for social data mining research. A basic intuition is that a link from one web site to another may indicate both similarity of content between the sites and an endorsement of the linked-to site. Various clustering and rating algorithms have been designed to formalize this intuition. Pirolli (1996) developed a categorization algorithm that used hyperlink structure (as well as text similarity and user access data) to categorize web pages into various functional roles. Later Pitkow and Pirolli (1997) experimented with clustering algorithms on the basis of co-citation analysis (Furnas, 1986), in which pairs of documents were clustered on the basis of the number of times they were both cited by a third document.

Kleinberg formalized the notion of document quality within a hyperlinked collection using the concept of authority (Kleinberg, 1998). At first pass, an authoritative document is one that many other documents link to. However, this notion can be strengthened by observing that links from all documents aren't equally valuable – some documents are better hubs for a given topic. Hubs and authorities stand in a mutually reinforcing relationship: a good authority is a document that is linked to by many good hubs, and a good hub is a document that links to many authorities. Kleinberg developed an iterative algorithm for computing authorities and hubs. He presented examples that suggested the algorithm could help to filter out irrelevant or poor-quality documents (i.e. they would have low authority scores) and identify high-quality documents (they would have high authority scores). He also showed that his algorithm could be used to cluster pages within a collection, in effect disambiguating the query that generated the collection. For example, a query on "Jaguar" returned items concerning the animal, the car, and the NFL team, but Kleinberg's algorithm splits the pages into three sets, corresponding to the three meanings.

Several researchers have extended this basic algorithm. Chakrabarti (1998) weight links on the basis of the similarity of the text that surrounded the hyperlink in the source document to the query that defined the topic. Bharat and Henzinger (1998) made several important extensions. First, they weighted documents on the basis of their similarity to the query topic. Second, they count only links between documents from different hosts, and average the contribution of links from any given host to a specific document. That is, if there are k link from documents on one host to a document D on another host, then each of the links is assigned a weight of $1/k$ when the authority score of D is computed. In experiments, they showed that their extensions led to significant improvements over the basic authority algorithm.

PageRank (Page, 1998) is another link-based algorithm for ranking documents. Like Kleinberg's algorithm, this is an iterative algorithm that computes a document's score on the basis of the scores of documents that link to it.

To summarize, much recent research has experimented with algorithms for extracting information from web structure. A major motivation for these algorithms is that they can be used to compute measures of document quality. Yet there is little empirical evidence that what these algorithms compute (in-links, authority scores, PageRank scores) actually correlates with human quality judgements. We will report on an experiment that investigates this issue.

9.2.3 Information Workspaces

Once information has been extracted, it must be presented in a user interface. Users must be able to evaluate collections of items, select items they find useful, and organize them into personally meaningful collections. Card, Robertson, and Mackinlay (1991) introduced the concept of information workspaces to refer to environments in which information items can be stored and manipulated. A departure point for most such systems is the file manager popularized by the Apple Macintosh and then Microsoft Windows. Such systems typically include a list view, which shows various properties of items, and an icon view, which lets users organize icons representing the items in a 2D space. Mander, Salomon, and Wong (1992) enhanced the basic metaphor with the addition of "piles". Users could create and manipulate piles of items. Interesting interaction techniques for displaying, browsing, and searching piles were designed and tested.

Bookmarks are the most popular way to create personal information workspaces of web resources. Bookmarks consist of lists of URLs; typically the title of the web page is used as the label for the URL. Users may organize their bookmarks into a hierarchical category structure. Abrams, Baecker, and Chignell (1998) carried out an extensive study of how several hundred web users used bookmarks. They observed a number of strategies for organizing bookmarks, including a flat ordered list, a single level of folders, and hierarchical folders. They also made four design recommendations to help users manage their bookmarks more effectively:

• Bookmarks must be easy to organize, e.g. via automatic sorting techniques.
• Visualization techniques are necessary to provide comprehensive overviews of large sets of bookmarks.
• Rich representations of sites are required; many users noted that site titles are not accurate descriptors of site content.
• Tools for managing bookmarks must be well integrated with web browsers.

Many researchers have created experimental information workspace interfaces, often designed expressly for web documents. Card, Robertson, and York (1996) describe the WebBook, which uses a book metaphor to group a collection of related web pages for viewing and interaction, and the WebForager, an interface that lets users view and manage multiple WebBooks. In addition to these novel interfaces, they also presented a set of automatic methods for generating collections (WebBooks) of related pages, such as recursively following all relative links from a specified web page, following all (absolute) links from a page one level, extracting "book-like" structures by following "next" and "previous", and grouping pages returned from a search query. Mackinlay, Rao, and Card (1995) developed a novel user interface for accessing articles from a citation database. The central UI object is a "butterfly", which represents an article, its references, and its citers. The interface makes it easy for users to browse among related articles, group articles, and generate queries to retrieve articles that stand in a particular relationship to the current article. The Data Mountain of Robertson et al (1998) represents documents as thumbnail images in a 3D virtual space. Users can move and group the images freely, with various interesting visual and audio cues used to help users arrange the documents. In a study comparing the use of Data Mountain to Internet Explorer Favorites, Data Mountain users retrieved items more quickly, with fewer incorrect or failed retrievals.

Marshall and Shipman's (1994) VIKI system lets user organize collections of items by arranging them in 2D space. Hierarchical collections are supported. Later extensions (Shipman, 1999) added automatic visual layouts, specifically non-linear layouts such as fisheye views (Furnas, 1986).

Other researchers have created interfaces to support users in constructing, evolving, and managing collections of information resources. SenseMaker (Baldanado, 1997) focuses on supporting users in the contextual evolution of their interest in a topic. It attempts to make it easy to evolve a collection, e.g. expanding it by query-by-example operations or limiting it by applying a filter. Scatter/ Gather (Pirolli, 1996) supports the browsing of large collections of text, allowing users to iteratively reveal topic structure and locate desirable documents. Hightower et al (1998) addressed the observation that users often return to previously visited pages. They used Pad++ (Bederson, 1996) to implement PadPrints, browser companion software that presents a zoomable interface to a user's browsing history.

9.3 PHOAKS

Our initial attempt at automatically mining social information used the Usenet news repository. In this section we will describe how we gathered recommendations for web sites from Usenet news and some of the lessons we learned that led to our most recent system, TopicShop.

Usenet news is full of pointers to useful resources but because of its immense size it is not always easy to find the best and most reliable ones, without manually sifting through many non-relevant messages. The PHOAKS (People Helping One Another Know Stuff) system has been developed at AT&T Labs to address the problem of constructing collections of web pages by scouring Usenet news and keeping a database of all web pages that have been mentioned in its everyday conversations. The basic premise of PHOAKS is that an effective way to find good information resources (web sites) about a given topic is to ask experts in that topic. Since users of Usenet newsgroups are already carrying on discussions about thousands of topics, there is a large body of information available to find recommendations for quality resources (web sites, downloadable files, etc.) available on the internet, without requiring any additional work from the users.

The typical user searching for information could, as one of many search methods, read through a newsgroup and look for relevant resources. But newsgroups have enormous amounts of traffic and this could be a time-consuming task. Some of the more active newsgroups have thousands of posted messages per day. Most people do not want to sift through so many messages to find what they are looking for. An agent such as PHOAKS eliminates much of this work by automatically sifting out resources from all the messages posted and presenting them to the user.

9.3.1 Usenet News

Usenet is a large distributed depository for message exchange among interested users on the internet. It can be thought of as a global internet bulletin board. It is subdivided into many topic areas and users posting messages decide where their message fits in best (see discussion of Usenet in earlier chapters).

Social filtering can help determine which web sites mentioned in the messages are most important in the topic they are posted. By systematically counting the number of times a web site is mentioned within a newsgroup, we can gather a list of the most talked-about sites for each newsgroup. This list can be used to rank the sites and show a user which sites were most highly recommended by the community of users participating in the newsgroup discussion. PHOAKS was developed to implement this idea by constantly monitoring newsgroups and storing in a database all web resources mentioned in the discussions.

9.3.2 Frequency of Mention in Public Conversation

The metric PHOAKS used to determine which web sites are the most popular within a newsgroup is frequency of mention. The social data provided in Usenet news in the form of messages posted by users can be used to determine what URL mentions the users of each newsgroup have referenced most often. Counting one vote per distinct person posting a message with the URL mention provides a frequency count for URL mentions. This prevents users from posting multiple times about a site to try to manipulate the system and cause their favourite page to move higher on the recommended resource list for a newsgroup. Currently, PHOAKS requires a threshold of only one vote to make it into the frequency page, which is a list of the top 40 resources for a newsgroup ranked by frequency of mention. A better way to do this might be to accept a resource only when at least two distinct people have recommended it. This will help eliminate the spam (unwanted junk mail postings, advertisements, etc.) and automatic posts that are found throughout Usenet. The main presentation page of PHOAKS shows frequency counts for web resources gathered from newsgroups.

Another order of presentation is recency of mention. Using this ordering, PHOAKS presents the web resources that users are currently talking about in a newsgroup. The recency view of PHOAKS lists all the resources recommended in the most recent posts that PHOAKS has come across in descending order by date and time of the post.

A combination of recency and frequency is also available in PHOAKS. This allows a moving time window that causes only resources that were recommended somewhere within a specified time period to be included in the presentation of the top recommended resources list. Since PHOAKS started running in October 1997, many pages have built up a large number of recommendations. This makes it more difficult for newer resources to reach the top of the frequency ordered list of pages in high traffic newsgroups. A moving time window allows a user to specify that they would rather see more current recommendations and information. Since web sites for many topics are rapidly changing, the best pages may be ones that have a fair number of recent recommendations instead of a large number of old recommendations. Of course, some pages that remain around for a long time are still the best source of information available, but that means that they will probably be recommended continually.

9.3.3 Classification Rules: Development and Iterative Refinement

Each URL mention in a Usenet news post is classified by PHOAKS into one of a number of categories, by applying a set of classification rules. By manually reading through a few thousand posts, we generated an initial representative set of categories:

- **Private:** mentions in messages with the private header field set to true (used to mark messages as private and not publicly archivable)
- **PHOAKS URL:** any mention of a PHOAKS web page
- **Spam:** URLs mentioned in more than 40 newsgroups in the same message
- **Kill:** mentions of an URL on a list of system definable undesirable sites
- **Quoted:** mention was inside a quoted area of text
- **Code:** mention was part of a source code sample
- **Signature:** mention was part of a user's signature
- **Organization Signature:** mention was part of a user's signature and was of the posting organization
- **URL in Signature:** mention was part of a user's signature and contained the user's email name
- **Approved FAQ:** mention within an approved FAQ
- **Unapproved FAQ:** mention within an unapproved FAQ
- **URL in FAQ:** mention in message that appears to be a FAQ but is not specifically tagged as one
- **Self Recommendation:** mention is a recommendation of the user's own site
- **Recommendation List:** mention is a recommendation within a list of two or more
- **Recommendation:** mention is a recommendation
- **Other.**

PHOAKS uses categorization to determine which URLs will be counted as a recommendation. Currently the categories used in frequency calculations are recommendation, Approved/Unapproved FAQ, and URL in FAQ. Each of these categories consists of times when the message poster is recommending an URL. For example, in a list of FAQs, the URLs found there are usually answers to specific questions that can be considered recommendations.

The rule set that PHOAKS uses to determine an URL's category has gone through three iterations. An initial set of rules was created using rule learning software called RIPPER (Cohen, 1995). This software takes as input a set of text samples along with a list of features and a result to conclude about each sample (in our case, categories). RIPPER then analyses the features and develops a Boolean combination of features that best predicts the desired result for each sample. Two independent raters manually classified a set of 200 URL mentions. Then, 10% of these URLs were used to initialize RIPPER, and the rest used by RIPPER to learn the rule set that produced similar results to the examples given. Once these initial rules were created, they were applied to another independent set of URLs randomly sampled from PHOAKS. These URLs were also manually classified and the results were compared to the automated classification, leading to a more refined set of rules. Finally, one more iteration was performed and after the rules were able to predict the URL mentions accurately within about 85%, they were used in the PHOAKS system.

There are two aspects of rule accuracy: precision (percentage of URLs that rules classify into a certain category that actually belong in that category) and recall (percentage of URLs that belong to a category that rules classify into that category). For the current set of rules in PHOAKS, the precision is 88% and the recall is 87%, with an inter-rater reliability of 88% as determined by applying the rules to a sample set of URLs and comparing to human categorization performed by two independent raters. It is much more important that the rules filter out false positives. A few false negatives are OK, because there are enough data coming through Usenet daily that these will tend to be overcome. But false positives lead to incorrect recommendations and must be kept to a minimum.

9.3.4 PHOAKS Architecture

The PHOAKS system architecture was carefully designed to be general enough to support many different text filtering and collection tasks. There are three main parts of PHOAKS: filtering, categorizing, and disposition. New functions can be plugged in to perform these three tasks to create a new system with different behaviours. Examples of different tasks this architecture is capable of supporting are URL filtering from Usenet news (described below), FAQ collection, or personal mail filtering.

9.3.5 PHOAKS News Agent

Filtering

The first part of PHOAKS extracts the recommendations of web resources from Usenet messages. To do this, PHOAKS searches through every message of Usenet news looking for a pattern (http://) that indicates the following text is an URL. Any message that contains binary data is ignored because these messages are typically long and take too much time to filter. Messages containing binary data do not normally contain URL mentions other than in the message header, so not many mentions are missed.

To allow general searching in the filtering module, PHOAKS searches for a textual pattern or a regular expression. The pattern recognizers allow Boolean operations so the pattern can consist of multiple phrases each assigned different weights. Also, different sections of the message or text can be specified to reduce search time. Sometimes it may only be necessary to search for patterns in the subject header while other times they should be looked for throughout the entire message body, depending on the application.

Categorization

Next, PHOAKS must classify every URL mention into one of the categories described above. This is done by first performing a sort of tokenization of the message. We developed a set of features about each message that describes aspects of the message we thought were important for determining the category of URL mentions in a message (i.e. the URL Block feature corresponds to the block of text surrounding an URL mention). While the rules described above were being developed, additional features were added so messages could be classified into the most appropriate categories. These features are used in conjunction with the rules to categorize the URL mentions.

Combining these syntactic features into rules gives a systematic method of categorizing URL mentions from the messages. For example, if the URL is within 20 lines of the end and occurs after a double dash, the category is a signature. If there are no special characters to set off the signature, there is another rule that looks for standard signature items such as email addresses, phone numbers, etc. If the URL occurs toward the end of a message and contains any of the signature items, it is also categorized as a signature.

Disposition

Finally, after all other processing is finished, the message data and its category are stored in a database for later retrieval. At this point the HTML code for each URL mention in the message is fetched. A title is taken from the page text and stored for use as the display name for the resource. Also, a reduced representation of the page text is kept so that a search index can be built on this text. This process not only provides this valuable information but also allows PHOAKS to ensure that the URL is a valid resource. If not, it is marked as unfetchable and not checked until the next iteration of the system. The web pages for each URL mention are continually checked to make sure that they are current. There is also an occasional problem of network lag and unavailable servers where a resource may appear to be invalid. If a resource once existed and is no longer available it must be confirmed five times before the resource is dropped from PHOAKS.

Since the web is constantly changing, sites tend to move frequently. If a site move is done in a standard way, such as adding a field in the http header, or using a meta-refresh tag, PHOAKS can determine that the two sites should be equated and combine the data for the two records. If on the other hand, no forwarding information is left or some non-standard method of guiding users to the newly moved site is used, then PHOAKS will track two different sites. Since the title of the web pages is usually the same in these cases, PHOAKS can infer that the sites are the same, and will list the sites together when presenting the information to users. However, site information is not combined and will not affect the frequency count for the site.

9.3.6 Web Interface

The last component of PHOAKS deals with displaying information from the database to users in the form of web pages (shown in Figure 9.1). This system was

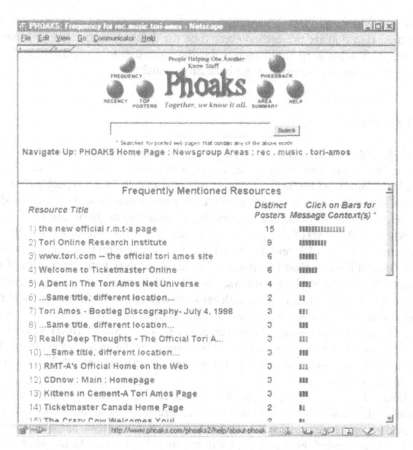

Figure 9.1 PHOAKS Web Interface.

developed to be easily extendable and updated. It incorporates a template language so site maintainers can build page templates to dynamically generate web pages on the basis of the templates. This page definition language is an extension of HTML that adds iteration and conditional constructs and a set of variables specific to PHOAKS data. The language makes it easy to describe, for example, a resource summary page as an iteration over all recommended resources for a newsgroup.

There is also a software layer in PHOAKS that fills database requests from the dynamically created web pages. When a page is requested by a PHOAKS user, the template is checked and any constructs and variables are translated into database requests. Then the database layer makes queries to the database and returns all requested items and finally a page is created. Since speed of presentation of web pages was important, we developed a caching feature to pre-cache popular pages for each newsgroup and keep a cached copy of any page that a user has requested (as long as it is still valid). Now, when a page is requested, the system first checks to see if the page has been cached. If it has, then the page is simply displayed in the browser. If not, the page is generated, cached, and displayed. Since 75% of the pages accessed by users of PHOAKS are resource summary pages and index pages, these are the pages that are pre-cached every time the database is updated for a newsgroup. This helps keep simultaneous database accesses to a minimum and lets users get commonly accessed pages back immediately.

9.3.7 Usage

The PHOAKS system has been available to the public since February 1996. It contains about 74,000 pages of recommendation data for about 2,300 newsgroups. About 400,000 people used PHOAKS during its first year and about 5,000 people continue to use PHOAKS each weekday. As shown by this usage data, people are interested in finding recommendations for resources about topics they might be interested in.

When PHOAKS was first made available, the only form of feedback we allowed was email messages. We read, evaluated, and responded to each message manually. Over time it became clear that much of the feedback dealt with the content of the pages. This should not be surprising: what PHOAKS provides are many organized sets of pointers to content (along with associated contextual information), and it is the content that people really care about. Analysis of PHOAKS access records support this interpretation. People typically don't access many PHOAKS pages at a time; rather, they seem to go to the PHOAKS page for the topic they are interested in, then follow links to the content. So, people don't engage in extended interactions with PHOAKS per se.

Detailed content analysis has shown that the concept of recommendation is difficult to define algorithmically; specifically, there are hard, ambiguous, or controversial cases. There are rare cases when a web resource is warned about, rather than recommended. For example, someone posted a message to soc.culture.african-american condemning the contents of an URL operated by a hate group. He was drawing his community's attention to the hate group, making it aware of its activities, but was he recommending it? More prosaically, it is sometimes hard to detect when an URL is being advertised by someone with a personal or organizational connection with the URL, rather than being recommended by a disinterested third party. And finally, sometimes a web resource is of only ephemeral interest to a community. For example, when one of the stars of *The X-Files* was scheduled to appear on the *Tonight* show, someone posted a message announcing this and included the URL for NBC. This URL was recommended and was relevant, but only for a short time. In addition, since content is generated by re-using information that people have posted, it is not surprising that some of the original producers want to express their opinions, both on the content itself and on how it is reused.

Over the years that PHOAKS has been running, we have received much user feedback in the form of email messages. The number of "topic related questions", messages about the topic dealt with by a newsgroup, particularly surprised us. Among the many examples are messages sent from the PHOAKS pages for:

- rec.antiques, asking for information about pricing and selling antique adding machines;

- rec.video, asking for help in setting up a camcorder as a video source for a PC videophone;
- rec.music.indian.classical, asking for help in finding musical notation for playing karnatic ragas on an electronic keyboard.

Another surprising type of message was what we describe as a "question about or to a person". The people who sent such messages either wanted to contact an individual mentioned on a PHOAKS page (often because they shared the same last name and were searching for relatives), or thought they were in fact sending email to an individual mentioned on a PHOAKS page. Both categories pointed out several things to us. First, they suggest that our interface is not clear. PHOAKS reuses and repackages information produced by many different individuals. It was one of our design goals to make this fact apparent, i.e. to communicate the context in which recommendations were produced, including some information about the producer. However, it seems that we may have achieved this goal at the expense of obscuring the role of computational mechanisms in extracting information from its original sources.

These messages remind us how much people want to talk to other people. We might call what's going on here "information-based introduction". It's the opposite of social filtering: rather than using people to filter information, these PHOAKS users used (or tried to use) information as a pointer to appropriate people. Note that there is a tension between this desire and the PHOAKS design goal of preserving the privacy of the original producers of information. If we had included a mailto: link to each information producer, we would have greatly helped information seekers; however, we were pretty sure that at least some information producers would not be happy about this sort of contact.

A more interesting use of access data that deals directly with page content is on the basis of "jump -off" information, a record of each click on a link on a PHOAKS page. By analysing this data, we can determine that, on average, the first ranked link on a page is clicked on (say) 35 out of 100 times, the second ranked link 20, the third ranked link 15, etc. Now, if we see that on some pages the second ranked link is never clicked on, or the eighth ranked link is clicked on 25 times out of 100, we know this is anomalous, and we can investigate these links.

9.3.8 Lessons Learned

PHOAKS effectively solved the problem of automatically collecting quality web sites about a topic. In addition, we showed that Usenet messages are an abundant source of recommendations of web pages, that recommendations could be recognized automatically with high accuracy, and that there is some correlation between the number of recommenders of a web page and other metrics of web page quality. However, there were a number of aspects of PHOAKS that needed improvement.

The basic unit of the items recommended by PHOAKS was the web page. However, for many purposes, the web page is the wrong unit of information. The World Wide Web consists of many web sites, coherent, structured multimedia documents consisting of many individual web pages. Many times PHOAKS would contain recommendations of multiple web pages within a single web site. Clearly, recommendations for these pages could be aggregated to count as recommendations for the common web site that they are a part of. We want to group web pages into sites and present the consolidated structure of the web site to users. But, we also must keep the original pointers to individual parts of the web site so that we may indicate which areas of a web site might have been more popular.

A general goal of PHOAKS was to collect as many relevant web pages as possible while including few non-relevant pages. Because PHOAKS monitored newsgroup discussions and there were some off-topic web pages mentioned within newsgroups, PHOAKS sometimes collected web pages that did not concern a particular newsgroup's topic directly. Another common occurrence in newsgroups is the posting of general publications across many newsgroups. These publications may contain a few resources relevant to the newsgroup and many that are not. The opposite situation also arose. Since PHOAKS had a "no self promotion" rule, web pages mentioned by the site maintainer were not included. In a few of these cases, since the page was already mentioned in the discussion, additional users felt no need to repeat the recommendation and therefore the page was not included in PHOAKS. In future designs, we want to filter out irrelevant resources and include more relevant resources.

PHOAKS was based mainly on a single ranking metric, the number of distinct individuals who recommended an item. This metric is useful for many purposes, but situations arise where users need additional metrics to evaluate sites. By including numerous ways of comparing web sites we can meet this need, plus help to eliminate the case where a quality site is excluded because of a low ranking within a single metric. The main representation of a web page in PHOAKS is the title, which may not always be the best way to communicate what a page is useful for. It is our goal to construct representative profiles of web site content and structure that make it easy for users to evaluate sites, helping them to determine both site quality and function.

Finally, no information workspace was included in PHOAKS. We found that users had a desire to define and organize personal collections of web resources. In future interfaces we want to implement an information workspace that allows users to easily manage their resources and make it easy for them to share their collections with others.

We have addressed these issues in a new system called TopicShop. Instead of looking at Usenet news for social information mining, TopicShop crawls the Web and utilizes the hierarchical link structure inherent in the Web to gather recommendations for web sites. The next section describes TopicShop and the empirical studies we have done, in detail.

9.4 TopicShop

9.4.1 The Webcrawler

Topic management begins with the identification of a collection of relevant resources. We have developed an algorithm (Terveen, 1998) that takes as input a user-specified set of web sites (the "seeds") and follows links from the seeds to construct a graph of the seed sites and closely connected sites. All seed sites are fetched and included in the collection. It is likely that sites reached by following links from the seeds are on the same topic as the seeds and are also included in the collection on the basis of the relevance metrics we employ to ensure that highly relevant sites are visited during the early stages of a crawl. These metrics are used to prioritize the list of potential URLs so that our crawler can find the best pages in the shortest amount of time.

- First, a weighted sum of the number of in-links of all sites that point to a page is used to rank a page on its potential not only for being a quality site but for recommending other quality sites.
- Second, the text of each page is analysed and compared to a topic centroid – a weighted vector of keywords – computed on the seed pages and used to represent the terms that are central to the topic. The potential linked-to URLs that are closest to this centroid are ranked higher and therefore fetched earliest in the crawl.
- In addition, anchor text is searched for keywords related to the crawl. Anchor text is the text description, written by the site designer, that is displayed for each link and is what the user clicks on to visit the site linked to. This text is usually highly related to what the site contains and can be used to instil further order on the list of pages the crawler will visit.

For purposes of this chapter, however, the discovery of new sites is not relevant because the crawls in our studies were kept within the seed pages to ensure accurate comparisons with other interfaces; what is relevant is that our webcrawler heuristically groups web pages into web sites and builds profiles of the sites it fetches.

Pages are grouped into sites using heuristics that look at the directory structure of URLs. For example, if the crawler encounters a link to the URL http://a/b/page1.HTML, and http://a/b/index.HTML is a site known to the crawler, it records this URL as part of the site. Further, if the link was encountered while the crawler was analysing the site http://x/y/, a link is recorded from the site http://x/y/ to the site http://a/b/index.HTML. A number of specific heuristics handle large hosting sites such as geocities, tripod, etc.

Site profiles are built by fetching a large number of pages from each site. Profiles contain the following data:

- title (of the site's root page)
- a thumbnail image (of the site's root page)
- links to and from other sites
- internal HTML pages, images, audio files, and movie files.

9.4.2 The TopicShop Explorer: Evaluating, Managing, and Sharing Collections of Resources

Topic collections can be viewed and managed using the TopicShop Explorer, an interface modelled on the normal Macintosh file manager/Windows file explorer. The TopicShop Explorer is a Windows application, written in C++/MFC that interprets and processes site profile files. (Figure 9.2)

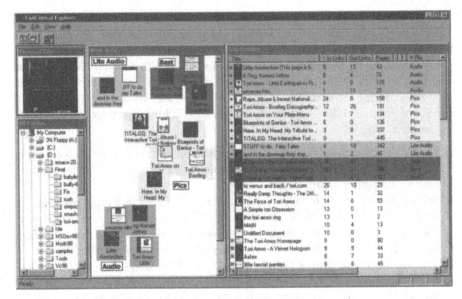

Figure 9.2 TopicShop Explorer.

There are two major linked views, the Site Profiles View and the Work Area. The other two views show a thumbnail and folder navigation interface. Users can show/hide whichever views they choose to help them in accomplishing their tasks. The main feature of the Site Profiles View is the ability to see the profile information our crawler has collected for each site. The Work Area is a view where users can arrange the site icons spatially. We will explain the user interface further as we consider some of the main design goals of the TopicShop Explorer.

9.4.3 Initial Design Goals

Make Relevant but Invisible Information Visible

The first goal of TopicShop is to help users evaluate and identify high-quality sites. We sought to achieve this goal by providing site profile data and interface mechanisms for viewing and exploring the data. Making this data visible means that users no longer had to select sites to browse based solely on titles and (sometimes) brief textual annotations. (A chief complaint of subjects in the study by Abrams et al (1998) was that titles were inadequate descriptors of site content – and that was for sites that users already had browsed and decided to bookmark.) Instead, users may visit only sites that have been endorsed (linked to) by many other sites or sites that are rich in a particular type of content (e.g. images or audio files). Users can sort resources by any property (e.g. number of in-links, out-links, images, etc.) simply by clicking on the label at the top of the appropriate column. Users can "drill down" to investigate the profile data in detail, for example, to see a list of all the audio files on a site and all the other sites that it links to or that link to it. And users can browse the site in their default web browser just by double-clicking it.

Make it Simple for Users to Explore and Organize Resources

The second goal is to make it easy for users to organize collections of sites for their own future use and to share with others. TopicShop lets users organize sites spatially in the Work Area. Nardi and Barreau (1995) found that users of graphical file systems preferred spatial location as a technique for organizing their files. We believe spatial organization is particularly useful early in the exploration process while users are still discovering important distinctions among resources and user-defined categories have not yet explicitly emerged. Thumbnail images also serve as effective memory aids to help users identify sites they already have visited.

These two design goals were maintained throughout the iterations of TopicShop development. The results of our user studies also helped to shape the design of TopicShop.

9.4.4 Features Resulting from User-centred, Iterative Design

We developed TopicShop using an iterative design process, gathering user feedback early in the design process, conducting pilot studies to gain insights into user requirements for the task of topic management (Amento, 1999), and incorporating our findings into further design iterations. The primary modifications to our initial design were incorporated to fulfil the following user needs.

Two Always Visible, Linked Views Support Task Integration and a Cleaner Definition of Each Task

The initial version of TopicShop contained two alternate views. In one view, users could evaluate sites using the detailed site profile information (similar to the current Site Profiles View). In the other view, users could spatially organize larger thumbnail icons representing each site (similar to the Work Area view). Both were views on to the same collection of sites, but only one view was available at a time and users were forced to choose which view they wanted to see. However, we found much evidence that users wanted to integrate work on the evaluation and organization tasks.

- First, they wanted to be able to organize items without losing sight of the detailed information contained in the site profiles. One subject commented:

    I really want to organize the large icons, but don't want to lose the detailed information. Switching all the time is too painful, so I have to settle for the details view only.

- Second, we realized that most items in a collection never needed to be organized, because users would not select them as worthy of further attention. Thus, most of the icons were useless and were just in the way of the user's task.

Rather than supporting a single collection, a better design would support two data sets. Users can evaluate the initial, machine-generated collection on the basis of the site profiles shown in the interface and select promising items for additional in-depth analysis. In this case, organization will only be done for the selected items, saving the user valuable time for further browsing.

We have adapted the interface so that the site profile data and a work area for organizing sites are visible at all times. Items in the initial collection are displayed in the Site Profiles window, and the Work Area is initially empty (unlike Figure 9.2, which shows the results of a subject from the user study). As users evaluate items and find good ones, they select them simply by dragging them and dropping them in the Work Area. Since icons are created just for selected items, the Work Area is uncluttered, and provides a clear picture of the sites users care about.

"Piling" Icons Makes It Easy to Create First-Class Groups by Spatial Arrangement

The original grouping method in TopicShop gave users the ability to create explicit folders. While this supported spatial organization, the groups were not first class objects. We wanted to explore spatial techniques to make it easy to create and manipulate groups.

In the current design, groups can be formed in the Work Area by simply dragging icons. When a user positions one icon "close enough" to another, a group is automatically formed. (How close two icons must be before a pile is formed is a system parameter, set by default to occur just when their bounding boxes touch.) Each group is assigned a colour. As the views are linked, both the group of icons in the Work Area and the features for sites in that group in the Site Profiles window are displayed using the colour as a background. To help users better organize their groups, they can perform operations on piles (i.e. move, name/annotate, arrange, and select) as well as the normal operations on single sites.

Multi-level sorting is a useful operation that can be applied to a pile; it also illustrates how the linked views support task integration. In the Site Profiles View, users can reorder the sites on the basis of primary and secondary sort keys. In the earlier version of TopicShop, users commonly sorted first by the groups they defined in folders and then by some additional feature, such as in-links or number of pages. To support this operation in the new design, we built in a multi-level sorting technique that lets users evaluate and compare sites within a single group. Figure 9.2 shows just such a sort. In fact, users can sort by any two keys by simply defining the primary and secondary sort keys with simple mouse clicks on the header fields.

Visual Indicators Make the Task State Apparent

The status of the user's task must be manifest. Most important, it has to be clear which items in the initial collection users have already evaluated and which they have not. Unevaluated items are a kind of agenda of pending work. Subject comments made this clear:

An indication of whether or not I visited the site would be useful. I can't tell what I've already seen.

It's hard to know what you've looked at and what you haven't?

Any site included in the Work Area is marked with a green diamond in the site profile view and kept at the top for easy reference. Users can mark irrelevant or low-quality sites for "deletion"; this marks the sites with a red X and moves them to the bottom of the list to get them out of the way. Thus, users quickly see which sites they have already processed (selected or deleted) and which need additional evaluation.

Annotations and Large Thumbnails Support Reuse and Sharing

Subjects observed that including more graphical and textual information could improve site recall. Many subjects asked for the ability to annotate both individual sites and groups of sites. (Note that annotations also make collections more informative for others.) And other subjects asked for a larger thumbnail image to provide a better visual cue:

A larger thumbnail would be nice – It can be used to refresh your memory, and would be more effective if it looked more like the site.

The Focused Site window (upper left of Figure 9.2) displays a large thumbnail of the most recently clicked-on site. Users can create textual annotations for piles or individual sites in the Work Area. Annotations become visible as "pop ups" when the user lets the cursor linger over an object (pile or individual thumbnail) for a second or two.

9.5 Research Question I: Can We Predict Human Quality Judgements?

The primary question we are interested in answering is whether or not the features that TopicShop computes are useful. In particular, we want to know if they can be used to predict quality.

Link analysis algorithms (described previously in Related Work) have received much attention recently, in large part for their potential to help with this problem. To review, the basic intuition is that a hyperlink from document A to document B implies that the author of document A thinks document B contains worthwhile information. Thus, counting the links to a document may yield an estimate of the document's quality. More sophisticated algorithms have been developed that build on this intuition. These link-based algorithms are all good candidate metrics for indicating quality.

However, there has been little empirical evaluation of these algorithms. This leaves a fundamental issue unresolved – do link-based metrics work, i.e. do they correlate with human judgements of quality? We're actually interested in a more general question, namely whether any metrics we can compute for web documents are good predictors of document quality. Accordingly, we investigate content-based as well as link-based metrics.

We encountered several other questions while investigating this issue.

- First, we wondered to what extent topic experts agree on the quality of items within a topic. If human judgements vary widely, this suggests limits on the utility of automatic methods (or perhaps that collaborative filtering, which can personalize recommendations for an individual, may be more appropriate). More fundamentally, it would call into question whether a shared notion of quality even exists. Conversely, if experts do tend to agree in their quality judgements, our confidence in the concept of quality will be bolstered, even if it is difficult to give a precise definition.
- Second, we wondered whether there were any significant differences between various link analysis algorithms – for example, would one score documents D_1, D_2, and D_3 highly, while another scored D_4, D_5, and D_6 more highly? If there are no such differences, then an algorithm can be chosen for other factors, such as efficiency.

9.5.1 Relevance Versus Quality

Finding documents on the World Wide Web relevant to a given interest typically is easy. Suppose you're interested in a television show such as *The Simpsons*. Search engines such as Google or AltaVista return tens of thousands of items, and even human-maintained directories like Yahoo or UltimateTV contain dozens to hundreds of items. However, these items vary widely in quality, ranging from large, well-maintained sites to smaller sites that contain specialized content to nearly content-free, completely worthless sites. No one has the time to wade through more than a handful of items.

The quality of a web site inherently is a matter of human judgement. Major factors influencing quality judgements include site organization and layout, as well as the quantity and uniqueness of information. Note that even small sites may be judged high quality if they cover a particular sub-area well.

We treat quality and relevance as distinct notions, rather than viewing quality as just an aspect of relevance judgements. Perhaps an example can clarify the distinction. It seems natural to view a student paper and a collection of literary criticism as equally relevant to their topic, e.g. Shakespeare's sonnets, while allowing that the latter is of much higher quality.

9.5.2 Experiment

In order to determine how well we can predict human quality judgements, we carried out a large-scale empirical investigation of how web users look for quality items and what sort of support system could help users with this task.

We selected five popular entertainment topics for the study, the television shows *Babylon 5*, *Buffy The Vampire Slayer*, and *The Simpsons*, and the musicians Tori Amos and the Smashing Pumpkins. Popular entertainment is one of the main interests people follow on the web. A study of 1.1 million queries issued to the Magellan search engine between March 1997 and April 2000 supports this claim. We found that 42% of the queries were about popular entertainment. Its popularity alone makes this domain worthy of investigation. Further, we believe that it is representative of other domains characterized by rich content and many links between sites, including popular scientific topics such as Mars exploration.

Features Computed for the Study

To compute link and content-based metrics to compare with the expert ratings, we had to analyse the web neighbourhood surrounding the items. We did this by applying our webcrawler/analyser to each collection of items we obtained from Yahoo.

Starting from these seeds, the crawler constructs the surrounding neighbourhood. Link and text similarity heuristics are used to select URLs to fetch and add to the neighbourhood. In addition, for the purposes of this experiment, we limited the crawler to consider only URLs on the same site as one of the seeds; we did this by accepting only URLs which contained some seed URL as a prefix.

When the crawling is complete, URLs are aggregated into sites (as described above). In addition to the basic URL graph – whose nodes are URLs, and whose edges represent hyperlinks between URLs – this results in a site graph – whose nodes are sites, and whose edges represent a hyperlink from (any URL on) one site to (any URL on) another.

From these graphs, we computed five link-based features: in and out degree, Kleinberg's authority and hub scores, and the PageRank score. In all cases, we computed features for both the site and the root URL of the site. Computing these metrics at the site level was straightforward. When we computed at the URL level, we followed Bharat and Henzinger (1998) by (1) counting only links between URLs on different sites, and (2) averaging the contribution of links from all the URLs on one site to an URL on another.

The crawler also computes a set of content-based features for each URL. Page size and the number of images and audio files are recorded. This information is aggregated to the site level, and the total number of pages contained on each site also is recorded.

Finally, the crawler computes text similarity scores. Although we consider relevance and quality to be different notions, we wanted to test whether relevance would help predict quality. The crawler uses the Smart IR System (Buckley, 1985) to generate a centroid – a weighted vector of keywords – from the content of the seed items for each topic. The relevance score of each page is on the basis of the inner product similarity of the page's text to the centroid. And for each site, the relevance score of the root page, the maximum relevance score of any contained page, and the average relevance scores of all contained pages are recorded.

Each of the features induces a ranking of the items in our dataset. In subsequent analysis, we examine how well the various rankings match human quality judgements. To summarize, here is a list of all the features we used:

- in-degree – number of sites that link to this page/site
- Kleinberg's authority score
- PageRank Score – link-based score used in Google (Page, 1998)
- Out degree – number of pages/sites this site links to,
- Kleinberg's hub score
- text relevance score – similarity to topic seed text
- size (number of bytes and number of contained pages)
- number of images
- number of audio files.

9.5.3 Results

Do Experts Agree?

We first investigated how much experts agreed in their quality judgements. To the extent they do agree, we gain confidence that there is a shared notion of quality within the topic areas we investigated. We did two computations to measure agreement. First, we correlated the scores assigned to items by each pair of experts for each topic. (Recall that we had four experts for *The Simpsons* and three for all other topics.) We used the Pearson product-moment correlation since the expert averages represent interval data, ranging from 1 to 7. Table 9.1 presents the results. It shows that almost all pairs of experts were highly correlated in their judgements of item quality (all correlations were significant, $p < 0.01$).

We did a second analysis that abstracted the expert judgements a bit. Rather than using the exact scores that experts assigned to items, we categorized each item into one of two bins – "good" items were those that an expert rated 5, 6, or 7, and "other" items were all the rest. (We use this categorical notion of quality in many of the remaining analyses.) For each topic, we computed the set of items that all experts assigned to the same category, as well as pairwise agreement (shown as Avg PW Agr in Table 9.2) between each pair of experts. Table 9.2 presents the results, which are quite similar to the correlations presented above. On average,

Table 9.1 Expert agreement, using correlation

Topic	Correlations between pairs of experts						
	1–2	2–3	1–3	1–4	2–4	3–4	Avg
Babylon 5	0.91	0.92	0.76				0.87
Buffy	0.75	0.79	0.83				0.79
Smashing Pumpkins	0.80	0.73	0.69				0.74
Tori Amos	0.61	0.63	0.50				0.58
Simpsons	0.52	0.59	0.50	0.75	0.59	0.59	0.59
Total							0.71

Table 9.2 Expert agreement, using categories

Topic	# items	#Agr	%Agr	Avg PW #Agr	Avg PW %Agr
Babylon 5	40	31	0.78	34.0	0.85
Buffy	41	28	0.68	32.3	0.79
Simpsons	39	24	0.62	30.7	0.79
Smashing Pumpkins	41	28	0.68	32.3	0.79
Tori Amos	42	21	0.50	28.0	0.67
Average	40.6	26.4	0.65	31.5	0.78

across topics, all experts agreed on the category for 65% of items. Pairs of experts agreed 78% of the time.

These results suggest that experts agree on the nature of quality within a topic, and that the expert judgements thus can be used to evaluate rankings obtained by algorithms. However, there is some variation between topics; *Babylon 5* experts agreed the most, Tori Amos experts the least, and the other three topics were in the middle. Some lack of agreement may be due to properties of the topics. For example, we noticed that one or two Tori Amos sites were of quite high quality, but somewhat tangential relevance to the topic. Some experts' quality judgements may be influenced by the relevance. Second, some variation in opinions is inevitable, particularly in the area of popular entertainment, where there is no objective quality standard. Thus, results might be slightly different in a technical domain, where there are more objective quality standards. One expert may be more interested in one type of content than another (e.g. song lyrics vs. tour schedules). Some experts may have highly idiosyncratic tastes. Where tastes do differ significantly, a collaborative filtering approach (see Chapter 10) may ultimately be necessary. To get the best information for you, you may have to inform the system about your preferences, so it can find experts with similar preferences, and recommend items that they like.

Are Different Link-based Metrics Different?

The second issue we investigated was whether the three link-based metrics – in degree, authority, and PageRank – ranked items differently.

Since the different metrics use different scales that do not maintain a linear relationship, we converted raw scores into ranks and used Spearman's rho rank correlation on the resulting ordinal data. We computed correlations between each pair of metrics. Table 9.3 presents the results. The correlations were extremely high (and were all significant, $p < 0.01$). We also computed the Kendall tau rank correlation. Correlations again were high, although not quite as high as Spearman's rho; the final row in Table 9.3 presents the average Kendall correlations.

Second, we computed the intersections between the top 5 and top 10 items as ranked by the three metrics. Table 9.4 presents the results. Again, there is great agreement. For example, in-degree and authority have an average intersection of 8.4 of the top 10 items, and all three metrics agree on an average of 6.4 of the top 10 items.

Table 9.3 Metric similarity, using correlations

Topic	In/Auth	In/PR	Auth/PR
Babylon 5	0.97	0.93	0.90
Buffy	0.92	0.85	0.70
Simpsons	0.97	0.99	0.95
Smashing Pumpkins	0.95	0.98	0.92
Tori Amos	0.97	0.92	0.88
Average (Spearman)	0.96	0.93	0.87
Average (Kendall)	0.86	0.83	0.75

These results (and results we present below) show no significant difference between the link-based metrics. In-degree and authority are particularly similar. This should be surprising – the primary motivation for the authority algorithm was that in-degree isn't enough, that all links are not equal. Do our results prove this assumption false? No – but they require further consideration. The discussion below illuminates where and why more sophisticated algorithms are needed.

By starting with items from Yahoo, we almost guaranteed that items in the neighbourhood graph we constructed would be relevant to the topic. In contrast, other evaluations of Kleinberg's algorithm (Bharat, 1998; Chakrabarti, 1998; Kleinberg, 1998) have begun with much noisier neighbourhoods. Typically, they have started with a base set of items returned by a search engine, many of which are of dubious relevance, and then added items that link to or are linked to by items in the base set. This sort of neighbourhood is likely to contain many pages that are not relevant to the original query. Kleinberg argued that although some of these irrelevant pages have high in-degree, the pages that point to them are not likely to have high out-degree; in other words, they don't form a coherent topic. In such cases, the authority/hub algorithm will assign low scores to some items with high in-degree.

To follow through with this argument, we see that two processes are going on:
- obtaining a set of relevant items
- rating the quality of the items in this set

As commonly conceived, the authority algorithm helps with both. However, our experiment shows that if one already has a set of relevant items, in-degree alone may be just as good a quality measure. Many manually constructed collections of topically relevant items are available from general purpose or topic-oriented directories.

Table 9.4 Metric similarity, intersection of top 5 and 10

Topic	I/A 5	I/P 5	A/P5	All 5	I/A 10	I/P 10	A/P 10	All 10
Babylon 5	5	4	4	4	9	7	6	6
Buffy	4	4	3	3	7	5	5	4
Simpsons	3	3	3	2	8	8	7	6
Smashing Pumpkins	5	4	4	4	9	9	9	9
Tori Amos	5	4	4	4	9	9	8	7
Total	4.4	3.8	3.6	3.4	8.4	7.6	7	6.4

A further note is that the in-degree metric we're using is site in-degree. By aggregating links to the site level, we avoid the problems Bharat and Henzinger identified (links between pages that belong to a common site, and mutually reinforcing relationships between two sites). They showed that solving these problems resulted in significant improvements to the basic authority algorithm. The site in-degree metric accrues the same benefits.

Can We Predict Human Quality Judgements?

We tested how well the rankings induced by each of the features listed in section 9.5.2 matched expert quality judgements. We wanted to compute the precision of each ranking; to do this, we needed the set of good – high quality – items for each topic. We defined the good items as those that a majority of experts rated as good (i.e. scored 5, 6, or 7). Table 9.5 shows the total number of items for each topic, number of good items, and proportion of good items. The proportion of good items serves as a useful baseline; it tell us that, across all topics, if you picked a set of 10 items at random, you would expect about 3 to be high quality.

For ease of presentation, we present results for 10 metrics. The same 5 metrics performed best in all analyses, so we include them. We also found that all site-based metrics outperformed their URL-based counterparts in all cases (e.g. number of images on the entire site was better than number of images on the root page), so we omitted the URL-based versions. None of the text relevance metrics performed well, but we include the best – maximum relevance score – for the sake of comparison.

Using the set of good items, we computed the precision at 5 and at 10 for each metric. Table 9.6 presents the results, with metrics ordered by average precision at 5. The table shows that the top 5 metrics all perform quite well. For example, the in-degree metric has a precision at 5 of 0.76 – on average, nearly 4 of the first 5 documents it returns would be rated good by the experts. This is more than double the number of good documents you would get by selecting 5 at random from the expert dataset. And recall that most of the items in the expert dataset probably are of pretty good quality, since they were selected by multiple subjects in phase 1 of our experiment. Thus, we speculate that in a larger dataset, that contains items of more widely varying quality, the improvement obtained by using these metrics would be even greater.

Table 9.5 Number and proportion of good items

Topic	Total	# good	Proportion good
Babylon 5	40	19	0.48
Buffy	41	15	0.37
Simpsons	39	10	0.26
Smashing Pumpkins	41	7	0.17
Tori Amos	42	13	0.31
Average			0.32

Table 9.6 Precision at 5 and 10

Metric		B5	Buffy	Sim	Sm P	TA	Avg
In degree	at 5	0.8	0.8	0.8	0.8	0.6	0.76
	at 10	0.6	0.7	0.6	N/A	0.5	0.6
# Pages on site	at 5	0.8	1	0.6	0.6	0.6	0.72
	at 10	0.8	0.8	0.5	N/A	0.4	0.63
Authority score	at 5	0.8	0.6	0.8	0.8	0.6	0.72
	at 10	0.7	0.7	0.5	N/A	0.5	0.6
Pagerank score	at 5	1	0.8	0.6	0.8	0.4	0.72
	at 10	0.7	0.6	0.6	N/A	0.4	0.58
# Images	at 5	1	0.6	0.6	0.6	0.4	0.64
	at 10	0.8	0.7	0.5	N/A	0.5	0.63
Out degree	at 5	0.8	0.4	0.4	0.4	0.6	0.52
	at 10	0.5	0.5	0.5	N/A	0.5	0.5
# Audio files	at 5	0.2	0.4	0.6	0.6	0.8	0.52
	at 10	0.2	0.2	0.5	N/A	0.6	0.38
Hub score	at 5	0.8	0.2	0.4	0.4	0.6	0.48
	at 10	0.4	0.5	0.4	N/A	0.5	-[a]
Max rel score	at 5	0.4	0.6	0.6	0.2	0.4	0.44
	at 10	0.7	0.5	0.5	N/A	0.4	0.53
Root page size	at 5	0.6	0	0.4	0.4	0.2	0.32
	at 10	0.5	0.2	0.3	N/A	0.2	0.3

[a]Since there were only 7 high quality items for Smashing Pumpkins, we could not compute precision at 10 for this topic. Accordingly, the average precision at 10 is for the other four topics.

Since the link-based metrics were highly correlated, it should be no surprise that they have similar precision. However, it is surprising how well a very simple metric performs: in this dataset, simply counting the number of pages on a site gives as good an estimate of quality as any of the link-based computations (and number of images isn't bad, either). We speculate that the number of pages on a site indicates how much effort the author is devoting to the site, and more effort tends to indicate higher quality.

The precision analysis abstracted away from the item scores, which could conceal significant differences. For example, suppose that two metrics have identical precision. In principle, they could return completely different sets of items; further, one metric could return the best – highest ranked – of the good items, while the second returned the worst of the good items. Thus, we wanted to do another analysis using item scores to check for this possibility.

We experimented with two different item scoring schemes, the average of all expert scores and a majority score – (number of experts rating item as good / number of experts rating the item). The two methods yielded similar results, and for the sake of consistency with previous analysis, we used majority score. Table 9.7 presents the results. For reference, we present the average scores for the top 5 and 10 items as ranked by the expert majority score itself. This is the ideal – no metric can exceed it. A score of 1 (e.g. for majority score at 10 for *Babylon 5*) means that all experts rated all items as good. A score of 0.8 (e.g. in-degree at 5 for Smashing Pumpkins) means that 80% of experts rated all 5 items as good. The best metric is in-degree. It performs about 74% of the ideal at 5, and 68% at 10.

Table 9.7 Majority score at 5 and 10

Metric		B5	Buffy	Sim	Sm P	TA	Avg
Majority score	at 5	1	1	1	0.9	1	0.96
	at 10	1	0.9	0.7	0.7	0.9	0.84
In degree	at 5	0.8	0.7	0.7	0.8	0.5	0.71
	at 10	0.6	0.7	0.6	0.4	0.6	0.57
Authority score	at 5	0.8	0.5	0.5	0.5	0.5	0.69
	at 10	0.7	0.6	0.5	0.4	0.5	0.57
PageRank score	at 5	1	0.7	0.5	0.8	0.4	0.69
	at 10	0.7	0.6	0.6	0.4	0.4	0.53
# Pages on site	at 5	0.7	1	0.6	0.6	0.4	0.66
	at 10	0.8	0.8	0.5	0.4	0.3	0.56
# Images	at 5	0.9	0.7	0.6	0.6	0.3	0.62
	at 10	0.8	0.7	0.5	0.4	0.5	0.56
# Audio files	at 5	0.3	0.5	0.4	0.6	0.8	0.52
	at 10	0.2	0.3	0.4	0.4	0.6	0.39
Out degree	at 5	0.7	0.4	0.4	0.4	0.5	0.49
	at 10	0.5	0.5	0.4	0.4	0.5	0.45
Hub score	at 5	0.7	0.3	0.4	0.4	0.5	0.47
	at 10	0.4	0.5	0.4	0.4	0.5	0.44
Max rel Score	at 5	0.3	0.5	0.6	0.2	0.3	0.39
	at 10	0.6	0.4	0.5	0.3	0.4	0.43
Root page size	at 5	0.5	0.1	0.2	0.5	0.3	0.31
	at 10	0.4	0.2	0.3	0.3	0.3	0.28

The same metrics – in-degree, authority, page rank, number of pages, and number of images – are in the top five slots in each of the four analyses (precision/majority score at 5/10), although their order varies a little. Its not immediately obvious which of these differences are significant, so we applied a t-test to each pair of metrics, for each analysis. This will give us further insight into which of these metrics is best at predicting quality. Table 9.8 presents the results of this analysis for majority score at 5 (results were similar for majority score at 10 and precision at 5 and 10). Metrics are ordered by their average majority score at 5; this score is given in italics in the diagonal cells. All other cells contain the p-values returned by the t-test; a p-value is displayed in bold if it indicates a significant difference at the 0.05 level. All the comparisons for a particular metric are found by reading down a column; for example, the comparisons between in-degree and all other metrics are in the first column.

We highlight a few interesting results. First, there were no significant differences between any of the first five metrics. Second, in-degree was significantly better than the rest of the metrics (i.e. other than the top 5). Authority, PageRank, and number of pages were similar, except their advantage over number of audio files wasn't quite significant at the 0.05 level. Third, all of the top five methods are significantly better than text similarity. Perhaps text similarity fares so poorly because we started with a set of relevant documents; in other words, if there were more variance in relevance, higher relevance might indicate higher quality.

Table 9.8 Statistical significance for majority score at 5 ($p < 0.05$). Italics indicate average majority score.

	In degree	Authority score	Page rank score	#Pages on site	#Images	#Audio files	Out degree	Hub score	Max Rel score	Root page size
In degree	*0.71*									
Authority score	0.63	*0.69*								
PageRank score	0.70	0.93	*0.69*							
# Pages on site	0.43	0.63	0.69	*0.66*						
# Images	0.17	0.28	0.33	0.5	*0.62*					
# Audio files	0.01	0.05	0.07	0.13	0.32	*0.52*				
Out degree	0.01	0.03	0.02	0.04	0.09	0.76	*0.49*			
Hub score	0	0.01	0.01	0.04	0.05	0.57	0.75	*0.47*		
Max/rel Score	0	0	0	0	0	0.15	0.16	0.33	*0.39*	
Root page Size	0	0	0	0	0	0.01	0.03	0.02	0.29	*0.31*

9.5.4 Summary

We have investigated the utility of various computable metrics in estimating the quality of web documents. We showed that topic experts exhibit a high amount of agreement in their quality judgements; however, enough difference of opinion exists to warrant further study. We also showed that three link-based metrics and a simple content metric do a very good job of identifying high quality items.

Our results contained two main surprises – first, that in-degree performed at least as well as the more sophisticated authority and PageRank algorithms, and second, that a simple count of the pages on a site was about as good as any of the link analysis methods.

Now that we have shown that the features we have collected with TopicShop can be used to predict quality to some degree, we can move on and look at how presenting this information to the user can help improve their performance in web browsing tasks.

9.6 Research Question II: Can We Improve User Task Performance?

We have iteratively developed an interface to efficiently display web site features to users, allowing them maximum flexibility in gathering, evaluating, and organizing information resources for a given topic. To test the advantages of the latest design iteration, we carried out a large empirical investigation of how web users evaluate and organize collections of web sites.

Recall that the task of Topic Management is difficult and not well supported by current tools. A common way to find an initial set of (potentially) relevant resources is to use a search engine like AltaVista or a directory like Yahoo. At this point, however, a user's work has just begun: the initial set usually is quite large, consisting of dozens to hundreds of sites of varying quality and relevance, covering assorted aspects of the topic. Users typically want to select a manageable number – say 10–20 – of high-quality sites that cover the topic. With existing tools, users simply have to browse and view resources one after another until they are satisfied they have a good set, or, more likely, they get tired and give up. Browsing a web site is an expensive operation, in both time and cognitive effort. And bookmarks, probably the most common form of keeping track of web sites, are a fairly primitive organizational technique.

In an attempt to improve user task performance we have designed our TopicShop system to support the task of Topic Management directly, providing comprehensive, integrated support for this task. The lessons we have learned throughout the design process and various user studies have re-shaped our understanding of the task and led to a significant re-design.

9.6.1 Experiment

Design and Methodology

We needed a suitable yardstick of comparison for the user study. For the task of exploring and evaluating web sites, we chose Yahoo, the most widely used search tool on the web. For the task of organizing web sites, we chose Netscape Communicator bookmarks, since bookmarks and the equivalents in other browsers are the primary means by which users organize web sites.

Using the same five popular entertainment topics from the previous experiment, (the television shows *Babylon 5*, *Buffy The Vampire Slayer*, and *The Simpsons*, and the musicians Tori Amos and the Smashing Pumpkins), we again compared TopicShop to Yahoo+ Bookmarks, obtaining collections from Yahoo and applying our webcrawler to obtain site profiles and thumbnail images for use in TopicShop.

The experiment was a 2×5, between-subjects design with topic and user interface as factors. We recruited 40 subjects from a local university. The key metrics we wanted to measure were the quality of sites that users selected and the amount of effort required.

To give a quality baseline, three experts (four for *The Simpsons*) for each topic were presented a list of the sites (in random order) on that topic. Experts had to browse each site, and evaluate it on the basis of its content and layout. Experts rated site quality on a scale of 1 (worst) to 7 (best). For our studies, we define "best" as a set of sites that collectively provide a useful and comprehensive overview for someone wanting to learn about the topic. The topic collections for this study ranged from about 90 to over 250 sites. Since we wanted to limit the number of sites experts rated to about 40, it was impossible for experts to rate all the sites. It wasn't even possible to rate all the sites that any subject selected. Instead, experts rated all the sites selected by multiple subjects and a sample of sites selected by one or no subjects. During analysis, we used the "expert intersection", the set of sites that all experts for each topic selected, as the yardstick for measuring the quality of sites selected by the subjects.

Subjects were assigned a topic and interface at random. To begin the experiment, subjects received 15 minutes of instruction and training in the task and user interface. For the main task, subjects investigated the sites for their assigned topic by using the interface (TopicShop or Yahoo) and browsing sites. They were asked to choose the 15 best sites (as defined previously). Subjects were given 45 minutes to complete the task and were kept informed of the time, although they could take more time if they chose. We also instructed subjects to organize their selected sites into groups and annotate the groups with descriptive labels. All subject actions were recorded and stored in log files.

There is a relationship between time on task and quality of results: the more time spent, the better results one can expect. By limiting the amount of time, we hoped to focus on any differences in the quality of results (i.e. the selected sites) between the two interfaces. And people do not spend unlimited amounts of time browsing, so we wanted to see whether users could find high-quality sites in a limited amount of time.

Results

Our results showed the benefits of TopicShop in supporting both the evaluation and organization tasks and in enabling task integration. We present quantitative data and subject comments to illustrate these benefits.

Supporting the evaluation task TopicShop subjects selected significantly higher quality sites than did Yahoo subjects. We generated the set of high-quality sites for each topic by sorting sites by their average expert score and selecting the top 15 (since subjects selected 15 sites). The quality of each subject's sites is measured by counting how many were among the top 15 expert sites. Table 9.9 shows the results for each topic and interface condition. On average, TopicShop subjects selected 76% more high quality sites ($p < 0.05$) – 7.4 of the expert sites vs. 4.5 for Yahoo subjects.

We wanted to be sure that users didn't gain quality by putting in more effort, so we measured the amount of time subjects spent on their task and the total number of sites they browsed. Again, TopicShop subjects had the advantage. They took about 72% of the time of Yahoo subjects (38 vs. 53 minutes), and they browsed about 67% as many sites (27 vs. 40). This latter fact showed that they were basing their judgements on the data presented in the TopicShop interface.

In summary, TopicShop subjects selected higher quality sites, in less time and with less effort. We believe these benefits are due to TopicShop's site profile data. User comments and survey responses support this belief.

TopicShop subjects commented on the utility of the information they saw:

> It presented me with lots of information very quickly. I could get a feel for what the site had to offer before visiting it, saving time to find the info that interested me. I got more than a site description, I got site facts.

> The different sorting methods make it very easy for you to find what you're looking for.

And Yahoo subjects asked were near unanimous in asking for more information to judge sites:

> [Show] some sort of popularity information to evaluate the sites.

> [Show] something like an indication of how popular [the sites] were. Some rating of content.

> Add some sort of ranking, that would be nice.

Table 9.9 Intersection between users' selections and top 15 expert rated sites

Topic	TopicShop	Yahoo	% Increase
Babylon 5	7.00	5.75	22
Buffy	7.25	3.50	107
Simpsons	6.50	5.25	24
Smashing Pumpkins	8.50	5.00	70
Tori Amos	7.75	3.00	158
Average	7.40	4.50	76

[Show] number of web pages, top 10 most visited.

List the type of audio or video offered on the multimedia pages.

I would add the approximate graphic level [i.e. number of images on a site] (so as to be able to judge the worthiness).

Subjects also were given a survey. It included a question asking them to rate the utility of the site profile features. Number of in-links was first, and number of pages was second (responses were similar in the pilot study). Interestingly, our results, presented above, showed that both in-links and number of pages are good predictors of site quality (Amento, 2000). Thus, subjects proved accurate in their utility judgements.

Supporting the organization task   The second part of the subjects' task was to organize their selected sites into groups and to name the groups. Recall that in the TopicShop condition, subjects grouped items by piling them together, while Yahoo subjects created folders in the Netscape Communicator Bookmarks window and placed items in the folders.

We defined a number of metrics to measure performance on the organization task. The metrics characterize the effort involved, the level of detail of the organization, and the amount of agreement between subjects on how sites should be grouped.

- We examined the log files to compute how much time subjects spent on the organization task. TopicShop subjects spent 18% of their total time, but Yahoo subjects spent 36% of theirs. Since TopicShop subjects spent less time organizing sites, they were able to devote more time to evaluating and understanding the content of sites and selecting the good ones. Yet, even while taking less time, TopicShop users still created finer grained and more informative organizations, as we discuss next.
- We computed the number of groups subjects created. TopicShop subjects created 4 groups on average, and Yahoo subjects created 3. Thus, TopicShop subjects articulated the structure of the topic somewhat more. In addition, TopicShop subjects grouped nearly all of their selected sites (3% were left ungrouped), but Yahoo subjects left more ungrouped (15%).
- TopicShop subjects created more site annotations, thus making their collections more informative for their own use or for sharing with others. The experiment didn't require subjects to annotate sites. Yet 10 of 20 TopicShop subjects did so, annotating a total of 15% of their selected sites. Two Yahoo subjects annotated a total of 4 sites.
- TopicShop subjects tended to agree more about how sites should be grouped. This is a difficult issue to investigate; in general, it requires interpreting the semantics of groups. We computed a simpler metric: for each pair of subjects within a topic and interface condition, for each pair of sites that they both selected, did they group the sites together or not? If both subjects grouped the pair of sites together, or both grouped them separately, we counted this as agreement; otherwise, we

counted it as disagreement. Table 9.10 summarizes the results. It shows that TopicShop subjects agreed 68% of the time on average and Yahoo subjects agreed 43% of the time; thus, TopicShop subjects agreed 61% more.

Taken cumulatively, the results show that TopicShop subjects appear to do a better job of organizing the items they select – they create more groups, they annotate more sites, and they agree in how they group items more of the time – and achieve these results in half the time Yahoo subjects devote to the task. We believe these results are because TopicShop makes grouping and annotation very easy, because of the rich information about sites that is available and remains visible while users organize sites, Subject comments support these beliefs.

TopicShop subjects found it easy to group sites:

Piling web sites and annotating them makes grouping easy. You can easily see an overview of the organization.

Easily viewing category annotations and collared groups in the Work Area helps when attempting to determine what the important areas within a topic are.

Thumbnail images and textual annotations were effective memory aids for identifying sites and recalling their distinctive properties; TopicShop users commented on their utility, and Yahoo users expressed a desire for these types of functionality.

Treating a site as a graphical object that can be dragged and dropped like anything else in your normal windows environment was much easier to conceptualize than treating sites as text links that required cutting, pasting, editing [TopicShop subject].

A thumbnail of the site would help the user who has been using several sites remember the site by looking at its thumbnail [Yahoo subject].

I used annotations to remind me about a site so I could tell the difference from the many other sites that I looked at [TopicShop subject].

Some way to take notes while surfing would be useful [Yahoo subject].

Relationship between evaluation and organization tasks We also studied the relationship between the evaluation and organization tasks. The TopicShop Explorer allows the

Table 9.10 Agreement in grouping items

Topic	Avg. agreement		Avg. % difference
	TopicShop	Yahoo	
Babylon 5	0.78	0.39	100
Buffy	0.59	0.44	34
Simpsons	0.78	0.36	116
Smashing Pumpkins	0.75	0.53	40
Tori Amos	0.48	0.41	17
Total	0.68	0.43	61%

Table 9.11 Interleaving tasks

| | TopicShop | | Yahoo | |
Quartile	# of actions	% of total	# of actions	% of total
Quartile 1	125	23	2	1
Quartile 2	138	26	31	18
Quartile 3	110	21	50	29
Quartile 4	160	30	89	52
Total	533		172	

tasks to be integrated, but doesn't force it. On the other hand, in the Yahoo+bookmarks condition, browsing sites and organizing bookmarks are separate tasks.

The log files contain data that let us quantify the relationship between tasks. Each user action is time stamped, and we know whether it was an evaluation or organization action. Evaluation actions included visiting a page in a web browser and sorting data in the Site Profiles Window. For TopicShop, organization actions included moving or annotating icons or groups in the Work Area. In the Yahoo+bookmarks condition, organization actions included creating a bookmarks folder, naming a folder, naming a bookmarked item, and placing an item in a folder.

We computed how many actions of each type occurred in each quartile of the task, i.e. how many occurred in the first 25% of the total time a subject spent on task, how many in the second 25%, etc. Table 9.11 shows the results for organizational actions.

- It shows how much more organizational work TopicShop users did – 533 actions vs. 172. (And recall they did this in half the time.)
- As expected, TopicShop users integrated organization and evaluation to a much greater extent than did Yahoo users. They did about a quarter of their total organizational work in each of the first two quartiles, dipped slightly in the third quartile, then increased a bit in the final quartile. Yahoo users, on the other hand, did virtually no organizational work in the first quartile of their task, then ended by doing more than 50% in the last quartile. We should emphasize that TopicShop does not force task integration; rather, it enables it. And when users had the choice, they overwhelmingly preferred integration.

We also can construct detailed timelines of user activity. Figure 9.3 shows such timelines for two Yahoo and two TopicShop subjects. They provide vivid illustrations of the overall results. TopicShop users interleaved the two tasks throughout the course of their work and performed many more organization actions. On the other hand, Yahoo users began by focusing exclusively on evaluation; then, toward the end of the task, they shifted to focus mostly on organization. And they did much less organization.

Several comments showed that subjects appreciated the ability to integrate tasks and having the state of their task made visible.

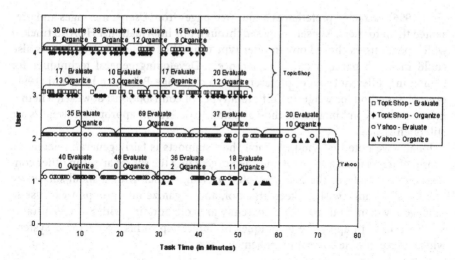

Figure 9.3 Timelines of user activity. TopicShop users do more organization actions and interleave organization with evaluation. Yahoo/bookmarks users did less organization, and did it at the end of their task.

- Linked views helped users integrate the evaluation and organization tasks. In particular, they could evaluate within groups they created.

  > Colouring was nice, because it gives me the ability to quickly SEE what was in what pile. Sorting within a pile was helpful for picking things out of each pile.

- TopicShop made the state of the task apparent, allowing users to treat the initial collection of sites as an agenda of items to be processed.

  > The graphics indicators let you quickly see what's left, because they show what you've already picked and what you didn't like.

9.7 Future Work

There are a number of important issues that deserve further investigation. One direction is to seek new sources for mining information about user preferences. As we have discussed, researchers have investigated hyperlink structure, electronic conversations, navigation histories and other usage logs, and purchasing history. One area we have been looking at recently is electronic media usage, in particular, listening to digital music. By observing what music someone is listening to, a system can infer the songs, artists, and genres that person prefers, and use this information to recommend additional songs and artists, and to put the person in touch with other people with similar interests.

As user preferences are extracted from more and more sources, the issue of combining different types of preferences becomes important. For example, PHOAKS

(Hill, 1996) extracted preferences about web pages from Usenet messages and presented them to users. As users browsed through this information, PHOAKS tracked which pages users clicked on (another type of implicit preference), and users also could rate web pages (explicit preferences). Developing general techniques for combining different types of preferences is a challenge. Billsus and Pazzani (1998) present a method for weighting different types of contributions; however, whether this is the best combination method and how to determine appropriate weights are still open issues.

Finally, we note that the task TopicShop supports is fairly general: selecting a subset of items from a large set and then organizing the subset arises in other contexts. For example, of the many people I exchange email with, a small subset are "contacts" whom I wish to keep track of, and organize into groups I can use to manage my communication. We currently are collaborating with Steve Whittaker of AT&T Labs to apply the techniques of TopicShop to his ContactMap system, which addresses the contact management task.

9.8 Summary

The popularity of the World Wide Web has made the problems of information retrieval and management more acute. More people than ever before face the problems of identifying relevant and high quality information and organizing information for their own use and for sharing with others.

The TopicShop systems improve people's ability to solve these problems.

- The features collected in TopicShop can be used to predict which web sites will be the highest quality sites.
- The TopicShop interface provides information and interaction techniques that help people select the best sites from large collections of web sites. Two user studies have demonstrated that users can select better sites, more quickly and with less effort. It also offers 2D spatial arrangement techniques for creating groups of sites, and thumbnail images and annotations that enhance site recall and make the collections more informative. A study showed that users found it easy and fast to create groups and annotate their work.
- Finally, TopicShop makes it possible to integrate the two major tasks of evaluating and organizing web sites. A user study showed that users preferred to integrate these two tasks when permitted by the interface.

References

Abrams, D., Baecker, R., and Chignell, M. (1998) Information Archiving with Bookmarks: Personal Web Space Construction and Organization, in Proceedings of CHI'98 (Los Angeles CA, April 1998), ACM Press, 41–48.

Ackerman, M.S. (1994) Augmenting the Organizational Memory: A Field Study of Answer Garden, in Proceedings of CSCW'94 (Chapel Hill NC, October 1994), ACM Press, 243–252.

Ackerman, M.S. and McDonald, D.W. (1996) Answer Garden 2: Merging Organizational Memory with

Collaborative Help, in Proceedings of CSCW'96 (Boston MA, November 1996), ACM Press, 97–105.

Aggarwal, C.A., Wolf, J.L., Wu, K-L., and Yu, P.S. (1999) Horting Hatches an Egg: A New Graph-Theoretic Approach to Collaborative Filtering, in Proceedings of ACM SIGKDD International Conference on Knowledge Discovery and Data Mining, 1999.

Amento, B., Hill, W., Terveen, L., Hix, D., and Ju, P. (1999) An Empirical Evaluation of User Interfaces for Topic Management of Web Sites, in Proceedings of CHI'99 (Pittsburgh, PA, May 1999), ACM Press, 552–559.

Amento, B., Terveen, L., and Hill, W. (2000) Does "Authority" Mean Quality? Predicting Expert Quality Ratings of Web Documents, in Proceedings of SIGIR'2000 (Athens Greece, July 2000), ACM Press.

Amento, B., Terveen, L., Hill, W. (2000) TopicShop: Enhanced Support for Evaluating and Organizing Collections of Web Sites, in Proceedings of UIST 2000 (San Diego, CA, November 2000), ACM Press, 201–209.

Balabanovic, M. and Shoham, Y. Fab (1997) Content-Based, Collaborative Recommendation, in Resnick and Varian (eds,), 66–72.

Baldonado, M.Q.W., and Winograd, T. (1997) An Information-Exploration Interface Supporting the Contextual Evolution of a User's Interests, in Proceedings of CHI'97 (Atlanta GA, March 1997), ACM Press, 11–18.

Bederson, B.B., Hollan, J.D., Perlin, K., Meyer, J., Bacon, D., and Furnas, G. (1996) Pad11: A zoomable graphical sketchpad for exploring alternate interface physics. J. Visual Lang. Comput. 7, 3–31.

Billsus, D. and Pazzani, M. (1998) Learning Collaborative Information Filters, in Proceedings of the International Conference on Machine Learning (Madison WI, July 1998), Morgan Kaufmann Publishers.

Bharat, K. and Henzinger, M.R. (1998) Improved Algorithms for Topic Distillation in a Hyperlinked Environment. ACM SIGIR Conference on Research and Development in Information Retrieval.

Buckley, C. (1985) Implementation of the SMART Information Retrieval System, Department of Computer Science, Cornell University, TR85–686.

Bush, V. (1945) As We May Think. The Atlantic Monthly, July 1945.

Card, S.K., Robertson, G.C., and Mackinlay, J.D. (1991) The Information Visualizer, an Information Workspace, in Proceedings of CHI'91 (New Orleans LA, April 1991), ACM Press, 181–188.

Card, S.K., Robertson, G.C., and York, W. (1996) The WebBook and the Web Forager: An Information Workspace for the World-Wide Web, in Proceedings of CHI'96 (Vancouver BC, April 1996), ACM Press, 111–117.

Chakrabarti, S., Dom, B., Gibson, D., Kleinberg, J., Raghavan, P., Rajagopalan, S. (1998) Automatic Resource Compilation by Analyzing Hyperlink Structure and Associated Text. Computer Networks and ISDN Systems 30, 65–74.

Chalmers, M., Rodden, K., and Brodbeck, D. (1998) The Order of Things: Activity-Centred Information Access, in Proceedings of 7th International Conference on the World Wide Web, (Brisbane Australia, April 1998), 359–367.

Cohen, William. (1995) Fast Effective Rule Induction, in Proceedings of the 12th International Conference on Machine Learning. (Lake Tahoe CA, 1995), 115–123.

Dourish, P. and Bly, S. (1992) Portholes: Supporting Awareness in a Distributed Work Group, in Proceedings of CHI'92 (Monterey CA, May 1992), ACM Press, 541–547.

Dourish, P. (1999) Where the Footprints Lead: Tracking Down Other Roles for Social Navigation, in Munro, Höök, and Benyon (Eds.), 15–34.

Furnas, G.W. (1986) Generalized fisheye views. in Proceedings of CHI'86, (Boston, MA April 1986), ACM Press, 16–23.

Garfield, E. (1979) Citation Indexing. ISI Press, Philadelphia, PA, 1979.

Goldberg, D., Nichols, D., Oki, B.M. and Terry, D. (1992) Using Collaborative Filtering to Weave an Information Tapestry. Communications of the ACM, 35, 12 (December 1992), 51–60.

Good, N., Schafer, J.B., Konstan, J., Borchers, A., Sarwar, B., Herlocker, J., and Riedl, J., (1999) Combining Collaborative Filtering with Personal Agents for Better Recommendations, in Proceedings of AAAI'99 (July 1999).

Herlocker, J., Konstan, J., and Riedl, J., (2000) Explaining Collaborative Filtering Recommendations. Proceedings of CSCW 2002 (Philadelphia PA, December 2000), ACM Press.

Hightower, R.R., Ring, L.T., Helfman, ,J.I., Bederson, B.B., and Hollan, J.D. (1998) Graphical multiscale Web histories: A study of PadPrints. in Proceedings of Hypertext '98 (Pittsburgh PA, June 1998). ACM Press, New York, NY.

Hill, W.C., Hollan, J.D., Wroblewski, D., and McCandless, T. (1992) Edit Wear and Read Wear, in Proceedings of CHI'92. (Monterey CA, May 1992), ACM Press, 3-9.

Hill, W.C., Hollan, J.D. (1994) History-Enriched Digital Objects: Prototypes and Policy Issues. The Information Society, 10, 2 (1994), 139-145.

Hill, W.C., Stead, L., Rosenstein, M. and Furnas, G. (1995) Recommending and Evaluating Choices in a Virtual Community of Use, in Proceedings of CHI'95 (Denver CO, May 1995), ACM Press, 194-201.

Hill, W.C. and Terveen, L.G. (1996) Using Frequency-of-Mention in Public Conversations for Social Filtering. in Proceedings of CSCW'96 (Boston MA, November 1996), ACM Press, 106-112.

Katz, J. (1999) Here Come The Weblogs, Slashdot May 24, 1999. http://slashdot.org/features/99/05/13/1832251.shtml.

Kleinberg, J.M. (1998) Authoritative Sources in a Hyperlinked Environment, in Proceedings of 1998 ACM-SIAM Symposium on Discrete Algorithms (San Francisco CA, January 1998), ACM Press.

Konstan, J.A., Miller, B.N., Maltz, D., Herlocker, J.L., Gordon, L.R., and Riedl, J. (1997) GroupLens: Applying Collaborative Filtering to Usenet News, in Resnick and Varian (Eds,), 77-87.

Mackinlay, J.D., Rao, R., and Card, S.K. (1995) An Organic User Interface for Searching Citation Links, in Proceedings of CHI'95 (Denver CO, May 1995), ACM Press, 67-73.

Maglio, P.P., Farrell, S., and Barrett, R. (2000) How to Define "Place" on the Web, in CHI 2000 Workshop Social Navigation: A Design Approach?, edited by Höök, K., Munro, A., and Wexelblat, A.

Maltz, D. and Ehrlich, K. (1995) Pointing the Way: Active Collaborative Filtering, in Proceedings of CHI'95 (Denver CO, May 1995), ACM Press, 202-209.

Mander, R., Salomon, G., and Wong, Y.Y. (1992) A 'Pile' Metaphor for Supporting Casual Organization of Information, in Proceedings of CHI'92 (Monterey CA, May 1992), ACM Press, 627-634.

Marshall, C., Shipman, F., and Coombs, J. (1994) VIKI: Spatial Hypertext Supporting Emergent Structure, in Proceedings of ACM ECHT '94, (Edinburgh, Scotland, September 1994). ACM Press, 13-23.

McDonald, D. and Ackerman, M. (1998) Just Talk to Me: A Field Study of Expertise Location, in Proceedings of CSCW'98 (Seattle WA, November 1998), ACM Press, 315-324.

Munro, A.J, Höök, K., and Benyon, D (Eds.) (1999) Social Navigation of Information Space. Springer, 1999.

Nardi, B. and Barreau D. (1995) Finding and Reminding: File Organization from the Desktop. ACM SIGCHI Bulletin, 27, 3, July 1995.

Page L., Brin S., Motwani R., and Winograd T. (1998) The PageRank Citation Ranking: Bringing Order to the Web. Stanford Digital Libraries Working Paper.

Pirolli, P., Pitkow, J., and Rao, R. (1996) Silk from a Sow's Ear: Extracting Usable Structures from the Web, in Proceedings of CHI'96 (Vancouver BC, April 1996), ACM Press, 118-125.

Pirolli, P., Schank, P., Hearst, M., and Diehl (1996) Scatter/Gather Browsing Communicates the Topic Structure of a Very Large Text Collection, in Proceedings of CHI'96 (Vancouver BC, April 1996), ACM Press, 213-220.

Pitkow, J., and Pirolli, P. (1997) Life, Death, and Lawfulness on the Electronic Frontier, in Proceedings of CHI'97 (Atlanta GA, March 1997), ACM Press, 383-390.

Resnick, P., Iacovou, N., Suchak, M., Bergstrom, P., Riedl, J. (1994) GroupLens: An Open Architecture for Collaborative Filtering of Netnews. in Proceedings of CSCW'94 (Chapel Hill NC, October 1994), ACM Press, 175-186.

Resnick, P., and Varian, H.R., guest editors, (1997) Communications of the ACM, Special issue on Recommender Systems, 40, 3 (March 1997).

Resnick, P. and Varian, H.R., (1997) Recommender Systems, in Resnick and Varian (eds.), 56-58.

Robertson, G., Czerwinski, M., Larson, K., Robbins, D.C., Thiel, C., van Dantzich, M. (1998) Data Mountain: Using Spatial Memory for Document Management, in Proceedings of UIST'98 (San Francisco CA, November 1998), ACM Press, 153-162.

Shardanand, U., and Maes, P. (1995) Social Information Filtering: Algorithms for Automating "Word of Mouth". in Proceedings of CHI'95 (Denver CO, May 1995), ACM Press, 210-217.

Shipman, F., Marshall, C., and LeMere, M. (1999)Beyond Location: Hypertext Workspaces and Non-Linear Views, in Proceedings of ACM Hypertext '99, ACM Press, 121-130.

Terveen, L.G., and Hill, W.C. (1998) Finding and Visualizing Inter-site Clan Graphs, in Proceedings of CHI'98 (Los Angeles CA, April 1998), ACM Press, 448–455.

Terveen, L.G., and Hill, W.C. (2001) Beyond Recommender Systems: Helping People Help Each Other, in Carroll, J. (ed.), HCI In The New Millennium, Addison-Wesley, 2001.

Viegas, F.B. and Donath, J.S. (1999) Chat Circles, in Proceedings of CHI'99 (Pittsburgh, PA, May 1990), ACM Press, 9–16.

Wexelblat, A. and Maes, P. (1999) Footprints: History-Rich Tools for Information Foraging, in Proceedings of CHI'99 (Pittsburgh PA, May 1990), ACM Press, 270–277.

Chapter 10
GroupLens for Usenet: Experiences in Applying Collaborative Filtering to a Social Information System
Bradley N. Miller, John T. Riedl and Joseph A. Konstan

10.1 Introduction

We live in the information overload age. Don't believe that? Here is some evidence:

> The world's total yearly production of print, film, optical, and magnetic content would require roughly 1.5 billion gigabytes of storage. This is the equivalent of 250 megabytes per person for each man, woman, and child on earth. (Lyman and Varian, 2000)

The massive amount of content produced each day is changing the way each of us lives our life. Historically, society has coped with the problem of too much information by employing editors, reviewers, and publishers to separate the signal from the noise. The problem is that we do not have enough editors, publishers, and reviewers to keep up with the volume of new content. One solution to this problem is to use technology to allow each of us to act as an editor, publisher, and reviewer for some subset of the rest of society. The technology that enables us to work together to solve the information overload problem for each other is called collaborative filtering.

Our society already uses a basic form of collaborative filtering, it is called "word of mouth". Here are some examples:

- We consult with gastronomically inclined friends to gather opinions about a new restaurant before reserving a table.
- We consult with literary colleagues before plunking down £19.99 for a new hardcover book.
- We pay attention to the opinions of our musically gifted friends before ordering a new compact disc.

In the information overload age, collaborative filtering is taken to the next level by allowing computers to help each of us be filters for someone else, even for people that we do not know. To do this requires that each of us be willing to provide the collaborative filtering system with our expression of value for a particular information item. The expression of value by a user for an item is called a rating.

The rating will typically be on the scale of 1–5 or 1–7 and will reflect whether the user thought the item was good or bad. The computer's role is to predict the rating a user would give for an item that he or she has not yet seen. The first step in calculating a prediction is to find a group of individuals that have rated information items similarly. This group of individuals is called a neighbourhood. Once a neighbourhood is formed a prediction is calculated for an item by looking at how the user's neighbours have rated that item. The intuition behind collaborative filtering is that if the user has agreed with their neighbours in the past, they will continue to do so for future items.

Collaborative filtering allows both humans and computers to do what they do best. Humans are good at reading and reacting to information items. Humans can make judgments about the value of information items. Humans can evaluate the quality of information. Computers excel at crunching data. Computers can store and retrieve data quickly. Computers can find patterns in data. Collaborative filtering combines the qualitative judgments of humans with the data crunching capabilities of computers to make predictions about things humans will value.

One of the sources for the vast amount of new information generated each day, is the worlds largest online bulletin board system, Usenet. At any one time there are hundreds of thousands of ongoing discussions on almost any imaginable topic. The Usenet news system brings people together from around the world and forms social groups on the basis of common interest. Usenet news is a domain that is suffering badly from information overload. Each day more than a million new articles are posted, but most of the articles are not relevant to any one particular reader. This is where collaborative filtering can work to help each user find the news that they will value most each day.

In this chapter we will describe a trial of a collaborative filtering system applied to Usenet news, called GroupLens. The GroupLens trial service was launched in February 1996 for two dozen Usenet newsgroups. The trial involved over 200 users and continued through April 1996. The project had four main goals.

- To test whether collaborative filtering could work with a large number of users where many new items were created and rated each day.
- To learn whether or not users valued the ability to read filtered news.
- To test the accuracy of our prediction algorithms.
- To create a dataset of ratings and information items that could be used to investigate and compare new algorithms and filtering techniques.

We were at least partially successful in achieving all four goals. Moreover, since the end of the trial collaborative filtering has gained popularity with online retailers as a mechanism for helping shoppers find products they may be interested in buying. The structure of the rest of the chapter is as follows. First, we look at the problem created by the popularity of Usenet news, and some of the other approaches to solving the information overload problem within Usenet. Then we look at the GroupLens architecture designed to solve the problem, and the experimental design used during the 1996 trial. Next we look at what we learned about users and their behaviour during the trial, and present our findings on the accuracy of the underlying filtering algorithms. Finally, we will survey a number of interesting problems that collaborative filtering can help address and briefly survey the work that has been done since 1996, including the application of collaborative filtering to a number of problems outside the domain of Usenet news.

10.2 The Evolution of Usenet

Usenet was not the first method of electronic communication, but early ARPANET researchers realized that they needed to find a more efficient way of disseminating and managing email discussions. Usenet was born in the late 1970s as a way for users to communicate over a highly distributed network of news servers. In the beginning Usenet traffic was transferred independently of the Internet. Vast volumes of messages were transferred via UUCP over modem to modem connections between UNIX computers. In order to send and receive news you had to know somebody who was willing to give you "a news feed". Getting a working feed required system administrator level privileges and skill to configure your modem and computer to talk to another news server.

In 1996, Usenet had grown to around 8,000 newsgroups, with an average of 130,000 new messages posted each day. In the 5 years from 1996 to 2001 the volume of Usenet news has grown by an order of magnitude to 1.3 million messages per day. In addition, the number of individual newsgroups has expanded to over 60,000. In, 1996 Usenet was still mostly non-commercial and although the level of spam seemed high then, was nowhere near the levels today. The GPU project at the University of Toronto tracks (and cancels) Usenet spam (http://cns.utoronto.ca/abuse/Usenet/index.HTML). The latest statistics from the project show that they classify nearly 130,000 messages per day as spam.

Table 10.1 Top 10 Newsreaders in 1996 and 2001. Statistics are based on the optional X-Newsreader header and so should be taken only as a guide

Rank	Reader	Share in February 1996 (%)	Rank	Reader	Share in March 2001 (%)
1	Mozilla	29.00	1	Microsoft	52.40
2	TIN	22.30	2	Mozilla	16.40
3	Forte	13.10	3	Forte	15.70
4	NN	4.70	4	TIN	1.50
5	WinVN	4.10	5	MicroPlanet	1.50
6	gnus	3.20	6	Xnews	1.20
7	News	3.00	7	slrn	1.10
8	Pipeline	2.50	8	MT	1.10
9	slrn	2.50	9	gnus	0.90
10	knews	1.50	10	MacSOUP	0.70
			14	News	0.37
			21	WinVN	0.19
			25	NN	0.17
			36	knews	0.07

It is almost hard to imagine, but in 1996 Microsoft wasn't even a significant player in web browsing, or newsreading. Table 10.1 illustrates the dominant newsreaders both then and now. Notice that in 1996 Microsoft doesn't even make the top 10!

Looking more deeply at the platforms that the top 10 newsreaders run on reveals some interesting trends. In 1996 UNIX was the platform of choice for about 58% of the Usenet newsreading public with Windows accounting for 39% and Macintosh 3%. In 2001 Windows accounts for 93%, with Macintosh and UNIX each garnering only 3%. Looking at Mozilla alone we see that the percentage of users running Mozilla on a UNIX platform has dropped from 9.8% in 1996 down to 1.4% in 2001.

Another clue to the changing dynamics of Usenet can be found by looking for the source of the 1.3 million messages. Each Usenet message contains a header field that contains the address of the server that originally posted the message. Looking at the top level domains for a random sample of messages from 1996 we see that the com domain accounted for 30.8% of the news, edu 19.0%, and net 11.9%. In 2001 the top three domains are net with 19.8%, com with 18.5% and tw at 7.8%. The edu domain is far down the list with only 1.5%.

What we conclude from all of this is that Usenet is no longer dominated by the researcher or hacker running UNIX. Most people participating in Usenet are doing so on common desktop hardware found in most corporate or home offices. We can also conclude that even though the web has become more important in online communication, Usenet has continued to grow and flourish. Because of the continued growth, users need even more help filtering their messages than they did 5 years ago.

As the user base has grown and changed over the years, so have the alternatives for communicating. In the last 6 years we have seen an increasing number of web-based message systems, see for example http://www.thewell.com for one of the oldest online communities. In addition to the discussion online communities like The Well, many commercial web sites provide message boards for product support, tip sharing, and product comparison.

Web-based message systems duplicate much of the functionality of Usenet, but have the following advantages:

- All you need to participate is a browser.
- The owner of the system has control over the content.
- The message boards have more focused content.
- The discussion is often associated with a web site containing information on the topic.
- It is harder for spammers to post inappropriate messages.

Will web based message boards eventually replace Usenet? Just recently Microsoft announced that MSN would be dropping support for newsgroups in favour of their own online message boards. The demise of Usenet seems very unlikely to us. The highly distributed nature, and relatively little formal oversight, make Usenet an ideal place for new discussion groups to flourish. In any case, the technology we are studying applies equally well to message boards or Usenet.

10.3 Filtering on Usenet

Although the volume of Usenet news has increased dramatically over the last 5 years, very little has been done to help users efficiently find good articles to read. Since the early days of Usenet people have tried to find ways to reduce the number of messages they must view each day. In this section we consider some of the methods that have been employed over the years to reduce the amount of noise on Usenet. Note that many of the techniques could be equally applied to web-based messaging boards, or email discussion lists.

10.3.1 Moderated Newsgroups

One approach to reducing the noise level on Usenet is the creation of moderated newsgroups. In a moderated newsgroup one person, the moderator, must approve each article before it is distributed throughout Usenet. The moderator is responsible for rejecting articles that are off-topic, inflammatory, or generally of poor quality. The problem with moderated groups is that they require a large time commitment from the moderator, and the quality judgment is left up to a single person.

10.3.2 Kill Files/Score Files

Another method introduced to the Usenet community to reduce the noise level was the killfile. Recently scorefiles have been introduced as a more general mechanism. A killfile allows the user to specify certain subjects or authors that they never wants to see; a scorefile allows the user to give interesting subjects and authors high scores and uninteresting subjects and authors low scores (Magne-Ingebritson, 2000). The problem with these techniques is their coarseness. Not all articles containing a desired keyword are interesting, and even generally poor writers occasionally produce an article worth reading. Additionally, keywords are difficult to identify in the presence of aliases, synonyms, and misspelled words.

10.3.3 Programmable Agents

Programmable agents are simple programs that perform actions on behalf of users. Programmable agents have been used in information filtering to prioritize messages, gather messages into folders by keyword, or even reply to messages. For instance, the Information Lens system enables even unsophisticated users to automatically perform actions in response to messages (Malone, Grant, Turbak, Brobst and Cohen, 1987). Object Lens extends the Information Lens to other domains, including databases and hypertext (Lai and Malone, 1988).

10.3.4 Intelligent Agents

The July 1994 issue of *Communications of the ACM* was devoted to the state of the art in intelligent agent research. This issue includes discussions of several agents designed to reduce information overload. (Maes, 1994). The agents address meeting scheduling, email handling, and netnews filtering. The netnews agent is known as NewT (Sheth and Maes, 1993). A user trains NewT by showing it examples of articles that should and should not be selected. The agent performs a full text analysis of the article using the vector-space model (Salton and McGill, 1983). Once the agent has gone through initial training it starts making recommendations to, and accepting feedback from the user. On the basis of user feedback NewT is able to make weighted judgments about news articles containing keywords. More recently, an agent for automatically detecting flames has been investigated. (Spertus, 1997). In addition the Amalthaea system (Moukas and Zacharia, 1997) investigates a multi-agent environment for filtering on the World Wide Web. Although Amalthaea was developed for the web, its approach could be used for Usenet. Intelligent agents for information filtering suffer from the same drawbacks as keyword based techniques. An additional problem is that agents must be trained. Norman (1994) points out that interaction with and instruction of agents is a difficult problem that has not been solved satisfactorily, 7 years later this is still true.

10.3.5 NoCeM

NoCeM (no see 'em) is a system that makes it possible for anyone to attempt to cancel an article that is widely cross-posted or seen as a blatantly commercial posting. Under the NoCeM model, any person on the net who sees something they think shouldn't have been posted can issue a NoCeM notice. However, just as with any other type of Usenet message, the weight the notice carries will be no greater than the poster's reputation in the community. If people agree with the issuer's criteria and also feel that he or she is a good judge of that standard, then they will accept that person's notices. When a NoCeM notice is accepted by a user it will typically mark the message as read in the user's history file, and the user will not see the message. NoCeM notices could instead be used to remove the message from the local database of articles, thus keeping all users on the local system from seeing the article. The NoCeM system also lends itself to some degree of automation. To that end some automated spam detectors have been written. The most famous of these is the Cancelmoose system. One of the problems with NoCeM is that it must be integrated into the newsreader, which limits the newsreaders that are supported to the UNIX crowd or gnus which will run on any platform that supports GNU Emacs. See http://www.nocm.org for more information about NoCeM.

10.3.6 Newsreader Support

What is interesting is that the most popular newsreaders, Microsoft Outlook Express, and Netscape (Mozilla), provide very little functionality for filtering news articles. The Microsoft Outlook newsreader contains a simple rule that allows the user to filter news articles on the basis of keywords in the subject line, who the message is from, the age of the message, or how long the message is. If a message matches one of the rule criteria the user can choose to delete the message, colour it a specific colour, or download it for reading. Outlook also provides the equivalent of the kill file functionality with its blocked senders list. Netscape 4.7 provides users with the ability to watch or ignore individual topic threads, but no general rule capability, and no killfile capability.

10.4 GroupLens Architecture

Now we will look how collaborative filtering can be applied to the problem of information overload on Usenet.

10.4.1 A Brief Introduction to Collaborative Filtering

The goal of applying collaborative filtering to Usenet news is to provide users with a prediction of how much value they will find in each news article. Figure 10.1 helps illustrate the basic algorithm used to compute a prediction for a fictitious user, Al. The basic collaborative filtering algorithm can be divided into roughly three main phases: neighbourhood formation, pairwise prediction, and prediction aggregation. In Figure 10.1 the shadows represent users, and the distance between each shadow indicates how similar one user is to another user. The closer the shadows, the more similar the users. In neighbourhood formation the trick is to select the right subset of users that are most similar to Al. The GroupLens algorithm uses Pearson correlation (Devore, 1995) as the measure of similarity. Once the algorithm has selected a neighbourhood, represented in Figure 10.1 by the users in the circle, it can use the Pearson similarity measure to make an estimate of how much Al will value a particular item. Once it has made an estimate using each user in the neighbourhood, the final step is to do a weighted average of all the

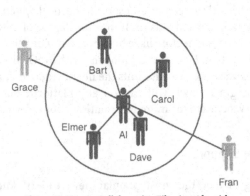

Figure 10.1 Basic Collaborative Filtering Algorithm.

estimates to come up with a final prediction. For a more detailed explanation of the algorithm see Herlocker, Konstan and Riedl (2000).

10.4.2 The GroupLens System Architecture

The GroupLens system was designed to be scalable so that eventually it could support the filtering of news for all newsgroups and users. To achieve our scalability goals we implemented two different strategies for distributing the load on the system.

- First, we implemented an architecture that would distribute the computational load on a machine.
- Second, we implemented a partitioned data architecture that would allow many machines to handle different newsgroups. The original design of the GroupLens architecture is shown in Figure 10.2.

On the right-hand side of Figure 10.2 you can see that the three different recommendation engines are storing data, and making predictions for news articles within three different Usenet hierarchies. This is an example of data partitioning. The design of the recommendation engine itself allows for a multi-process architecture, as implemented in 1995, or a multi-threaded architecture, as it is implemented today. For a more detailed description of the original GroupLens recommendation engine architecture see (Miller, Riedl and Konstan, 1997).

To further illustrate the operation of the GroupLens system, let's examine a typical newsreading session for a GroupLens enhanced newsgroup. The user starts up a newsreader, which creates a connection to both the NNTP server and the rec-

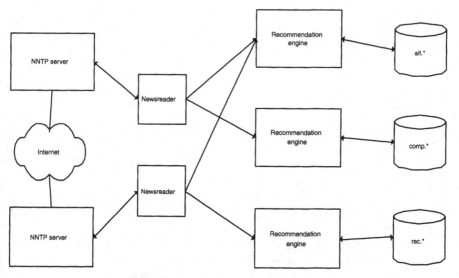

Figure 10.2 Grouplens Architecture Overview.

ommendation engine (RE). The newsreader authenticates itself to the RE by using a pseudonym chosen, and registered with the RE through our web site. The RE makes no association between a user's pseudonym and their real identity.

The user selects a newsgroup to read, and "enters" the newsgroup. The newsreader contacts the NNTP server and obtains header information for articles the user has not read yet. The newsreader contacts the RE and requests predictions for the unread articles. The RE calculates personalized predictions for the user and returns the predictions to the newsreader. Figure 10.3 illustrates what the predictions look like to the user using the GNUS newsreader. Support is available for the other popular UNIX-based newsreaders, tin, slrn, and xrn.

Once a user has the predictions they can pick and choose which articles they want to read on the basis of the subject lines and the predictive scores supplied for each article. In Figure 10.3 a prediction of "NA" indicates that the RE could not calculate a prediction for the article. When a user selects an article to read, the newsreader sets a timer to keep track of how much time the user spends reading the article. After the user has read some or all of the article they give the article a rating

Figure 10.3 The GNUS newsreader with Grouplens predictions.

on a scale from 1 to 5. To make rating articles as easy as possible we have designed the interface so that a rating can be entered with a single extra keystroke.

Once users have read and rated the articles they are interested in, they "leave" the newsgroup. When a user leaves a newsgroup the newsreader sends all the ratings and times collected for the read articles to the RE.

Once the rating and timing information is back at the RE, it is stored in two databases. One database is used for the online system, and the other is a relational database used for analysis and offline experiments. Using our relational database it is possible to recreate a sequence of rating and prediction events in a controlled manner. This enables us to compare the predictions calculated against the ratings entered by the user. This setup allows us to test and compare a variety of algorithms under controlled conditions.

10.5 User Behaviour

We were able to learn much about our users during the course of the trial on the basis of the ratings they submitted, the behaviours we were able to observe through the log files, and the written comments we received on our email list. This section discusses three main results:

- how users rated news articles in different groups and what that tells us about the overall quality of articles on Usenet
- the impact the collaborative filtering system had on the users' reading habits
- one particularly effective way to infer how a user would rate a news article on the basis of their behaviour.

10.5.1 The Ratings Game

The first question to ask in the ratings game is "What am I rating?" With Usenet news there are several dimensions along which a user could decide to rate an article. To simplify the problem, participants were told to rate articles according to the following definitions:

1 This article is really bad! a waste of net bandwidth.
2 This article is bad.
3 This article is neither good nor bad.
4 This article is good.
5 This article is great, I would like to see more like it.

During the course of the trial over 300 users registered to participate, and rated over 40,000 articles. In Table 10.2 we show the number of ratings received for the 10 most active groups in the trial.

If we break our analysis of the ratings down into three representative newsgroups we can see how users actually rated articles, and whether or not our users tended to agree on the messages they rated.

Table 10.2 Number of ratings received in the 10 most active trial groups

Newsgroup	Number of Ratings
rec.food.recipes	1063
comp.human-factors	1265
comp.lang.java	1339
comp.groupware	1569
comp.os.linux.announce	1828
comp.lang.c++	2212
comp.os.linux.development.system	2935
comp.os.linux.development.apps	3833
mn.general	4253
comp.os.linux.misc	5319
rec.humor	17313

Figure 10.4 summarizes the distribution of ratings across all newsgroups, and within each group. In rec.humor, 83% of the ratings are 1 or 2. This reflects the paucity of funny articles and the overabundance of cascades, name-calling, flaming, trolls, and completely unfunny discussions of World War II. rec.humor is a good example of a newsgroup where there is a clear metric for determining a rating: "Is it funny?" The fact that there is a clear metric for judging each article, and the fact that there is so much noise leads to a high level of correlation between pairs of users. This is illustrated in Figure 10.5 where we can see that most pairs of users have a high positive correlation.

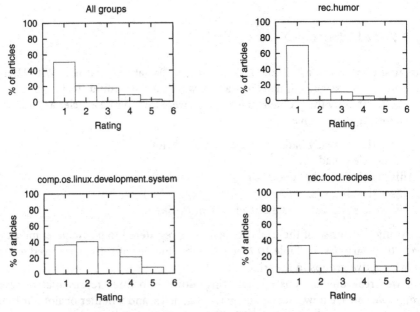

Figure 10.4 Rating profiles for newsgroups.

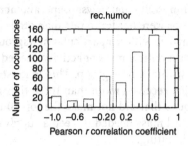

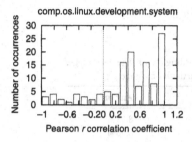

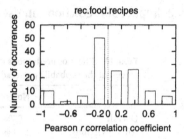

Figure 10.5 User agreement on ratings.

In comp.os.linux.development.system, and rec.food.recipes we see that the ratings are more evenly distributed (see Figure 10.4). rec.food.recipes is a moderated newsgroup, so all of the posts are on topic, and there is no name calling or spamming. In addition users once again have a clear metric for rating an article: "Would I like to cook this?" However, as Figure 10.5 shows, users in rec.food.recipes have a lower correlation. The reason for this is that ratings are based literally on taste. For example, two users may agree all the time on dessert recipes, but one may be a vegetarian who rates all recipes with meat low, and the other may be a carnivore who rates recipes with meat high.

Determining what to rate an article in comp.os.linux.development.system is more difficult than either of the two previous newsgroups. When rating an article in this group a user must weigh several factors:

- Is the article appropriate for this newsgroup?
- Is the topic of the article interesting to me?
- Is the article well written?
- Is the article factually correct?

Despite all of these factors, the readers of comp.os.linux.development.system have a high degree of correlation. This may be because the early adopters of the GroupLens system are all likely to be unusually sophisticated Linux users.

The ratings profile data confirms what many Usenet users have believed for a long time; there is more noise than quality information being posted on Usenet. This is illustrated in Figure 10.4 where we see that ratings of 1 and 2 dominate both within individual newsgroups, and across all newsgroups. We speculate that some groups were harder to rate than others, due to the clarity of the metric used to rate an article within a particular newsgroup. We would also observe that there appears to be a critical mass of activity needed to sustain both prediction and rating activity within a newsgroup. This is illustrated by the results in the rec.humor group, which received more than three times the ratings of the next most active group. Groups that did not make the top 10 usually did not get enough users to achieve critical mass needed to keep a supply of predictions, and users quickly lost interest in rating.

10.5.2 Impact of Predictions on User Behaviour

Table 10.3 Effect of predictions on users' reading habits. The percentages represent the probability of reading any particular message

	No prediction	Any prediction
Overall	6.02%	8.35%
After 5 sessions	6.94%	8.98%
After 25 sessions	8.54%	10.19%

One may ask whether or not the presence of predictions influenced a user's decision to read an article. Table 10.3 shows that the presence of any prediction for an article makes it more likely that a user will take the time to read it. It also shows that this effect persists over many newsreading sessions, suggesting that it is not just a novelty effect of seeing a prediction.

Another question is whether a "good" prediction has more influence than a "bad" prediction. For our purposes here, and later in this chapter we define a "good" prediction to be a one in which the collaborative filtering system has predicted that the user would rate the article a 4 or 5. A "bad" prediction assumes that the user would have rated the article in the range 1–3. Table 10.4 shows that users are 3–4 times more likely to read an article with a good prediction than one with a bad prediction.

Table 10.4 Effect of good and bad predictions on users' reading habits

	Prediction < 1.5	Prediction < 2.5	Prediction > 3.5
Overall	5.81%	6.61%	16.55%
After 5 sessions	6.21%	7.02%	23.17%
After 25 sessions	6.97%	7.91%	21.81%

10.5.3 An Implicit Measure of Quality or Interest

Over the course of the trial, we observed that users were either dedicated readers and raters, or they became quickly disillusioned with the system because there were not enough predictions.

This led us to contemplate a system that would allow us to capture more data, and did not require active user participation in the ratings process. There are a number of possible actions that could be used to approximate a user's judgment of quality. For example, does the user:

- save the message
- forward the message to a friend
- post a response to the message
- print the message
- add the subject/author to a killfile
- spend a long time reading the article?

Many of the actions listed above would apply only to a "good" message, or a "bad" message. Time spent reading appears to be a good surrogate because it applies to all the messages a user chooses to read. Furthermore, we hypothesized that users would spend more time on the articles they found to be of value than those of little worth. This hypothesis was partially confirmed by an experiment (Morita and Shinoda, 1994). We further hypothesized that we could convert the time spent reading into a rating from 1–5 and use that rating in our collaborative filtering algorithm.

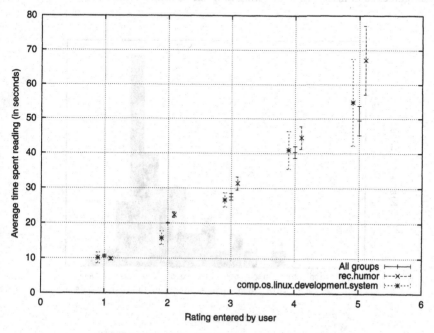

Figure 10.6 Correlation of ratings and time spent reading.

Table 10.5 Summary statistics

Group	No. data points	Correlation
All	25,249	0.36
humor	11,089	0.43
comp.os.linux.development.system	1,811	0.39

To test our hypothesis we collected both the time spent reading and explicit ratings from a number of users. From our test data gathered during the GroupLens trial we are able to segment article, rating, time triples into five groups according to how the user rated the article. To account for users walking away from their terminal, or getting distracted in other ways, we threw out any article where the time was more than 5 minutes. The number of articles removed by this criteria was less than 1%.

To help us create a table of times that we could use to convert to ratings, we calculated several summary statistics including mean, standard deviation, and the 95% confidence interval around the mean. In Figure 10.6 we show a graph of the mean time spent reading (TSR) for each of the five rating groups with the 95% confidence interval. In Table 10.5 we show the correlation coefficient from a regression analysis of ratings and TSR.

Finally, we wondered whether the correlation between ratings and time spent reading varied significantly by user. Figure 10.7 shows that there is indeed a range of correlations. Further analysis reveals that all users with more than 50 ratings are positively correlated. The variation by user suggests that a future project might investigate a customized time to rating map for each individual user.

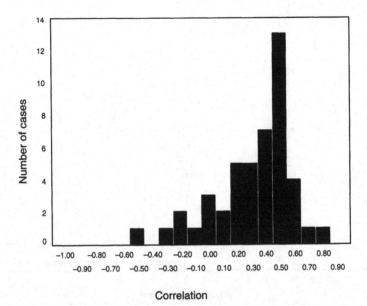

Figure 10.7 Distribution of Individual correlations with TSR.

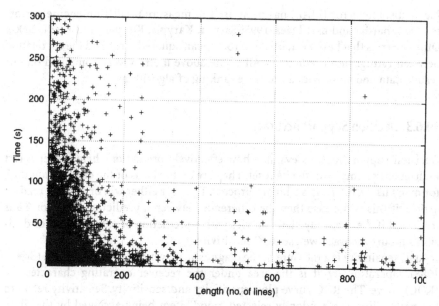

Figure 10.8 Distribution of time spent reading by article length.

The next question we considered was "what effect, if any, does article length have on TSR?" To investigate this question we looked to see if there was a correlation between article length, and time spent reading. Figure 10.8 illustrates that there is no correlation between TSR and length. The computed Pearson correlation between article length and TSR was 0.04.

These results are very encouraging and suggest that TSR might serve as the basis for a collaborative filtering system that places no additional burden on the user to rate news articles. Below, we discuss the results of implementing and algorithm using TSR as the basis for ratings.

10.6 Experimental Design

10.6.1 Metrics

There are three key dimensions along which we can measure the quality of recommendations: statistical accuracy, decision support accuracy, and coverage. We define each of them in the following paragraphs.

10.6.2 Statistical Accuracy

Statistical accuracy metrics evaluate the accuracy of a filtering system by comparing the numerical prediction values against the user ratings entered for the item.

Mean absolute error (MAE) has been used to measure prediction engine performance (Shardanand and Maes, 1995; Sarwar, Karypis, Konstan and Riedl, 2000). Other metrics that have been used are root mean squared error and the correlation between ratings and predictions. All of the above metrics were computed on our results data and all provided the same ranking of algorithms.

10.6.3 Decision Support Accuracy

Decision support metrics evaluate how effectively predictions help a user select high-quality items from the item set. They are on the basis of the observation that, for many users, filtering is a binary process. The user either will or will not read an article. If this is the case then the difference between a prediction of 1.5 or 2.5 is irrelevant if the user only views movies with a prediction of 4.0 or more. For decision support accuracy we use ROC sensitivity.

ROC sensitivity is a measure of the diagnostic power of a filtering system (Swets, 1988). Operationally, it is the area under the receiver operating characteristic (ROC) curve. The ROC curve plots specificity and sensitivity. Sensitivity refers to the probability of a randomly selected "good" item being accepted by the filter. Specificity is the probability of a randomly selected "bad" item being rejected by the filter. The ROC curve plots both sensitivity and specificity from 0 to 1. The area under the curve increases as the filter is able to retain more good items while accepting fewer bad items. For use as a metric, we must determine which items are "good" and which are "bad". For that task we use the user's own ratings. We consider a good article to be one the user has rated a 4 or 5, and a bad article to be one the user has rated less than 4. The area under the curve will be a value from 0 to 1, where 1 is perfect and 0.5 is chance.

10.6.4 Coverage

Coverage is a measure of the percentage of items for which a recommendation system can provide predictions. A basic coverage metric is the percentage of items for which predictions are available. We compute coverage as the percentage of items over all users for which a prediction was requested and the system was able to produce a prediction. Optimal coverage would be 100%, but because of the highly dynamic nature of Usenet our coverage results are far from optimal. The reason this is challenging for Usenet is that in order to compute a prediction for an article at least one user must rate it. Later in this chapter we discuss some ways to help increase the coverage in Usenet.

10.6.5 Post-hoc Evaluation Techniques

When we examine the accuracy of our algorithms we will report accuracy on the basis of post-hoc testing runs rather than simply reporting the accuracy the users experienced during the trial. This method has the advantage of allowing us to try many different algorithmic variations under controlled conditions. For our experimental runs we use the entire dataset as both training set and test set, but during the test we remove the rating for the item we are calculating a prediction for. The coverage metrics reported are on the basis of what we actually observed during the course of the trial.

10.7 Algorithmic Performance

In this section we look more carefully at the algorithmic performance of the system, focusing on the metrics defined above. First, we look at the accuracy of the algorithms broken out into the same three newsgroups used to analyse user rating patterns. Next we will look at the accuracy going across all newsgroups. Finally, we examine the accuracy of using time spent reading as a substitute for an explicit rating.

10.7.1 Results by Newsgroup

Given the different characteristics of each newsgroup, the results were different for each group. This section describes the results of applying the metrics defined in above for three representative newsgroups: rec.humor, rec.food.recipes, and comp.os.linux.development.system.

For each of the newsgroups we compare the accuracy of predictions for two different ways of calculating the predictions. First, a personalized prediction is calculated for each user for each article as described in the introduction. For comparison, the average rating entered for each article is also shown. We compare each prediction against the actual ratings entered by the users. It is useful to look at the average because it is fast to calculate and requires very little storage. On the other hand, the average does not allow for any personalization of the ratings.

Table 10.6 shows the comparison between average and personalized predictions for rec.humor. Because there is such a high degree of correlation between users the average is slightly better than the personalized algorithm in terms of the mean absolute error, though worse in mean squared error. One might think that given the ratings profile for rec.humor the best strategy to minimize error would be to simply predict 1 for every article. The row called "all-ones" in Table 10.6 shows that this is not a good strategy after all.

Table 10.6 Summary of results in rec.humor

Method	$\bar{E}^2$	$\bar{E}$	σ	r
Average	1.1	0.63	0.88	0.49
Personalized	0.94	0.67	0.68	0.62
All-ones	2.01	0.78	1.18	NA

Table 10.7 Summary of results in rec.food.recipes

Method	$\bar{E}^2$	$\bar{E}$	σ	r
Average	2.65	1.29	0.97	0.05
Personalized	1.94	1.09	0.86	0.33

Table 10.7 summarizes the results for rec.food.recipes. The errors in this group are uniformly higher than for rec.humor. This can be attributed to the fact that the correlation between users is low for this newsgroup. However, for this group, the personalized predictions are better than average predictions for all of our error metrics.

Table 10.8 summarizes the results for comp.os.linux.development.system. Once again the personalized predictions are more accurate than the average. In addition, due to the better correlation among users, the errors are smaller than in rec.food.recipes.

As mentioned above, statistical accuracy is only one piece of the puzzle. We next turn to decision support accuracy. Figure 10.9 shows the ROC curve that illustrates the decision support accuracy for our three reference newsgroups. This curve illustrates that decision support accuracy is best in rec.humor, where there was the highest degree of user correlation, and worst in rec.food.recipes, where there was a low degree of user-user correlation.

The curve also illustrates why users might choose to read all articles with a prediction of 3 or greater. Every user is going to make a trade-off between the number of false alarms they are willing to tolerate and the increased efficiency they get by only reading those articles above their threshold.

Figure 10.9 shows that if a user read only articles predicted 3 or above, they will read only 3% of the articles that they would have classified as bad, whereas in "colds" a user will read 19% of the articles they would have classified as bad. On the upside, a threshold of 3 in "colds" ensures that the user will read 57% of the articles they would have classified as good, whereas in rec.humor a threshold of 3 will only net that user 20% of the articles they would have rated as good.

An ideal ROC curve would have a very steep slope that maximizes the hit rate, but minimizes the false alarm rate for some threshold. As mentioned above, decision support accuracy can be represented either graphically, or by the area under the curve. The rest of the statistical accuracy results will be reported by the area under the curve.

Table 10.8 Summary of results in comp.os.linux.development. system

Method	$\bar{E}^2$	$\bar{E}$	σ	r
Average	1.28	0.78	0.82	0.41
Personalized	0.91	0.71	0.64	0.55

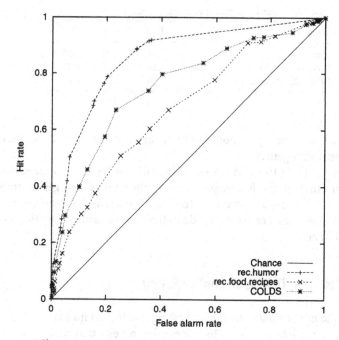

Figure 10.9 Comparison of decision support accuracy by newsgroup.

The final metric is coverage. Coverage is largely driven by the number of ratings you can collect, so the coverage was better for newsgroups that got a large number of ratings. The coverage for rec.humor with 19,380 ratings was the best at 25%. For comp.os.linux.system.development with 9,337 ratings it was 16%, and for rec.food.recipes with 1,705 ratings it was 13%.

10.7.2 Results Using a Single Virtual Newsgroup

A hypothesis that was implicit in the design of our Usenet trial was that the ratings should be partitioned according to newsgroup. In other words, your ratings in rec.humor probably don't help us make good predictions for you in comp.os.linux.development.system.

To test this hypothesis we ran a post-hoc test that combined all the ratings into a single virtual group and constructed neighbourhoods for the users from the virtual group. To make the comparison, we combined the predictions and ratings from each newsgroup together and calculated our summary statistics on this combined group. This aggregation of groups is called "personalized partitioned", and single combined group is called "personalized virtual". Table 10.9 shows that combining data from all groups together reduces the statistical accuracy of the algorithm.

Looking at decision support accuracy, for "personalized partitioned" the area under the ROC curve is 0.82, while the area under the curve for personalized

Table 10.9 Summary of results across newsgroups

Method	$\bar{E}^2$	$\bar{E}$	σ	r
Average	1.39	0.91	0.74	0.55
Personalized virtual	1.35	0.86	0.78	0.57
Personalized partitioned	1.15	0.75	0.76	0.6

virtual is 0.72. Once again partitioning the ratings provides better accuracy than combining them all together.

Taken together, Table 10.9 and the significant difference in area under the ROC curve support our hypothesis that partitioning the ratings into genres improves accuracy. We further hypothesize that this result extends into the e-commerce world and indicates that merchants will do better to keep ratings partitioned along departmental lines.

10.7.3 Results Using Time as an Implicit Rating

We return to the use of time as an implicit rating and look at how accurate a system based solely on implicit ratings is. To test our hypothesis that time spent reading would be a good substitute for explicitly rating an article, we ran a post-hoc experiment using ratings obtained by converting from time as discussed in the previous section. In this experiment time converted ratings were used as input to our algorithm in place of explicit ratings. The area under the ROC curve for the algorithmic results using ratings converted from time is 0.81. There is only 0.012 difference in the total area under the curve from the "personalized partitioned" data reported above.

In looking at coverage it is important to note that because we were able to capture many additional ratings using an implicit capture mechanism, we were able increase the number of ratings in rec.humor to 22,516, comp.os.systems.linux.development.system to 12,182, and rec.food.recipes to 1,935. Because we were not using the implicit ratings during the trial we cannot report comparable coverage measurements.

10.7.4 Summary

In this section we have demonstrated three key points:

- There is a good correlation between explicit ratings and time spent reading.
- The accuracy of the recommendations obtained using implicit ratings is nearly identical to explicit.
- We can capture more data from users by measuring their behaviour, which leads to increased coverage, and potentially even greater accuracy.

These three points lead us to believe that additional research around filtering Usenet news should focus on using implicit ratings.

10.8 What Did We Learn? Where Has the Research Gone?

10.8.1 The First Rater Problem

One of the key questions we asked ourselves about during the trial was "what motivates a user to rate?" The question is particularly important for collaborative filtering because if nobody rates an article, the recommender system cannot make a prediction for anybody. Avery has investigated the question of motivating users to rate from an economic point of view (Avery and Zeckhauser, 1997). The problem of needing a rating first in order to make a prediction, has come to be known as the "first rater" problem.

One solution to the first rater problem is to create a program that rates everything, automatically. We have investigated such a solution employing a simple form of agent known as a filterbot (Sarwar, Konstan, Borchers, Herlocker, Miller and Riedl, 1998). The work in the filterbot area has shown that simple agents that rate articles on the basis of their length, the number of spelling errors, or the amount of included text will correlate with users and provide increased utility. In addition we have found that collaborative filtering can be used to create a personal combination of agents that give even better results.

10.8.2 Combining CF and Content

Pure collaborative filtering is impractical in many domains because of the rate that new items are created and because too few ratings are available for the items. Domains where items are created frequently but have a short useful life span are particularly problematic because the first rater problem mentioned above becomes very obvious under these conditions. This problem limits the effectiveness of recommender systems for news, live discussions, and live or scheduled entertainment.

Several researchers are examining approaches to better integrate content filtering with collaborative filtering to take better advantage of the strengths of each. The Fab system, developed by Marko Balabanovic at Stanford (Balabanovic and Shoham, 1997) was one of the first systems to investigate the combination of content and collaborative filtering. The filterbots work described above is another example. Other examples include Claypool et al's online newspaper project (Claypool, Gokhale, Miranda, Murnikov, Netes and Sartin, 1999) and Baudisch's TV-Scout system (Baudisch1998). The key challenge is to develop a system that uses the best information available, relying more heavily on collaborative filtering when there is a lot of data from reliable predictors, and falling back to content filtering otherwise.

10.8.3 Algorithms

Another key problem in the field of collaborative filtering is to make algorithms ever faster, more scalable, and more accurate. In this section we will look at the work that has been done to improve collaborative filtering algorithms over the last 5 years.

Many different approaches have been applied to the basic problem of making accurate and efficient recommender systems, ranging from nearest neighbour algorithms to Bayesian analysis. The earliest recommenders used nearest-neighbour collaborative filtering algorithms (Resnick, Iacovou, Sushak, Bergstrom and Riedl, 1994; Shardanand and Maes, 1995). Nearest-neighbour algorithms work on the basis of computing the distance between users on the basis of their preference history. Predictions of how much a user will like an item are computed by taking the weighted average of the opinions of a set of nearest neighbours for that product. Opinions should be scaled to adjust for differences in ratings tendencies between users (Herlocker, Konstan, Borchers and Riedl, 1999).

Bayesian networks create a model on the basis of a training set with a decision tree at each node and edges representing user information. The model takes hours or days to build, but is very small, very fast, and essentially as accurate as nearest neighbour methods (Breese, Heckerman and Kadie, 1998). Other model-based techniques include dimensionality reduction using eigenvectors (Goldberg, Roeder, Gupta and Perkins, 2000) and singular value decomposition (Sarwar, Karypis, Konstan and Riedl, 2000). These techniques have the advantages of creating very compact models, and of creating a low-dimensional space within which latent relationships between users or items can be discovered. Clustering techniques work by identifying groups of users who appear to have similar preferences. Clustering techniques have fast online performance, but usually produce less personal recommendations than other methods, and in some cases, the clusters have worse accuracy than nearest neighbour algorithms (Dewan and Shen, 1998). Horting is a graph-based technique in which nodes are users, and edges between nodes indicate degree of similarity between two users. Predictions are produced by walking the graph to nearby nodes and combining the opinions of the nearby users. In one study using synthetic data, Horting produced better predictions than a nearest neighbour algorithm (Aggarwal, Wolf, Wu and Yu, 1999). In addition to "pure" collaborative filtering algorithms, researchers have experimented with combining collaborative and content filtering (e.g. (Sarwar, Konstan, Borchers, Herlocker, Miller and Riedl, 1998) with some success.

10.8.4 Implicit Ratings

As we mentioned above, one of the barriers to user acceptance of collaborative filtering is that in order to get the benefit they must provide the system information about their preferences in the form of ratings.

Finding ways to infer user ratings on the basis of their observed behaviour has been the subject of additional research. Terveen et al provided one of the early examples of using implicit data to make recommendations by mining Usenet postings for URLs to help users find high quality web pages (Terveen, Hill, Amento, McDonald and Creter, 1997). Claypool (Claypool, Le, Waseda and Brown, 2001) investigated browsing behaviour as an implicit measure of interest in web pages.

Many e-commerce sites make use of implicit data about their products, and the purchasing behaviour of their customers in order to make product recommendations (Schafer, Konstan and Riedl, 1999).

10.8.5 Explaining Recommendations

A frequently asked question for almost any collaborative filtering system is "why was this item recommended to me?"

Herlocker, Konstan and Riedl (2000) investigated the problem of explaining why a user was recommended an item on the basis of a conceptual model of collaborative filtering. They found that users were more apt to use a recommender system, and more likely to accept the system's recommendations when they were able to gain some insight into how the recommendation was arrived at.

They showed this by running user tests where the users were shown twenty-one different explanation interfaces. The interfaces ranged from showing the user an anonymous view of all of their neighbours ratings, to a confidence interval for the prediction. The interface that was the most compelling to the users was a simple histogram showing a summary of how the neighbours had rated the item.

10.9 Conclusion

In this chapter we have discussed collaborative filtering, one solution to the ever-increasing problem of information overload. We have seen that users can and will work with technology to help themselves overcome the flood of information that appears each day. We have demonstrated that we can predict, with some accuracy, how a user will rate a particular article. We have seen that a user's behaviour is affected by the presence of predictions, and that users are more likely to read articles with high predictions.

Our results in the area of using implicit ratings demonstrate that it is possible to create a collaborative filtering system that allows a user to reap the benefits of collaborative filtering with very little effort by using time as a surrogate rating.

We have also surveyed the wide variety of active research in the collaborative filtering area. We invite readers who are interested in trying out a collaborative filtering system to visit our research web site (http://www.movielens.org). Movielens provides users with recommendations for current movies, videos, and DVDs. The Movielens web site also serves as testbed and platform for our latest research.

From Usenet news, to electronic commerce, to bricks and mortar retailers, to knowledge management at Fortune 1000 companies; collaborative filtering technology is changing the way we shop and work. Each day, collaborative filtering systems are at work helping us wade through the mountains of information that are available to us at the touch of a button. As research in this area continues around the world, we look forward to many new and innovative applications that will continue to make life better for all of us.

References

Aggarwal, C., Wolf, J., Wu, K. and Yu, P. (1999), Horting hatches an egg: A new graph-theoretic approach to collaborative filtering, in "Proceedings of the Fifth ACM SIGKDD International Conference on Knowledge Discovery and Data Mining", pp. 201–212.

Avery, C. and Zeckhauser, R. (1997), "Recommender systems for evaluating computer messages", CACM 40(3), 66–72.

Balabanovic, M. and Shoham, Y. (1997), "Fab: Content based, collaborative recommendation as classification", Communications of the ACM.

Baudisch, P. (1998), Recommending tv programs on the web: How far can we get at zero user effort?, in "Recommender Systems: Papers from the 1998 Workshop", AAAI Press, pp. 16–18.

Breese, J.S., Heckerman, D. and Kadie, C. (1998), Empirical analysis of predictive algorithms for collaborative filtering, in "Proceedings of the 14th Conference on Uncertainty in Artificial Intelligence (UAI-98)", pp. 43–52.

Claypool, M., Gokhale, A., Miranda, T., Murnikov, P. and Matthew Sartin, D.N. (n.d.), Combining content-based and collaborative filters in an online newspaper, in "ACM SIGIR Workshop on Recommender Systems".

Claypool, M., Le, P., Waseda, M. and Brown, D. (2001), Implicit interest indicators, in "Proceedings of ACM Intelligent User Interfaces Conference (IUI)".

Dewan, P. and Shen, H. (1998), "flexible meta access-control for collaborative applications, in "Proceedings of the ACM 1998 Conference on CSCW", pp. 247–256.

Goldberg, K., Roeder, T., Gupta, D. and Perkins, C. (2000), Eigentaste: A constant time collaborative filtering algorithm, Technical Report M00/41, UCB.

Good, N., Schafer, B., Konstan, J., Borchers, A., Sarwar, B., Herlocker, J. and Riedl, J. (1999), Combining collaborative filtering with personal agents for better recommendations, in "Proceedings of the 1999 Conference of the American Association of Artificial Intelligence (AAAI-99)".

Herlocker, J., Konstan, J. and Riedl, J. (n.d.), Explaining collaborative filtering. recommendations, in "Proceedings of the ACM 2000 Conference on Computer Supported Cooperative Work". (acceptance rate: 18%).

Herlocker, J., Konstan, J., Borchers, A. and Riedl, J. (1999), An algorithmic framework for performing collaborative filtering, in "Proceedings of the 1999 Conference on Research and Development in Information Retrieval (SIGIR-99)".

Devore, J.L. (1995), Probability and Statistics for Engineering and the Sciences, fourth edn, Duxbury Press.

Lai, K.-Y. and Malone, T.W. (1988), Object lens: A "spreadsheet" for cooperative work, in "Proceedings of International Conference on Computer Supported Cooperative Work", ACM Press, New York, NY, Portland, OR.

Lyman, P. and Varian, H. (2000), How much information?, Technical report, University of California at Berkeley.

Maes, P. (1994), "Agents that reduce work and information overload", Communications of the ACM 37(7), 30–40.

Magne-Ingebritson, L. (n.d.), Gnus 5.0 Reference Manual. Available at: http://www.miranova.com/gnus-man/gnus.html.

Malone, T., Grant, K., Turbak, F., Brobst, S. and Cohen, M. (1987), "Intelligent information-sharing systems", Communications of the ACM 30(5), 390–402.

Miller, B.N., Riedl, J.T. and Konstan, J.A. (1997), Experience with GroupLens: Making Usenet useful again, in "Usenix 1997 Conference", Anaheim.

Morita, M. and Shinoda, Y. (1994), Information filtering based on user behavior analysis and best match text retrieval, in W. Croft and C. van Rijsbergen, eds, "Proceedings of 17th International Conference on Research and Development in Information Retrieval. SIGIR 94", Springer-Verlag; Berlin, Germany, p. 48.

Moukas, A. and Zacharia, G. (1997), Evolving a multi-agent information filteringg solution in amalthaea, in "Proceedings of Autonomous Agents 97".

Norman, D. (1994), "How might people interact with agents", Communications of the ACM 37(7), 68–71.

Resnick, P., Iacovou, N., Sushak, M., Bergstrom, P. and Riedl, J. (1994), Grouplens: An open architecture for collaborative filtering of netnews, in "Proceedings of CSCW 1994", ACM SIG Computer Supported Cooperative Work.

Salton, G. and McGill, M. (1983), Introduction to Modern Information Retrival, McGraw-Hill.

Sarwar, B., Konstan, J., Borchers, A., Herlocker, J., Miller, B. and Riedl, J. (1998), Using filtering agents to improve prediction quality in the grouplens research collaborative filtering system, in "Proceedings of the 1998 Conference on Computer Supported Cooperative Work".

Sarwar, B.M., Karypis, G., Konstan, J.A. and Riedl, J. (2000a), Analysis of recommender algorithms for e-commerce, in "ACM E-Commerce 2000".

Sarwar, B.M., Karypis, G., Konstan, J.A. and Riedl, J. (2000b), Application of dimensionality reduction in recommender system – a case study, in "ACM WebKDD 2000 Web Mining for E-Commerce Workshop".

Schafer, J.B., Konstan, J. and Riedl, J. (1999), Recommender systems in e-commerce, in "Proceedings of the ACM Conference on Electronic Commerce (EC "99)".

Shardanand, U. and Maes, P. (1995), Social information filtering: Algorithms for automating "word of mouth", in "Human Factors in Computing Systems CHI '95 Conference Proceedings", pp. 210–217.

Sheth, B. and Maes, P. (1993), Evolving agents for personalized information filtering, in "Proceedings of 9th IEEE Conference on Artificial Intelligence for Applications", IEEE Comput. Soc. Press; Los Alamitos, CA, USA.

Spertus, E. (1997), Smokey: Automated recognition of hostile messages, in "Proceedings of Innovative Applications of Artificial Intelligence (IAAI)", pp. 1058–1065.

Swets, J.A. (1988), "Measuring the accuracy of diagnostic systems", Science 240(4857), 1285–1289.

Terveen, L., Hill, W., Amento, B., McDonald, D. and Creter, J. (1997), "Phoaks: A system for sharing recommendations", Communications of the ACM.

Chapter 11

Exploring Interaction and Participation to Support Information Seeking in a Social Information Space

Christopher Lueg

11.1 Introduction

The amount of information available in electronic information spaces, such as Usenet or the World Wide Web, exceeds by far what a person could look at in a reasonable amount of time. Having access to this amount of information offers opportunities that were unimaginable a few decades ago. However, the sheer quantity involves the practical problem of finding the most interesting information without spending too much time investigating information that is less interesting (see also Chapter 10).

In this chapter, we look at ways to support users seeking information in electronic information spaces. By information seeking we mean all activities that a person may engage in to find and use information. This resembles what scholars in information science would call information behaviour (Wilson, 1999). An important difference is that we view information seeking as a situated activity, i.e. an activity that involves in a fundamental way interaction and participation. Following Clancey (1997), we argue that "[...] every human thought and action is adapted to the environment, that is, situated, because what people perceive, how they conceive of their activity, and what they physically do develop together".

In the context of this chapter, we use the term "interaction" to stress that people have to interact with tools, such as an information retrieval system, a web browser, or an Usenet news client, in order to access representations of information. Such representations would be text documents, web pages, or Usenet articles, respectively. We use the term "participation" to denote that information seeking is an intrinsically social activity. The course of information seeking is not only affected by explicit events, arising from activities such as using tools or communicating with others (e.g. Twidale et al, 1997; Ehrlich and Cash, 1999) but is also influenced by a person's culture and background knowledge. Moreover, information seeking is a generative activity by which we mean that the activity itself generates new interests and thus activities (see below).

In what follows, we explore support for interaction and participation as a way of allowing for the situated nature of human information seeking. We illustrate the issues by example of tools we developed in order to support information seeking in the global conferencing system Usenet news. This work is related to traditional information-seeking support (e.g. Marchionini, 1995), information retrieval research (e.g. Korfhage, 1997), and work on social navigation (e.g. Munro et al, 1999) but addresses issues in a different way due to the distinct point of view.

11.2 A Situated Perspective on Information Seeking

The term "situated" has its origins in the sociology literature in the context of the relation of knowledge, identity, and society (Clancey, 1997). These days, the term is used in a variety of different meanings in the literature. In particular, the over-whelming use of the term in research on artificial intelligence since the 1980s has reduced its meaning from something conceptual in form and social in content to merely "interactive" or "located in some time and place" (Clancey, 1997).

With respect to the core aspects of situatedness, researchers from fields as different as cognitive science, anthropology, and education are arguing in a similar direction although individual positions may still vary significantly. Lucy Suchman, for example, investigated situational aspects of human behaviour and has shown that the meaning of situations (and thus the significance of actions) is generated rather than given. The coherence of situated action is tied in essential ways to local interactions contingent on the actor's particular circumstances (Suchman, 1987). Bill Clancey argues in a similar direction emphasizing the relation of perception, action, and knowledge. As mentioned before, he claims that every human thought and action is situated, because what people perceive, how they conceive of their activity, and what they physically do develop together (Clancey, 1997). Jean Lave emphasizes that perception, action and even knowledge have to be considered in relation to identity and culture: "[…] learning, thinking, and knowing are relations among people engaged in activity *in, with, arising from the socially and culturally shaped world*. This world is itself socially constituted". (Lave, 1991).

In the context of this chapter, we refer to situatedness in order to stress that human thought and action are intrinsically bound to physical interaction as well as to social participation. In regard to information seeking, our understanding of situatedness calls into question the prevailing conceptualizing of information seeking as a goal-directed activity. We understand information seeking as a socially and culturally embedded activity with a scope beyond particular activities that could be described – from an observer's point of view – as information-seeking activities. Sitting down at a computer is rarely done with the intent of "using a computer"; usually there is some secondary cause (e.g. Kaptelinin, 1996). Similarly, the "purpose" of information seeking is not so much to find information but to be able to act in the world. For example, additional information may be required to understand and to solve a particular problem, detailed product information may be required to compare several products in order to buy the best, an address may be required to finish writing a letter, and author information listed on a web page may be required to add references to a bibliography. Regardless of the specific circumstances, information seeking is not just about finding information but about learning (about the world) in doing; "results" of information seeking activities are end and beginning at the same time, as the process of information seeking continuously changes the situation in which the information seeker is situated.

Exploring information-seeking support in the context of situatedness (and tool development in general) is a particular challenge. The nature of human cognition demands accounting for situatedness, but it is not yet clear how this could be accomplished. From a tool developer's point of view, the problem is that situatedness is not a property of a tool. Indeed, it would be a category error to claim that a tool is situated or that some tools are more situated than others. Tools can be supportive in terms of situatedness but situatedness is never a property of an artefact.

Developing tools for information-seeking support usually requires making strong assumptions about what the user is interested in. Typically, documents accessed by the user are analysed in order to find out why the user considered these documents interesting. Results of these analyses are then used to construct profiles that describe the user's information needs. The profile is used to filter or retrieve further documents. Modelling approaches tend to make strong assumptions about the user's information needs, and thus strong assumptions about how users perceive their environment. Also, strong assumptions about the significance of actions are made. An example of such an assumption would be that "selecting a document for reading" indicates interest in the document's content. Interpreting actions, however, has proved to be problematic. As Suchman (1987) argues,

> [...] an action's significance seems to lie as much in what it presupposes and implies about its situation, as in any explicit or observable behaviour as such. Even the notion of observable behaviour becomes problematic in this respect, insofar as what we do, and what we understand others to be doing, is so thoroughly informed by assumptions about the action's significance. In the interpretation of purposeful action, it is hard to know where the observation leaves off and where the interpretation begins.

Our understanding of situatedness suggests making as few assumptions as possible to avoid assuming the user's specific understanding of the information and the circumstances of the interaction with the information. Accordingly, we try to avoid modelling the user's information needs.

Clearly, trying to avoid strong assumptions about the user prevents us from developing more focused (and thus more restrictive) information-seeking support. However, we do not think that this conceptual restriction is indeed a limitation. Our understanding of situatedness suggests providing systems incorporating a broad selection of tools ranging from more focused to more "situated" approaches, by which we mean approaches that account for situatedness. In the end, it should be up to the user to select the tool that best fits their current preferences and capabilities.

11.3 Related Work on Information-seeking Support

Helping users find information in electronic information spaces is an active research area. In what follows, we briefly outline three of the most influential approaches. These approaches differ significantly in their assumptions and goals, and thus in the way they try to support users in accomplishing their tasks.

11.3.1 Information Retrieval

Most approaches to information-seeking support are on the basis of concepts originating from information retrieval research (e.g. Korfhage, 1997). As Jacob and Shaw (1998) outline, work in information retrieval has dominated research on the basis of the cognitive viewpoint in information science (Belkin, 1990). The basic assumption is that a user engages in information-seeking activities because he or she has information needs. The goal of the user's information-seeking activities is to find information that satisfies their information needs. Accordingly, support focuses on modelling these information needs and on automatically retrieving information that is supposed to satisfy the needs. As information needs cannot be investigated directly, information judged to be relevant by the user is used to infer underlying information needs. Research in interactive information retrieval (Belkin, 1993) and intelligent information retrieval (Belkin, 1996) are especially interesting in the context of this chapter as the user is considered to be an integral part of the retrieval process as opposed to a mere user of the system.

11.3.2 Collaborative Filtering and Social Navigation

A second major approach to information-seeking support is collaborative filtering (Goldberg et al, 1992; Resnick et al, 1994) or social filtering (Shardanand and Maes, 1995). Collaborative filtering aims at utilizing the collective knowledge of crowds of users to support individuals in finding the most interesting items which can be as different as Usenet messages, CDs, and movies. The general idea is that users help each other by providing ratings for items they have already investigated. Collections of these ratings can then be used by others to focus on those items collectively rated best (or at least rated acceptable). In addition, ratings can be used to construct rating profiles of individual users. Differences between profiles are being used to compute targeted or "personalized" recommendations. It has been argued that the term "collaborative filtering" seems to denote joint ventures among people sharing the same interests. However, as such relationships are not necessarily required in the case of fully automated collaborative filtering systems, Resnick and Varian (1997) proposed the term "recommender systems" in order to be able to generalize the approach. The term recommender system also allows for other technologies to be used for generating recommendations. Recently, collaborative filtering has been interpreted as a specific instance of a more general research direction called social navigation. According to Dourish (1999), the idea of collaborative filtering became "one of the key ideas that has driven subsequent work on social navigation". The idea behind social navigation is to support users in navigating information spaces by providing information about the activities of other users. Behaving in a particular way influenced by the activity of others would then be an instance of social navigation (Dourish and Chalmers, 1994). A broad overview of the social navigation field is to be found in Munro et al (1999).

11.3.3 Visual Information Seeking

Finally, the rapid progress in computer graphics has enabled information-seeking support that exploits patterns in information spaces. Information visualization interfaces make heavy use of human perceptual and cognitive characteristics, such as visual perception and spatial memory. Visual information seeking (Ahlberg and Shneiderman, 1994), for example, builds on the human capability to quickly recognize features in images, recall related images, and identify anomalies. Visual information seeking is mainly on the basis of browsing and emphasizes rapid filtering to reduce result sets, progressive refinement of search parameters, and visual scanning to identify results. A broad overview of the information visualization field is to be found in Card et al (1999).

11.4 Specific Characteristics of Usenet

In this chapter, we focus on Usenet news, the global conferencing system, which is a prime example for an (electronic) social information space. Usenet also offers the rare opportunity to investigate both interaction with a large "regular" information space and participation within a social information space at the same time.

11.4.1 Two Complementary Views on Usenet

Usenet can be seen as a large and dynamic regular information space and as a social information space which is shaped by social activity. The distinction between these two complementary perspectives on Usenet helps focus on different aspects of this global conferencing system. The distinction is valuable, although to some extent constructed, as the "regular" information space Usenet along with its standards and protocols is a result of social activities (see Pfaffenberger, this volume).

Usenet Viewed as a Self-contained Information Space

In technical terms, Usenet offers hundreds of thousands of messages per day that are filed into a hierarchy of several thousands of newsgroups. If Usenet is viewed as a regular information space, newsgroups are merely containers where messages related to a particular topic (the topic of the newsgroup) are stored.

The perception of Usenet as self-contained information space is reflected by its frequent usage as testbed for information retrieval and information filtering experiments (e.g. Fischer and Stevens, 1991; Morita and Shinoda, 1994; Lang, 1995; Mock, 1996).

Usenet Viewed as a Social Information Space

Apart from qualifying as a "regular" information space, Usenet is also a socially constructed space which is shaped by social activity and socially shared Netiquette rules that describe how to behave when participating in Usenet discussions. In fact, most newsgroups are the visible results of negotiations among netizens who care about Usenet's structure (see Pfaffenberger, this volume).

Many newsgroups are virtual places where people meet to exchange information and to share knowledge. Newsgroups are places where people discuss, communicate, exchange ideas, collaborate, hurl flames, and make friends. This means that Usenet newsgroups are not only collections of related messages, but also processes that are social by nature.

Another aspect of this social dimension is that Usenet discussions show some similarities to newspapers. Brown and Duguid (1996) point out that a newspaper does not just report news, it makes it. News items included in a newspaper gain social status and warrants that come from the combination of editorial selection, location on the page, and wide distribution. In a similar way, topics being discussed in Usenet newsgroups may gain social significance. Although, unlike newspapers, everybody may post a topic in a newsgroup, posting alone does not guarantee social significance. Gaining significance requires that the topic is "accepted" by other newsgroup participants who further elaborate on the topic.

11.4.2 What Does This Mean for Information-seeking Support?

Many participants do not specifically search for particular information when entering Usenet newsgroups. Statements collected during discussions and interviews with Usenet participants, as well as experiences reported in the literature, suggest that participants visit newsgroups for a variety of reasons, such as staying informed and knowing what is going on in a newsgroup. Other motivations may include relieving feelings, working off anger by flaming others, finding a hot topic to discuss with friends during lunch, or just looking what colleagues are talking about in their favourite newsgroups. This suggests that to a significant extent interests are generated in the interaction with Usenet newsgroups and in the participation in discussions. Of course, this is not the only way to make use of Usenet. Lots of people searching for specific information in newsgroups use specialized search engines, such as Google's newsgroup search.

However, for those people who are interested in interacting with newsgroups, traditional information filtering approaches (e.g. Fischer and Stevens, 1991; Morita and Shinoda, 1994; Mock, 1996) are unlikely to meet their needs. Such approaches focus on modelling the user's information needs and treat Usenet as if it were a "regular" information space. Newsgroups are treated as if they consisted of more or less isolated information items. The task of the filter – according to these approaches – is then to match models of information needs and information items stored in newsgroups. Of particular relevance in this context is Brown and Duguid's (1996) observation that personally tailored, genuinely unique electronic newspapers offer neither physical nor social continuity. Each individual output would be no more than that, individual, with little or no indication of its social significance. A traditional filtering system detaches messages from their discussion contexts and the social embedding of the newsgroup in a similar way.

11.5 Exploring Situated Aspects of Information Seeking in Usenet Newsgroups

Usenet's specific characteristics suggest that information-seeking support should account for Usenet's structure as well as for Usenet's social dimension. Furthermore, the previous discussion of situatedness suggests that we avoid making strong assumptions about the user's information needs (as this would involve making strong assumptions about how the user perceives their environment). In order to meet these requirements, we have explored two different approaches to information-seeking support in Usenet newsgroups which follow the two complementary views on Usenet outlined before. These approaches enhance interaction with Usenet discussions and support participation in Usenet newsgroups. The first approach, interactive filtering, monitors the user's interaction with discussions in order to find out which ones receive little attention. The second approach, personalized social navigation, complements the first one by visualizing which discussions received attention from other Usenet participants. In what follows, we discuss implementation details as well as practical experiences.

11.5.1 Interactive Filtering

This strand of work investigated how structures inherent in the "regular" information space Usenet could be used for information-seeking support. A unique characteristic of interactive filtering is that it is discussion-oriented instead of article-oriented.

Interactive filtering exploits the user's newsreading behaviour in order to help them choose between interesting and less interesting discussions. As we are exploring situatedness, we aimed at making as few assumptions about the user as possible. Clearly, there is no way to completely avoid assigning significance to actions. We decided to consider only the basic actions that are necessary when interacting with the news client; we do not analyse the content of messages selected (or not selected) by the user. Such an analysis is typically done by traditional approaches to information filtering, trying to construct models of the user's interests. This means that in the interactive filtering approach, any "filtering effect" is a direct result of the user's interactions with discussions; in other words, it is the user's perception of the newsreading situation, along with their interaction with discussions, that influence what the news client is going to do with discussions.

Figure 11.1 shows how interactive filtering relates to other work in information-seeking support. The dimensions are the use of meta-data provided by the user, the use of content-analysis, and the use of data about the user's behaviour. The most primitive filtering functionality is provided by so-called kill files that are typical functionalities provided by most news clients and mail tools. Kill files allow for the filtering ("killing") of messages on the basis of certain features, such as keywords, author, etc. On the meta-data axis, GroupLens (see also Miller et al, this volume) is

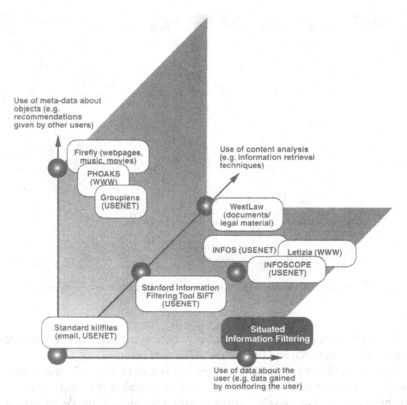

Figure 11.1 Classification of several information seeking support approaches (from Lueg, 1998 © 1998 ACM, Inc. Reprinted by permission).

shown as collaborative filtering systems make heavy use of meta-data. GroupLens has been extended to include content-based filtering agents. PHOAKS (Terveen et al, 1997; Amento et al, this volume) is a recommender system that extracts URLs from Usenet articles and then interprets the mentions as recommendations. On the content-analysis axis, two information retrieval-based systems can be found. WestLaw, in particular, is a sophisticated commercial retrieval system for legal material. Letizia (Lieberman, 1997) and WBI (Barrett et al, 1997) are located between the content-based axis and the user-data axis as they are using both content-analysis techniques and data about user behaviour. Both have been developed to filter web pages as well as to support the user in interacting with the web. Interactive filtering (formerly called situated filtering) is located on the user-data axis, as the approach uses neither meta-data nor content analysis.

We implemented interactive filtering as augmentation to the Knews news client. Knews was chosen because it runs on a variety of UNIX-style operating systems, it provides a graphical X11–based user interface and contemporary functionality such as kill files and threading, and its source code is freely available. Figure 11.2 shows how Knews uses threading information contained in the messages to display related messages jointly as threads or discussions (one discussion per row). From

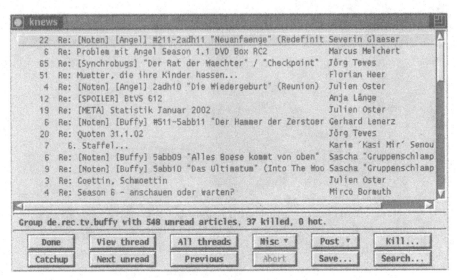

Figure 11.2 The news client Knews visualizes discussions in a newsgroup.

left to right, each row shows the number of unread messages in the discussion, the title of the discussion, and the author of the next message.

Interactive filtering works like this: the news client monitors the user's interaction with discussions available in a newsgroup. The metaphor is roughly one of floating air balloons which are slowly drifting downwards. Upward taps keep balloons floating; not touching them (or even giving them downward taps) allows them to drift and finally to disappear. We deliberately interpret "touching" as a notion of interest and not touching as a lack of interest. The metaphor is meaningful in the Usenet domain, as Usenet messages indeed "disappear" after some time: most Usenet servers expire incoming Usenet messages after a certain time in order to preserve storage capacity. Expire times are deliberately set by a server's administrator and are usually on the basis of a mixture of storage requirements (messages in high-traffic groups may be expired earlier than messages in low-traffic groups) and user interest, as reflected by user statements or by hits in the server's access logs.

Transferred to the realm of Usenet discussions, an "upward tap" becomes "entering" a discussion and "not touching" becomes "skipping" a discussion. (How we label the actions does not really matter, as the labelling is in the eye of the observer – we simply do not know what caused the user to act. Still, appropriate labels are important as labels are evocative.) "Downward taps" become manually marking discussions as read.

In the Knews interface, a graphical bar indicates the "current" discussion. In order to select a different discussion for reading, the bar has to be moved to this discussion. The bar can be moved by using the arrow keys on the keyboard or by clicking the discussion to be read next with the mouse. We refer to "skipping" a discussion when the user moves the bar over a discussion while moving the graphical bar to the discussion they want to read next. All discussions located between the discussion read previously and the discussion read next are interpreted as being "skipped". Consider, for example, the discussions shown in Figure 11.2. The graphical bar is located on the topmost discussion "[Noten] [Angel] [...]". If the user wants to proceed with the eighth discussion, "[Noten] [Buffy] [...]", they have to move the bar to this particular discussion, which implies that the seven discussions in between will be skipped.

On the basis of the monitoring of the user's actions, available discussions are augmented with tags representing the user's past interaction with the discussions. The shape of the tags is immediately adapted as soon as the user interacts with a discussion. Accordingly, a discussion's tag always indicates the current status of the discussion. "Skipping" a discussion causes the corresponding tag to "increase" towards the "probably less interesting" status, whereas "entering" a discussion resets the tag to its default status which is "potentially interesting". The fact that the tags always indicate the status of the discussions, and thus the actions that will be performed when the user leaves the newsgroup, ensures that the news client interface is commensurate with what Shneiderman (1997) calls a "comprehensible, predictable, and controllable user interface".

When the user enters a newsgroup, discussions are ordered according to the status of their tags. Discussions with "potentially interesting" tags are moved towards the top of the list and discussions tagged as "probably less interesting" are moved towards the bottom of the list. New discussions are also located near the top as the news client could not yet collect data suggesting a move towards the "less interesting" discussions at the bottom. Ultimately, the discussions at the top are either new or "ongoing", which means that the user recently interacted with the discussions. Conversely, the discussions at the bottom are those repeatedly skipped by the user. Figure 11.3, for example, shows five new discussions with + marks on the left, one ongoing discussion without any mark that yet has not been skipped,

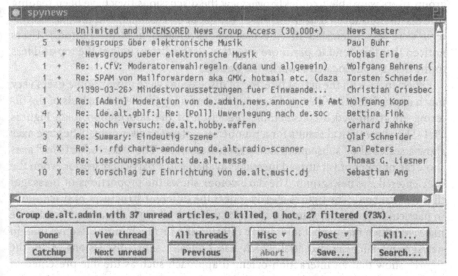

Figure 11.3 The news client Knews augmented with "interactive filtering" functionality.

and seven discussions with X marks on the left indicating that they have been skipped repeatedly. The discussions have been ordered according to the marks so that potentially interesting discussions are located near the top of the window and the supposedly less interesting discussions are located towards the bottom. In this particular session, seven discussions responsible for 73% of the messages in the newsgroup appear to be potentially less interesting. When the user leaves the newsgroup, the X-marked discussions will be processed such that they do not appear when the user enters the newsgroup the next time (technically, this filtering is done by marking the articles in the discussions as "read").

11.5.2 Experiences with Interactive Filtering

The modified news client has been used for more than 5 years. During the core evaluation period the modified news client was used by about half a dozen people for regular newsreading activities. We deliberately chose not to run controlled tests, as these would reveal little about the tool's usability in realistic settings. Moreover, artificially constructed settings would constrain the emergence of interests and thus violate some of our basic assumptions about situatedness.

Everyone involved had a computer science background and were familiar with Usenet. Some of the subjects used the client for their day-to-day Usenet activities; others used it for shorter periods of time. Log files generated by the news clients have been collected systematically over a period of more than 12 months. All subjects knew about the collection and the analysis of the log files.

We were specifically interested in the acceptance of the ordering of discussions and the filtering of discussions. Ordering of discussions according to the attention paid to them was generally considered quite useful. User feedback indicates that ordering helps users become aware of their own interests. When entering a newsgroup, users were able to quickly overview the discussions they have been reading (the discussions located near the top of the list of discussions) and the discussions they were less interested in (the discussions located near the bottom). Users noticed that they tend to pay more attention to the discussions at the top and less to the discussions located towards the bottom.

Experiences with the actual filtering of discussions were mixed. Some users very much appreciated the filtering functionality, and a log file-based analysis of the filtering effect showed a considerable reduction of the information load. Figures 11.4–11.6 show typical results for a number of different newsgroups. The time axes show a series of 60 subsequent newsreading sessions. The "#unread articles" axes show the number of yet unread messages available in a particular session when the user entered the newsgroup. The dark colour shows the proportions of messages that were filtered. The figures clearly reflect the different structures of discussions in particular newsgroups; in newsgroups such as de.alt.admin discussions tend to be massive, which means that interactive filtering can be much more effective than in newsgroups such as ch.general which has typically short discussions. Also, the figures show that an interaction-oriented approach such as the one presented in this chapter takes time to become effective: Figure 11.4, for example, shows a sig-

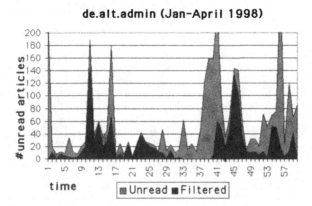

Figure 11.4 "Interactive filtering" applied to the German-language discussion group de.alt.admin. The time axis shows a series of 60 subsequent news reading sessions. The #unread articles axis shows the amount of yet unread messages available in a particular session when the user entered the newsgroup. The dark colour shows the proportion of messages that were filtered.

nificant number of messages that are not filtered between sessions 37 and 43; such a number of messages is typically due to the emergence of a new, highly controversial discussion, which is not unusual in this particular newsgroup. Shortly after that time, a large number of articles are actually filtered and it is reasonable to assume that the articles also belonged to the massive new discussion which in the meantime had proved to be of little interest.

The filtering functionality was also considered helpful in the sense that the discussions that turned out to be uninteresting during a newsreading session were deleted automatically when the user left the newsgroup. Finally, the permanent

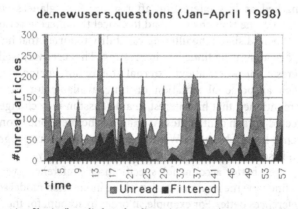

Figure 11.5 "Interactive filtering" applied to the discussion group de.newusers.questions. The time axis shows a series of 60 subsequent newsreading sessions. The #unread articles axis shows the amount of yet unread messages available in a particular session when the user entered the newsgroup. The dark colour shows the proportion of messages that were filtered.

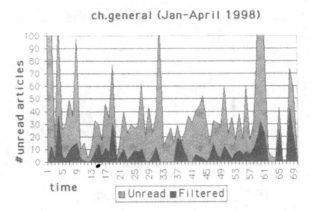

Figure 11.6 "Interactive filtering" applied to the discussion group ch.general. The time axis shows a series of 60 subsequent news reading sessions. The #unread articles axis shows the amount of yet unread messages available in a particular session when the user entered the newsgroup. The dark colour shows the proportion of messages that were filtered.

visual feedback and the chance to cancel indicated filtering actions increased trust in the filtering mechanism.

Other users, however, did not appreciate the automatic filtering and turned it off. An investigation of potential reasons showed that in these cases the interaction model failed to meet the way these users interacted with newsgroups. For example, one user reported he would frequently look into newsgroups without actually having the intention to read discussions at that time. The purpose of these "glances" is to quickly get an impression of "what's going on" in the newsgroups. The actual newsreading occurred later, when the user had sufficient time. The news client "mistook" these repeated glances as indicators that the user was less interested in the discussions available in the newsgroups. As a consequence, the discussions were marked as less interesting after a series of glances without actual reading, and after some time the user had to cancel the filtering actions indicated.

Another user who disliked the filtering capability reported that he likes to postpone reading discussions he finds less interesting. This user was well aware of his changing interests and knew about external effects influencing his newsreading behaviour, such as personal situation or time available for newsreading. Yet another user mentioned that his interest in a discussion may change significantly if a well-respected person contributes. As example, he mentioned contributions by computer science legend Nikolaus Wirth to a discussion about programming languages (which is something that indeed happens occasionally).

In order to even better account for specific user preferences, we subsequently added ways to fine tune the implementation of the interaction model so that it meets individual preferences better. For example, in order to account for the "contribution" effect, we modified the filtering algorithm in such a way that the existence of "highlighted" messages within a discussion (highlighting on the basis of certain criteria is a built-in Knews functionality) overrides the interactive filtering status. In addition, we implemented a variety of ways to customize the behaviour of the news client. For example, the number of "skips" required to render a discussion "less interesting" can be increased or decreased according to individual preferences.

11.5.3 Further Research in Interactive Filtering

We are pursuing two strands of work on the basis of our experiences with interactive filtering. First, we are investigating to what extent it is appropriate to automatically adjust the weights that are assigned to user actions. Implicit user feedback, such as skipping discussions or cancelling indicated filtering actions, could possibly be used for training a neural network using a supervised learning algorithm (e.g. Anderson, 1995). However, there is a considerable risk that incorporating such a learning algorithm would re-introduce assignments of significance to actions, which is exactly what we tried to avoid. Thus, the aim of this research is to find out to what extent automatic learning could be incorporated without conflicting with our other objectives.

Second, we are investigating to what extent interactive filtering could be applied to other structured information spaces, such as the World Wide Web. Despite significant structural differences between Usenet and the web, preliminary results suggest that interactive filtering can directly be applied to web-based discussion forums, such as the popular discussion forum on the web site Australien-Info. Using the list of topics, interactive filtering can be applied in such a way that links to topics not selected for a number of sessions are presented in a specific colour (or even removed). This would complement built-in browser capabilities, such as specific colouring of links already visited. Interactive filtering of web-based discussion forums could be implemented using IBM's WBI (Barrett and Maglio, 1999) proxy technology which provides all necessary means to count accesses to specific links and to alter the source code of pages retrieved by the user.

11.5.4 Personalized Social Navigation: Exploring Usenet as Social Information Space

In the previous section, we have shown that the user's interaction with Usenet discussions can be used to help users focus on the more interesting discussions without any modelling of the user's interests. According to our two complementary views on Usenet, this work explored Usenet as a self-contained information space. Supporting interaction with Usenet as social information space requires paying more attention to the people interacting in a newsgroup.

We already mentioned that interest in a discussion may be influenced by the contributors. A single contribution by a well-respected person could immediately raise interest in a whole discussion. The most frequent way that people participate in newsgroups, however, is not by posting new messages but by reading available messages. This is true even in the case of users who are actually contributing new messages, i.e. those users who are not just "lurking" (Lueg, 2000b). Lurking has

Table 11.1 Excerpt from a typical news server log file (from Lueg, 2000b)

NNRP			Readership statistics			
Client	Conn	Arts	Groups	Post	Rej	Elapsed
1	9	537	98	2	0	02:42:13
2	5	499	19	2	0	00:48:21
3	3	455	101	4	1	10:40:11
4	1	164	29	0	0	00:20:23
5	3	108	10	0	0	01:45:23
6	10	87	15	0	0	00:28:02
7	24	80	274	2	0	01:41:20
8	2	53	44	0	0	00:24:46
9	2	11	1	0	0	00:05:28
10	1	11	2	0	0	01:04:57
11	3	10	3	0	0	00:17:25
12	2	9	17	1	0	00:26:22

been widely viewed as less valuable than active participation in terms of posting new messages. A recent study of lurking behaviour in the context of mailing lists, however, suggests that lurking is a frequent and an important part of online communication (Nonnecke and Preece, this volume).

Table 11.1 shows an excerpt from a typical log file generated by a news server operated in an academic environment. Column 3 lists messages read by clients and column 5 lists new messages posted by clients. These data suggest that reading is an important way of interacting with Usenet newsgroups.

We have explored ways to use the newsreading behaviour of other newsgroup participants for information-seeking support. Generally, newsgroups do not reflect reading activities. We therefore implemented specific "reading indicators" that visualize newsreading behaviours of other users in a newsgroup. These indicators are the only approach we are aware of to visualize newsreading behaviours in the Usenet domain.

The problem with implementing reading indicators is that the actual requesting of messages from a news server is located in the private communication between the user's news client and their news server. In order to implement reading indicators, we had to modify both the user's news client and the news server. The server (a modified INN 2.1 server) now collects traces of newsreading behaviour and delivers this on request; modified Knews clients can request and visualize the data. We implemented the support for reading indicators as an application-specific extension to the Network News Transport Protocol (NNTP) (Kantor and Lapsley, 1986) which is now typically used for Usenet communication. The implementation is inspired by early work reported by Maltz (1994). On the client side, we modified the Knews news client to request and to visualize the trace data as reading indicators. Figure 11.7 shows how additional symbols in the third column indicate the discussions read by two particular users who are (from left to right) Peter (P) who has read two discussions and John (J) who has read five discussions.

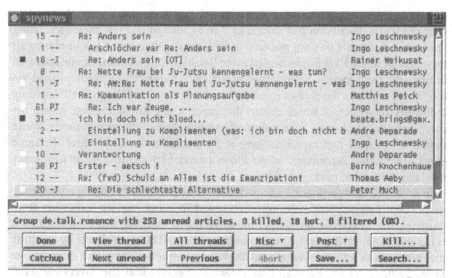

Figure 11.7 The news client Knews modified to visualize otherwise hidden newsreading activities.

11.5.5 Experiences with Personalized Social Navigation in Newsgroups

Reading indicators have been tested with a number of physically distributed users accessing the same news server remotely via NNTP. The number is not limited by server capabilities but by interface constraints, as it is difficult to incorporate a large number of indicators into the Knews interface.

Reports on experiences with reading indicators collected over a period of several months suggest that the additional information is contextually valuable in terms of who, when, and what. First of all, the indicators provide useful information about otherwise invisible activities within one's favourite newsgroups. It is helpful to see when a particular person reads which discussions. It is even somehow motivating to see that users keep reading discussions although they have seemingly disappeared from the newsgroup when they stopped contributing new messages. Moreover, seeing what others read allows users to refer to discussions without involving the need to provide the information again. For example, during a mail exchange that is related to a topic discussed in the newsgroup, it is not necessary to repeat all the information already discussed in the newsgroup; a reference to the discussion would provide the necessary context. Finally, sharing the interesting discussions with friends without explicitly pointing at them is straightforward: "see what I read".

11.5.6 Further Research in Personalized Social Navigation

The first generation of indicators was minimally implemented to show only whether or not a discussion had been read by others. Feedback has indicated that such indicators only partially meet user needs, as some users were observed to start reading a discussion but stop after having read only a few messages. Using Boolean indicators it was not possible to find out whether only a few or almost all messages were read. We implemented more flexible indicators that can be operated in three different modes. Selection of a particular mode can be accomplished via the "Misc" menu in the Knews interface. In the first mode, "Usage at all", reading indicators act as before which means that reading one single message causes the corresponding discussion to be indicated as being read. In the second mode, "More than one", at least two messages have to be read in order to produce the same effect. Finally, the "Percentage" mode allows a much better estimation of how many messages have been read.

In addition, user feedback indicated that the requirement of using a particular news client may prevent even users interested in using reading indicators from participating. Therefore, we further modified the news server in such a way that it is capable of delivering navigational information to all kinds of clients by injecting the information into the overview data that are requested by clients anyway (see Lueg, 2000a, 2002 for details). Our research suggests that the "overview data" concept is flexible enough to be used for the dissemination of additional information. Additional information transported as part of the overview data should be accessible by all clients that are in line with current Usenet standards. We did not experience significant performance problems during our experiments, as the time required to retrieve data from external information sources was similar to the time required to deliver overview data to clients.

So far the work on personalized social navigation indicates that knowing about the news reading behaviour of others provides some benefit. Reading and posting articles in newsgroups could be understood as peripheral participation; posting articles would resemble (visible) participation (Lueg, 2001).

In this context, we are investigating whether newsgroups may qualify as (virtual) communities of practice and what this would mean for information-seeking support. The term "communities of practice" refers to a theory that builds on learning as social participation (Lave and Wenger, 1991; Wenger, 1998). Social participation, in this perspective, is not just engaging in certain activities, such as working in a team, but actively participating in the practices of social groupings and constructing identities in relation to these groupings. Such participation not only shapes what participants do but also how they perceive themselves and how they understand what they are doing.

Legitimate peripheral participation denotes that a new member is able to observe how more experienced members perform tasks and how they deal with problems. It is important that the new member is not yet expected to be able to perform on a similar level. Rather, the new member might work on simplified versions or sub-tasks of complex tasks. However, despite peripheral and reduced responsibilities, the new member is participating in ongoing activities.

Becoming a fully accepted member of a newsgroup is actually a gradual process that is based on reading and posting articles. Indeed, many "regulars" are convinced that reading for several months before posting one's own first article is the best way to learn about Usenet newsgroups and their specific practices.

Participation in terms of contributing articles is essential as it is the only way to become visible and, moreover, to gain social status (which is on the basis of contributions to the newsgroup; jointly exploring a topic in a discussion could be viewed as a kind of shared "practice").

We are looking at ways to extend our work on delivering meta-information within the Usenet framework described previously to be used as a basis for (voluntary) visualizations of peripheral participation in newsgroups, in the tradition of work on social proxies (Erickson et al, 1999; Bradner, this volume). However, this would require us to generalize the approach as the current implementation only supports people willing to use the same Usenet news server. Also, it would demand that we drop the current focus on visualizing activities of particular people which would have implications for privacy.

11.6 Summary and Conclusions

In this chapter, we have presented work in the area of information-seeking support along with an interpretation of this and related work from a point of view inspired by "situated cognition". The two main components of our implementation work were interactive filtering and personalized social navigation. As discussed, interactive filtering provides useful support while avoiding some common pitfalls in the design of information filtering approaches. So far as we are aware, interactive filtering is the only filtering approach in the Usenet domain that features discussion-oriented filtering purely on the basis of the user's interaction with discussions. Although this work actually does filter information, interactive filtering seems to be more related to visual information seeking than to traditional information filtering. The second approach discussed in this chapter, personalized social navigation, provides further information-seeking support. We see this work as a first step in a novel research direction that considers not only the posting behaviour of other users but also their (typically hidden) reading behaviour. The importance of reading/lurking as been documented, but the insights have not yet had the practical impact they deserve.

The experiences reported in this chapter again suggest that designing support for information seeking in social information spaces (and probably information spaces in general as well) requires careful consideration of the many ways that users may interact with such spaces. In particular, attention should be paid to the extent to which apparently "neutral" implementations reinforce certain behaviours. In the case of interactive filtering, user feedback indicated that users tend to pay more attention to those discussions that drifted to the top of the page. Presumably, these discussions were the more interesting ones as they received more attention. However, we actually do not know to what extent the implementation reinforced this interest. Unfortunately, ways of investigating this issue in more detail are limited as the investigation of interests would itself change the object under investigation. Apart from the difficulties of testing novel approaches to information-seeking support in realistic settings, i.e. in settings that are not constrained by study conditions, the impact of the observer on the subject observed turned out to be the main problem in this research area.

Acknowledgements

A significant part of the work reported in this chapter was done while the author was with the Artificial Intelligence Lab, Department of Computer Science, University of Zurich, Switzerland. Funding was provided in part by the Swiss Federal Office for Education and Science under contract BBW No. 98.0065 (SELECT project in the EU Framework IV Telematics Programme). The author is grateful to Rolf Pfeifer for providing a stimulating research environment in Zurich and to Jim Underwood for his ongoing support in Sydney. Denis Antonioli, Stephan Lehmke, Jie Mei, Ralf Salomon and many others provided valuable feedback during the various stages of this research. Special thanks go to Karl-Johan Johnsson for permission to use and to modify his Knews news client and to Danyel Fisher, Simeon Simoff, and Jim Underwood for their comments on earlier drafts of this chapter.

References

Ahlberg, C. and Shneiderman, B. (1994), Visual information seeking: Tight coupling of dynamic query filters with starfield displays, in B. Adelson, S. Dumais and J. Olson, eds, "Proceedings of the Annual ACM SIGCHI Conference on Human Factors in Computing Systems", ACM Press, pp. 313–317.

Anderson, J.A. (1995), Introduction to Neural Networks, MIT Press, Cambridge, MA, USA.

Australien-Info. URL http://www.australien-info.de.

Barrett, R. and Maglio, P. (1999), "Intermediaries: An approach to manipulating information streams", IBM Systems Journal 38(4), 629–641.

Barrett, R., Maglio, P., and Kellem, D. (1997), How to personalize the web, in S. Pemberton, editor, "Proceedings of the Annual ACM SIGCHI Conference on Human Factors in Computing Systems", ACM Press, pp. 75–82.

Belkin, N. (1990), "The cognitive viewpoint in information science", Journal of Information Science 16, 11–15.

Belkin, N. (1993), Interaction with texts: Information retrieval as information seeking behavior, in "Information Retrieval '93: von der Modellierung zur Anwendung", pp. 55–66.

Belkin, N. (1996), Intelligent information retrieval: Whose intelligence?, in "Fifth International Symposium for Information Science", Universitätsverlag Konstanz, Konstanz, pp. 25–31.

Bradner, E. (this volume), Computer mediated communication among teams: What are "teams" and how are they "virtual", in C. Lueg and D. Fisher, eds, "From Usenet to CoWebs: Interacting with Social Information Spaces", Computer-Supported Cooperative Work, Springer, London, UK.

Brown, J.S. and Duguid, P. (1996), Keeping it simple: Investigating resources in the periphery, in T. Winograd, ed., "Bringing Design to Software", Addison-Wesley Publishing Company, New York, NY, pp. 129–145.

Card, S.K., Mackinlay, J.D. and Shneiderman, B., eds (1999), Readings in Information Visualization: Using Vision to Think, Morgan Kaufmann Publishers, San Francisco, CA, USA.

Clancey, W.J. (1997), Situated Cognition. On Human Knowledge and Computer Representations, Learning in Doing: Social, Cognitive, and Computational Perspectives, Cambridge University Press, Cambridge, UK.

Dourish, P. (1999), Where the footprints lead: tracking down other roles for social navigation, in A.J. Munro, K. Höök and D. Benyon, eds, "Social Navigation of Information Space", Springer, London, UK.

Dourish, P. and Chalmers, M. (1994), Running out of space: Models of information navigation, in "Proceedings HCI'94".

Ehrlich, K. and Cash, D. (1999), "The invisible world of intermediaries: A cautionary tale", Computer Supported Cooperative Work 8(1–2), 147–167.

Erickson, T., Smith, D.N., Kellogg, W.A., Laff, M., Richards, J.T. and Bradner, E. (1999), Socially translucent systems: Social proxies, persistent conversations and the design of 'Babble', in "Proceedings of the Annual ACM SIGCHI Conference on Human Factors in Computing Systems", ACM Press, New York, NY, USA, pp. 72–79.

Fischer, G. and Stevens, C. (1991), Information access in complex, poorly structured information spaces, in S.P. Robertson, G.M. Olson and J.S. Olsen, eds, "Reaching Through Technology: CHI 1991 Conference Proceedings", ACM Press, New York, NY, pp. 63–70.

Goldberg, D., Nichols, D., Oki, B.M. and Terry, D. (1992), "Using collaborative filtering to weave an information tapestry", Communications of the ACM 35(12), 61–69.

Google. URL http://groups.google.com.

Jacob, E. and Shaw, D. (1998), Sociocognitive perspectives on representation, in M.E. Williams, ed., "Annual Review of Information Science and Technology", Vol. 33, Published for the American Society for Information Science by Information Today, Inc., Medford, NJ, USA, pp. 131–185.

Kantor, B. and Lapsley, P. (1986), "Network News Transfer Protocol (NNTP)". Request for Comments (RFC) 977.

Kaptelinin, V. (1996), Computer-mediated activity: Functional organs in social and developmental contexts, in B.A. Nardi, ed., "Context and Consciousness. Activity Theory and Human-Computer Interaction", MIT Press, Cambridge, MA, USA, pp. 45–68.

Knews. URL http://www.matematik.su.se/~kjj/.

Korfhage, R.R. (1997), Information Storage and Retrieval, John Wiley & Sons, New York, USA.

Lang, K. (1995), Newsweeder: Learning to filter Netnews, in "Proceedings of the Twelth International Conference on Machine Learning", Morgan Kaufmann.

Lave, J. (1991), Situated learning in communities of practice, in L.B. Resnick, J.M. Levine and S.D. Teasley, eds, "Perspectives on Socially Shared Cognition", American Psychological Association, Washington, DC, pp. 63–82. Third Printing April 1996.

Lave, J. and Wenger, E. (1991), Situated Learning: Legitimate Peripheral Participation, Cambridge University Press, Cambridge.

Lieberman, H. (1997), Autonomous interface agents, in S. Pemberton, editor, "Proceedings of the Annual ACM SIGCHI Conference on Human Factors in Computing Systems", ACM Press, pp. 67–74.

Lueg, C. (1998), Supporting situated actions in high volume conversational data situations, in C.-M. Karat, A. Lund, J. Coutaz and J. Karat, eds, "Proceedings of the Annual ACM SIGCHI Conference on Human Factors in Computing Systems", ACM Press, pp. 471–479.

Lueg, C. (2000a), A flexible and non-intrusive approach to distribute context specific information to Usenet news clients, in "Proceedings of the Annual Conference of the Computer Human Interaction Special Interest Group of the Ergonomics Society of Australia", pp. 14–20. ISBN 0 643 06633 0.

Lueg, C. (2000b), Supporting social navigation in Usenet newsgroups, in "Proceedings of the Workshop "Social Navigation – A Design Approach?" (organized by K. Höök, A. Munro, and A. Wexelblat) at the Annual ACM SIGCHI Conference on Human Factors in Computing Systems", SICS, Box 1263, S-164 29 Kista, Sweden, pp. 25–26.

Lueg, C. (2001), "Newsgroups as virtual communities of practice". Paper presented at the Workshop "Actions and Identities in Virtual Communities of Practice" (organized by C. Lueg, E. Davenport, T. Robertson, and V. Pipek) at the 7th European Conference on Computer Supported Cooperative Work.

Lueg, C. (2002), "Enabling dissemination of meta information in the Usenet framework", Journal of Digital Information, to appear.

Maltz, D.A. (1994), Distributing information for collaborative filtering on Usenet net news, Master's thesis, Massachusetts Institute of Technology, Cambridge, MA, USA.

Marchionini, G. (1995), Information Seeking in Electronic Environments, Cambridge University Press, Cambridge, UK.

Miller, B.N., Riedl, J.T. and Konstan, J.A. (this volume), GroupLens for Usenet: Experiences in applying collaborative filtering to a social information system, in C. Lueg and D. Fisher, eds, "From Usenet to CoWebs: Interacting with Social Information Spaces", ComputerSupported Cooperative Work, Springer, London, UK.

Mock, K.J. (1996), Hybrid hill-climbing and knowledge-based techniques for intelligent news filtering, in "Proceedings of the National Conference on Artificial Intelligence", AAAI Press, Menlo Park, California.

Morita, M. and Shinoda, Y. (1994), Information filtering based on user behavior analysis and best match text retrieval, in "Proceedings of the Conference on Research and Development in Information Retrieval", Springer, London, UK.

Munro, A.J., Höök, K. and Benyon, D., eds (1999), Social navigation of information space, Springer, London, UK.

Nonnecke, B. and Preece, J. (this volume), Silent participants: getting to know lurkers better, in C. Lueg and D. Fisher, eds, "From Usenet to CoWebs: Interacting with Social Information Spaces", Computer-Supported Cooperative Work, Springer, London, UK.

Pfaffenberger, B. (this volume), "A standing wave in the web of our communications": Usenet and the socio-technical construction of cyberspace values, in C. Lueg and D. Fisher, eds, "From Usenet to CoWebs: Interacting with Social Information Spaces", Computer-Supported Cooperative Work, Springer, London, UK.

Resnick, P. and Varian, H.R. (1997), Recommender systems, Communications of the ACM 40(3), 56–58. Special Issue on Collaborative Filtering.

Resnick, P., Iacovou, N., Suchak, M., Bergstrom, P. and Riedl, J. (1994), GroupLens: An open architecture for collaborative filtering of Netnews, in R. Furuta and C. Neuwirth, eds, "Proceedings of the International Conference on Computer Supported Cooperative Work", ACM Press, pp. 175–186.

Shardanand, U. and Maes, P. (1995), Social information filtering: algorithms for automating "word of the mouth", in Irvin Katz et al., ed., "Proceedings of the Annual ACM SIGCHI Conference on Human Factors in Computing Systems", ACM Press, pp. 210–217.

Shneiderman, B. (1997), Direct manipulation for comprehensible, predictable, and controllable user interfaces, in "Proceedings of the International Conference on Intelligent User Interfaces", pp. 33–39.

Suchman, L.A. (1987), Plans and situated actions – The problem of human-machine communication, Cambridge University Press, Cambridge, UK.

Terveen, L., Hill, W.C., Amento, B., McDonald, D. and Creter, J. (1997), Building taskspecific interfaces to high volume conversational data, in S. Pemberton, ed., "Proceedings of the Annual ACM SIGCHI Conference on Human Factors in Computing Systems", ACM Press, pp. 226–233.

Twidale, M.B., Nichols, D.M. and Paice, C.D. (1997), Browsing is a collaborative process, Information Processing and Management 33(6), 761–783.

Wenger, E. (1998), Communities of practice: learning, meaning, and identity, Cambridge University Press, Cambridge, UK. First Paperback Edition 1999.

Wilson, T. (1999), Models in information behaviour research, Journal of Documentation 55(3), 249–270.

Appendix
Studying Online Newsgroups
Danyel Fisher and Christopher Lueg

This program posts news to thousands of machines throughout the entire civilized world. Your message will cost the net hundreds if not thousands of dollars to send everywhere. Please be sure you know what you are doing. Are you absolutely sure that you want to do this? [y/n]

Warning message displayed by original "nn" newsgroup program before posting

A.1 Introduction

Several of the chapters in this volume have discussed studying online newsgroups. The raw data they tap into is commonly available; however, it can be quite a challenge to mine that data for useful information.

This appendix is meant to serve two purposes. First, it is a basic introduction to the day-to-day structure of Usenet. It emphasises the threading structure of messages, and how those threads relate to news groups; it discusses the hierarchy of group names, and how those hierarchies are formed; and it discusses the life and death of newsgroups. It is meant as a general continuation of Pfaffenberger's chapter (this volume); it also draws on some of the information presented by Smith (this volume).

Second, it is a technical introduction to dealing with Usenet data. For many projects, it is easy enough to track some current messages from Google's "Groups" archive, or to count the number of posters at Netscan (Smith, this volume); however, to actually look at the content of messages still requires downloading and reading them all. This section briefly discusses some of the tools that can be useful in downloading and reading Usenet groups. It assumes some knowledge of programming – currently, to the best of our knowledge, there are no public domain tools for Usenet analysis – but may be of some use as a list of starting points.

Many of these facts may also be applicable to other online newsgroups and discussion boards; Usenet, as the granddaddy of so many of them, has been an important social shaper of the norms and understandings of these groups.

A.2 Posting to Usenet

Usenet is a distributed bulletin board: messages posted to one machine are sent around the world and readable on any other machine. Because of the Usenet propagation mechanism (discussed in section A.3), there is no definite order in which messages will arrive; however, almost all messages make it through. There are no central controls on who can post a message; rather, the system is open to all. Instead, site administrators have the ability to interrupt or drop messages.

This makes for a somewhat anarchic system; messages flow constantly from all over the world. But there is a way to organize to the messages. Each message is placed within one of more 'newsgroups;' software clients are designed to aid in reading those groups. A user might choose to read only the newest messages in comp.lang.python, for example, or rec.cooking.recipes. The former, by its name, is for discussion of the computer language Python; the latter is for exchange of recipes.

A.3 Usenet Propagation

Usenet is interesting partially in that it acts in a way fairly unlike other online sources. It is a fully decentralized system; there is no central authority of the Usenet system. Email messages, for example, are routed and then sent directly: my message to you goes through the smallest number of servers it can, Usenet messages, in contrast, are propagated indirectly from machine to machine. Using a protocol known as NNTP, each sites subscribes to one or more "feeds" from other sites. Each site, therefore, can only receive the messages that are sent on by the sites around them. There is no canonical central core of Usenet; rather, each site has a partial control of what is seen by those sites downstream from it. The impact of this is lessened slightly because each site can subscribe to feeds from several different sources. One of the implications of this is that it becomes important to know who is upstream of a site: because Usenet propagation is decided on a site-by-site basis, the messages that are visible from one site might be different than those from another; some upstream sites choose not to carry certain types of messages.

For example, Figure A.1 shows two headers of messages arriving at the University of California at Irvine

Paths are read backwards, and are separated by "!" marks. The first message has wound its way from Indiana to the University of Illinois, to Oregon, to Cal State Long Beach. The second was posted at Google.com, has passed through Syracuse university, San Diego State, and Cal State Long Beach before reaching Irvine.

In Figure A.2 we see the reverse – one author of this piece sent a message to a newsgroup to be checked by the other. The message originated at UC Irvine; it travelled a rather tortuous path to Switzerland, where it was read. In the meantime, it had passed through San Diego State and Oregon before going to Syracuse. This one spent more time at non-academic sites – the international networks icl.net and mediaways.net carried it – before sending it, at last, to the Swiss university.

```
news.service.uci.edu!csulb.edu!canoe.uoregon.edu
!logbridge.uoregon.edu!vixen.cso.uiuc.edu!news.indiana.edu!ahabig

news.service.uci.edu!csulb.edu!newshub.sdsu.edu
!news-spur1.maxwell.syr.edu!news.maxwell.syr.edu!feeder.qis.net
!sn-xit-02!supernews.com!postnews1.google.com!not-for-mail
```

Figure A.1 Paths of messages to California.

```
news.ifi.unizh.ch!news-zh.switch.ch!feedme.news.mediaways.net
!newsfeed.icl.net!news.maxwell.syr.edu!logbridge.uoregon.edu
!ihnp4.ucsd.edu!news.service.uci.edu!not-for-mail
```

Figure A.2 The path of a message from California to Switzerland.

Each of those servers had its own policy for which messages to pass on, and how often. Each of them cares about a different selection of newsgroups. With a web this tangled, it becomes clear why different sites can see a different selection. This also means that there is no canonical view of Usenet: the sites that Netscan sees on the Microsoft campus, and the order they arrive, may be quite different from the messages arriving at Google's headquarters in Palo Alto.

More confusingly, there are many different types of software meant to help handle administer Usenet traffic. Usenet traffic has always been extensive, and it has grown even more in the last few years. Unfortunately, much of that growth has been in spam – undesirable, off-topic advertisements – so a number of sites have started to carefully constrain which messages they pass on. There is no longer such a thing as an unconstrained Usenet feed of all groups.

A.4 The Birth and Death of Newsgroups

Pfaffenberger (this volume) gives a good overview of how groups are created. In classic Usenet fashion, there are three or four distinct methods. One of them is voting. To keep the hierarchy of important topics well-organized, there are specific conditions under which a new group can be added to the "big 8" hierarchy. Essentially, a new group requires a period of discussion and comments, followed by a period of online voting. Current members involved in the parent group are expected to vote on whether a new group would serve a distinct population, and whether the additional complexity in the hierarchy would be worth the additional specificity. (For example, a regular country music listener might vote against a new country music group because he wants to minimize the number of groups he checks daily for new messages, or might vote for it in order to ensure he has a community of dedicated fans to tap into.) Email votes for and against are counted, and if over half of the votes come out in favour, then the group is instituted. The voting is done, to some extent, on the honour system: although votes are kept and published by email address, there is no way to ensure that some addresses are not multiply maintained. Still, the system often works out to be a fair one, with the exception of some notable abuses.

One notable explosion was the notorious rec.music.white-power vote. When members of the newsgroup rec.music became irritated at certain political attitudes in their group, some members started a campaign to split off their own special interest. Unfortunately, word got out the net. Well-meaning net users, wanting to strike a blow against white separatists, sent in thousands of malformed "no" votes. The exhausted moderator eventually declared the election a failure, and rec.music.white-power was not created.

However, those parties did find other places to create their group. As Pfaffenberger explains, there are other hierarchies, not subject to votes. One, the alt groups, are collectively known as the alternet. Groups there are created informally, based on discussions in the group alt.config. Because anyone can create an alt group fairly easily, the propagation of those groups is much less standardized. It is impossible to keep up with the tens of thousands of groups that are created and destroyed constantly. Within the groups, many alt messages are not distributed very far, are filtered rapidly by destination sites, or are kept in a spool of far fewer messages than messages in the 'big 8.' There are many joke groups – alt.Swedish.chef.bork.bork.bork is named after a humorous character on a children's television show, and alt.fan.star-trek.sexy.bald.captain is a fan group for Patrick Stewart's role in the 1980s *Star Trek: The Next Generation* TV show. However, there are serious discussion groups, too, that for one reason or another have been placed in the alt hierarchy. Thus, there is an entire alt.legends sub-hierarchy, with alt.legends.urban being an active and ongoing group engaged in serious discussion, but alt.legeneds.ghost-stories being far quieter.

Last, there are regional hierarchies. System administrators at sites can set up groups that are designed only for the local site. These can be created by any mechanism desired. At many universities, for example, local groups carry class discussions; many cities and nations have local groups, and many corporations carry custom groups on their servers. These hierarchies may be carried locally, or distributed widely: for example, German de newsgroups are fairly widely propagated.

By some estimates, some 80,000 newsgroups are created and propagated for at least some distance on the net. On the other hand, the vast majority of them lie fallow: only 20,000 or so are actively used.

A.5 How Messages Look

Messages on Usenet are stored as raw text files. This means that it takes no special software to interpret the messages, once downloaded; any editor can read the messages. The messages are constructed of a header followed by a body. The body is the message text itself. In most messages, it is plain text: readable English (or other languages), presented in traditional text formats. However, in so-called "binary" newsgroups, messages may also contain attachments containing parts of images, programs, or audio files stored in one of several standard formats. (Information on this can be found in "requests for comments" or RFCs, a form of internet standard numbered 822, 1036, 2076, which are archived at web sites such as http://www.faqs.org)

The header provides contextual information about the message. Like email messages, the headers each carry a sender, a destination, and a subject line. Unlike email, they are also each assigned a globally unique identity (or GUID) by the local client;[1] this is understood to be a specific label that can represent only that

---

[1]GUIDs usually consist of two parts: a locally unique ID number, perhaps a serial number generated by a local machine, and a number unique to the client. For example, some messages are tagged with a serial number, the date, and the IP address of the server they originate from.

message. As Smith (this volume) points out, some messages violate the specifications: some ill-configured machines generate many identical unique IDs; some anonymous posters, hoping to cover their tracks, obliterate these IDs. Although the ID is a useful piece of data, then, it is unwise to depend on it too much.

Usenet messages always have a specific set of required headers, and a longer set of optional headers. Messages will be discarded by most servers without a "from" address telling who wrote the message, a "subject" line acting as a title to the message, and a "newsgroups" line, listing the groups that the message is to be sent to. They will also include a "date" (listing when the message was sent).

Of the optional fields, some are informative, such as "organization", which is used to store an affiliation for the message sender, and "X-complaints-to", which is used as a place to direct complaints about inappropriate messages – much like a "how's my driving" bumper sticker. Some are more technical, specifying information about the sort of client used to post the message, or its IP address ("NNTP-Posting-Host").

If a user wants to better direct where answers to their question will go, or wants to particularly influence a particularly bad "topic drift," the "followup-to" field can be used. A message posted to comp.math, for example, with the header followup-to: comp.groupware would propose to move an ongoing discussion from math to the group comp.groupware. This request can, of course, be either followed or violated. These relocations are most common when a topic drift – a change in the topic and meter of a conversation – is about to occur or already has occurred.

A unique aspect of the Usenet message is the "references" field. The references field lists the message IDs of several previous message, and allows the system to reconstruct a link to a previous message. The references field contains the ID of the immediate predecessor message, and often to previous messages before that, as well. Mail clients generate this field as they post the message; the field is considered optional, although most messages do comply.

That references field forms one of the fundamental aspects of Usenet organization, the message thread. Messages are either new messages – roots – or replies to old messages. The set of replies forms a tree-shaped message "thread": several users may respond to one message; each of those may or may not receive another reply in response, and so on. These trees are typically used to organize messages: users have the ability, in many clients, to navigate through the group, picking out threads and skipping across them individually.

Because there is little structure forced on the content of the fields – any of them might be forged, so long as they fit the form of the relevant guidelines – anonymous posting on Usenet has long been possible, and has been practiced frequently. When analysing Usenet messages it is important to know that almost all header information can be modified by users. The reason is that Usenet is based on trust; it was never intended as a secure system. Spammers, in particular, exploit these weaknesses when trying to hide their identities and the origins of their messages by modifying message headers. This is important as spam may be a significant part of the messages analyzed in a research project. Typically, spammers use fake From: entries (which can be set just as users want). Often, spammers also modify the Path: header information in order to hide where their messages have been injected into Usenet. Usually, Path: is set

```
Path:
news.ifi.unizh.ch!news-zh.switch.ch!feedme.news.mediaways.net!newsfeed.icl.net
!news.maxwell.syr.edu!logbridge.uoregon.edu!ihnp4.ucsd.edu!news.service.uci.edu
!not-for-mail
From: "Danyel Fisher" <danyelf@acm.org>
Newsgroups: rec.games.board
Subject: Re: Settlers Debate Rages On
Date: Tue, 12 Mar 2002 01:35:58 -0800
Organization: University of California, Irvine
Lines: 13
Message-ID: <a6ki83$rv5$1@news.service.uci.edu>
References: <u8pe8ebv8d4v6c@corp.supernews.com>
NNTP-Posting-Host: vp208299.reshsg.uci.edu
X-Newsreader: Microsoft Outlook Express 6.00.2600.0000
X-MimeOLE: Produced By Microsoft MimeOLE V6.00.2600.0000
Xref: news.ifi.unizh.ch rec.games.board:191208
```

Figure A.3 An entire message, sent from California and read in Switzerland.

by the server first accepting an article for distribution, i.e. where an article "enters" Usenet. Transit news servers only add their own identity to the Path: header to indicate that the article has passed through their sites. Listing server identities in the Path: header is used to prevent that the same article is being offered multiple times to a server. However, quite a few news servers accept articles where Path: is already set (so-called path preload) and just add their own identity to the Path:.

Figure A.3 highlights the major paths in a message posted by one of the authors; the message was then extracted by the other author, half-way around the world. The path shows that the message went through nine hosts on its way from California to Switzerland.

A.6 How Usenet Is Accessed

By and large, users read Usenet through specialized clients. Some of those are integrated into mail clients – for example, Microsoft's Outlook Express and Netscape's Messenger can both read Usenet News – or are standalone, such as the command line utility trn. Most clients present a view of a single Usenet newsgroup, with messages to that group threaded. Messages scroll back into history, disappearing into the past as they age. This gives the sense of a temporary nature to the medium. Messages disappear like bad memories, fading fast and away, and categorized by topic.

It has been a shock to many that this is not the only way of looking at the data. A reader calling himself James "Kibo" Parry was the first to publicly start searching through the incoming Usenet feed. He would post absurd comments, and then search out answers, responding to occurrences of his name wherever it appeared. It seemed nearly miraculous, in the early 1990s, that wherever Kibo's name appeared, Kibo's answer would follow. But that was a minor trick, quickly understood. Kibo searched through the text of the incoming mail feed with a simple program, searching out the single unique word. Because his name was unusual, it was easy to find.

If Usenet could be searched, though, Usenet could also be stored and kept for safekeeping. Various archives have kept subsets of Usenet posts: rec.food.recipes, for example, has long been a popular source for sharing recipes, and several people have archived it as "the internet cookbook". It was a largely manual task, copying relevant files as they sped by. So, too, was the archives that were built up for the "sources" groups. Those groups were dedicated to sharing code improvements to open source and shared projects; they were archived at ftp sites.

But many users continued the impression that their past mistakes remained theirs alone. Thus, it was a shock to many when the company Déjà announced, in 1997 that it had an archive of the last 2 years' network traffic. Supposedly secret posts from the past were dug up, and users were startled. Déjà ultimately promised to hide the archive again, making Usenet accessible only from the day they announced that they were storing messages. This limited archiving lasted for some time, but public demand also wanted to see an archive. This scenario repeated itself years later with Déjà's inheritors, Google. A powerful search engine, Google put together a display of Usenet's past, and then started working backward. By reconstructing tapes and collecting old entries, they were able to find a substantial slice of Usenet history through 1981. That was a full decade and a half of archives, suddenly exposed to the world. (One of the authors of this piece proudly discovered that the completion of this book coincides nicely with the tenth anniversary of his first post, in 1992.)

Today, Usenet can be reached through a variety of means. Users can follow their day-to-day groups with hybrid mail–news clients, or can search for information using the Google news archive.

A.7 Invisible Layers of Usenet

Because it is easy to send messages from Usenet clients, many users prefer to communicate in private to the authors of messages, rather than in the public eye. As Preece and Nonnecke point out (this volume), not all the action in newsgroups happens publicly. In fact, much of the vitality of some groups happens in the background, with users sending feedback and discussing articles with each other in the meantime.

There is, of course, no way to get these direct email messages. Past researchers have infrequently found surveying to be a successful technique; it can be seen as an invasion of privacy in some newsgroups, and may get intensely negative responses. A post from a stranger with a research project is almost always seen as undesirable. Anecdotal reports suggest that more successful estimates have come from qualitative studies, reading messages and looking for references to outside readers and so-called "offline" conversations. Personal email to key members of the group that carefully explain what is being asked and why may be seen as more useful.

A.8 Dealing with Usenet Data

There are a variety of ways to collect archived Usenet information. It depends on the technical ability of the collector, the purpose of the collection, and the size of the collection desired.

It is easiest, perhaps, to search down individual messages from Google's archive. This allows a refined search on some fronts, and the messages go back many years. With a little work, it is possible to find out exactly how many people referred to an issue of interest per month in the group; however, those messages are hard to save and in an inconvenient format.

A user already subscribed to several groups may find it easiest to simply copy interesting messages into a local archive through their reader. For example, Microsoft's Outlook Express allows users to copy messages en masse from newsgroups to a local folder. Folders can then be exported as text files, referred to as ".pst" and ".eml" format, to be read or analysed later. These text files match the header-and-body format discussed above, and can be searched with the usual set of qualitative text tools.

The more ambitious collector should look into tapping off a local news feed. It is comparatively easy to set up a news server; that server can then be set to keep an unlimited archive of potentially interesting messages. The messages kept in the server, again, would be text files, easy to search. It is outside the scope of this chapter to discuss how to set up a news server; however, the software is easily available for many types of machines (including both Windows and UNIX systems).

From this raw text format, many projects find it useful to build databases that index the content of the groups. Unfortunately, there are no current standards or off-the-shelf technologies for building such an index. The schema that Netscan uses is highlighted in Smith's chapter in this volume; however, that may not be appropriate for smaller-scale studies. Many researchers want to keep, for each message, the required fields – the "from" address, the date, and the newsgroup – and some information like the thread the message is embedded in.

A.9 Conclusion

Understanding Usenet can require a great deal of work: the technology is layered with social conventions and rules, and the quantity of data can be overwhelming. Understanding some of the technical measures that help support the technology can make it easier to follow the social movements that have emerged within the network. Similarly, because Usenet historically has been an influential system, the analytical methods that apply to Usenet can be used similarly on other bulletin boards and chat rooms.

Collection of data from Usenet newsgroups is a comparatively straightforward task for small projects, but becomes more challenging for large-scale projects. Still, it is fairly laborious; projects more sophisticated than word searches begin to require special-purpose scripts to be written anew. It is unfortunate that there are no off-the-shelf tools for managing this sort of research; we hope that more of them may be developed and made available in the near future.

Index